ROUTLEDGE LIBRARY EDITIONS:
AMERICA – REVOLUTION & CIVIL WAR

Volume 1

PHYSICIAN OF THE AMERICAN REVOLUTION

PHYSICIAN OF THE AMERICAN REVOLUTION
Jonathan Potts

RICHARD L. BLANCO

LONDON AND NEW YORK

First published in 1979 by Garland STPM Press

This edition first published in 2021
by Routledge
2 Park Square, Milton Park, Abingdon, Oxon OX14 4RN

and by Routledge
52 Vanderbilt Avenue, New York, NY 10017

Routledge is an imprint of the Taylor & Francis Group, an informa business

© 1979 Garland Publishing Inc.

All rights reserved. No part of this book may be reprinted or reproduced or utilised in any form or by any electronic, mechanical, or other means, now known or hereafter invented, including photocopying and recording, or in any information storage or retrieval system, without permission in writing from the publishers.

Trademark notice: Product or corporate names may be trademarks or registered trademarks, and are used only for identification and explanation without intent to infringe.

British Library Cataloguing in Publication Data
A catalogue record for this book is available from the British Library

ISBN: 978-0-367-54033-3 (Set)
ISBN: 978-1-00-312459-7 (Set) (ebk)
ISBN: 978-0-367-64232-7 (Volume 1) (hbk)
ISBN: 978-1-00-312362-0 (Volume 1) (ebk)

Publisher's Note
The publisher has gone to great lengths to ensure the quality of this reprint but points out that some imperfections in the original copies may be apparent.

This book is a re-issue originally published in 1979. The language used is a reflection of its era and no offence is meant by the Publishers to any reader by this re-publication.

Disclaimer
The publisher has made every effort to trace copyright holders and would welcome correspondence from those they have been unable to trace.

Physician of the American Revolution
Jonathan Potts

Richard L. Blanco

Garland STPM Press
NEW YORK & LONDON

ACKNOWLEDGMENT

The author wishes to thank the following for permission to quote from the following source: Princeton University Press, Lyman H. Butterfield, ed., *The Letters of Benjamin Rush,* 2 vols., *1*, © 1951.

Research funding for this publication was supported in part by NIH Grant LM 02597 from the National Library of Medicine.

Copyright © 1979 by Garland Publishing, Inc.
All rights reserved. No part of this work covered by the copyright hereon may be reproduced or used in any form or by any means—graphic, electronic, or mechanical, including photocopying, recording, taping, or information storage and retrieval systems—without permission of the publisher.

15 14 13 12 11 10 9 8 7 6 5 4 3 2 1

Library of Congress Cataloging in Publication Data
Blanco, Richard L
    Physician of the American Revolution, Jonathan Potts.
    Bibliography: p.
    Includes index.
    1. Potts, Jonathan, 1745-1781. 2. Physicians—Pennsylvania—Biography. 3. United States—History—Revolution, 1775-1783—Medical and sanitary affairs.
I. Title.
E283.P67   610'.92'4 [B]   79-10268
ISBN 0-8240-7104-2

Published by Garland STPM Press
545 Madison Avenue, New York, New York 10022

Printed in the United States of America

This book is dedicated to the memory of
my father,
Lidio Francis Blanco (1899–1939),
from Costa Rica.

Contents

List of Maps and Illustrations
ix

Preface
xi

I. An Apprenticeship in Philadelphia
1

II. A Term in Edinburgh
21

III. The Medical World of Jonathan Potts
35

IV. The Doctor as a Patriot
61

V. The Canadian Campaign and Fort Ticonderoga
83

Contents

VI. With Washington on the Delaware
113

VII. With Gates at Saratoga
133

VIII. The Valley Forge Hospitals
161

IX. Potts's Last Years
193

Appendix I
A Table of Fees and Rates
213

Appendix II
Illness in the American Ranks during the Revolution
223

Notes
227

Bibliography
251

Index
265

List of Maps and Illustrations

Following page 128

1. Pottsgrove Manor, the home of Jonathan Potts built by John Potts in 1752.
2. Dr. Jonathan Potts (1745–1781).
3. Surgical instruments in four inch silver case used by Dr. Jonathan Potts.
4. Appointment of Dr. Jonathan Potts by the Continental Congress to the rank of Deputy General of the Hospital in the Northern Department, April 11, 1777—signed by John Hancock.
5. Fort Ticonderoga.
6. Canada invasion, 1775–1776, and Burgoyne's offensive.
7. Campaign areas in New Jersey and Pennsylvania.
8. The medical chest of Dr. Willian Shippen, Jr. (1738–1808).

9. Field case of surgical instruments owned by Dr. Charles McKnight (1750–1791).
10. The surgical instruments of Dr. Charles McKnight (1750–1791).
11. The trepanning instruments of Dr. Charles McKnight (1750–1791).
12. A replica of the hospital hut at Morristown designed by Dr. James Tilton (1745–1822).

Preface

Although the War of American Independence has been studied intensively, relatively little information has been available about the medical problems of the Continental army. Although a few doctors recorded some incidents about the war, apparently no army physician or surgeon of the period left a detailed memoir providing an adequate account of the difficulties confronting medical personnel during the Revolutionary War. I have attempted to synthesize the activities of American doctors in this era by summarizing the career of Dr. Jonathan Potts (1745–1781), a key figure in the army medical department, whose work epitomizes developments in military medicine.

Potts first served in the army as a regimental surgeon. He later supervised army hospitals at Fort Ticonderoga, marched with Washington at Trenton and Princeton, established sanitary regulations for troops in New York, directed casualty evacuation during the fighting at Saratoga, and ministered to the sick at Valley Forge. Potts and his colleagues in the medical department frequently encountered debilitating diseases, such as smallpox, typhus, and dysentery, which took such a heavy toll of soldiers that regiments were often rendered inactive for months. Few American physicians in the northern campaigns from 1775 to 1780 experienced the problems on bloody battlefields and in pestilent-ridden hospital wards encountered by this dedicated and patriotic Quaker doctor from Pennsylvania, whose humanitarian creed was "to tenderly nurse the sick."

Potts, who died at the age of thirty-six, wrote little about himself that can be documented, and his contemporaries generally neglected to cite his accomplishments. Because of the scarcity of data about Potts's private life, aspects about his personality remain unresolved. As a result, I am unable to delineate Potts's character with the detail biographers normally assess their subjects. However, I have compiled sufficient material about his background, education, hospital training, civilian medical practice, and about his army activities to place Potts into the historical perspective that he merits.

I have been assisted in my study of Jonathan Potts by several institutions and many individuals. I acknowledge the financial support received in the summer of 1975 from the Research Foundation of the State University of New York which enabled me to initiate the project. A sabbatical leave in the autumn of 1975 from the College at Brockport, State University of New York, permitted me to continue the work. A research grant for the summer and fall of 1977 from the National Library of Medicine (the National Institutes of Health) allowed me to continue the research further and to begin writing the manuscript. I am deeply indebted to Dr. Albert W. Brown, President of the College at Brockport, State University of New York, for arranging a semester's leave for me in the spring of 1978 so that I could complete the manuscript.

I am particularly grateful to many individuals who encouraged me in my endeavors. Marjorie Potts Wendell, Pottstown, Pennsylvania, a descendant of Samuel Potts, a brother of Jonathan Potts, gave me invaluable insight into the Potts family and into Pottsgrove Manor. Ray Brown, Program Grants Officer (retired), the National Library of Medicine, suggested to me the need for a study of medical care in the Continental army during the American Revolution, and he

Preface

encouraged me to submit a grant proposal. Philip Weimerskirch, Research Librarian, History of Medicine Library, School of Medicine and Dentistry, University of Rochester, Rochester, New York has been a steady source of information and assistance. To Philip Cash, Department of History, Emmanuel College, Boston, Massachusetts, I am indebted for several incisive discussions about medicine in colonial America. Jane Lape, Curator-Librarian, Fort Ticonderoga Museum, Ticonderoga, New York, graciously located innumerable documents for me during my visit to the Fort. Linda Stanley, Archivist, Historical Society of Pennsylvania, located many items for me, even the long-lost Cash Book of Jonathan Potts. For many years, Robert J. Taylor, editor, The Adams Papers, Massachusetts Historical Society, has provided me with advice, encouragement, and inspiration. To him, I am especially obligated in many ways.

I also acknowledge the assistance of the following: Ross Beales, Jr., Department of History, College of the Holy Cross, Worcester, Massachusetts; Whitfield Bell, Jr., Executive Officer and Librarian, American Philosophical Society, Philadelphia; Janet Brady Berk, Librarian, History of Medicine Library, School of Medicine and Dentistry, University of Rochester, Rochester, New York; George Chalou, Archivist, Center for the Documentary Study of the American Revolution, National Archives; James Coleman, Superintendent, Morristown National Historical Park, Morristown, New Jersey; Thomas Dunnings, Jr., Assistant Curator of Manuscripts, New-York Historical Society; Charles Finalyson, Keeper of Manuscripts, Edinburgh University Library; J. William Frost, Director, Friends Historical Library, Swarthmore College, Swarthmore, Pennsylvania; Mary Gillett, Historian, Historical Unit, USAMEDD, Fort Detrick, Frederick, Maryland; Mary Belle Green, Supervising Hostess, Hugh Mercer Apothecary Shop, Fredericksburg, Virginia; Lucy Hrivnik, Archivist, Historical Society of Pennsylvania; William Joyce, Curator of Manuscripts, American Antiquarian Society, Worcester, Massachusetts; Susan A. Kopczniski,

Preface

Park Historian, Morristown National Historical Park; John Kramer, Registrar (retired), Philadelphia College of Pharmacy and Medicine; Charles H. Lesser, Assistant Director for Archives and Publications, South Carolina Department of Archives and History, Columbia; Jean McNeice, First Assistant, Manuscripts and Archives Division, New York Public Library; Frank Mevers, editor, The Papers of Josiah Bartlett, New Hampshire Historical Society, Concord; Caroline Morris, Librarian, Pennsylvania Hospital; Paul Nelson, Department of History, Berea College, Berea, Kentucky; John Parascandola, Director, American Institute of the History of Pharmacy, University of Wisconsin, Madison; Michael Philips, Park Historian, Saratoga National Historical Park, Stillwater, New York; John Reed, Director, Valley Forge Historical Society, Valley Forge, Pennsylvania; Carol Shiels Roark, Research Historian, Historic Yellow Springs, Chester Springs, Pennsylvania; David L. Salay, Curator of Library Resources, New York State Historical Association, Cooperstown; Mrs. Leroy Saunders, Director, Historical Society of Berks County, Reading, Pennsylvania; Richard Showman, editor, The Nathanael Greene Papers, Rhode Island Historical Society, Providence; Don Skemer, Keeper of the Manuscripts, New Jersey Historical Society, Newark; Paul Smith, Historian, American Revolution Bicentennial Office, Library of Congress; Thomas Smith, Librarian, Morristown National Historical Park, Morristown, New Jersey; Richard Sommers, Archivist, United States Military History Institute, Carlisle Barracks, Carlisle, Pennsylvania; Lee Stanton, Research Librarian, New York State Library, Albany; Ricardo Torres-Reyes, National Park Service, Boston; Albert Van Dusen, editor, The Papers of Jonathan Trumbull, Connecticut State Library, Hartford; Louis J. Venuto, Supervisory Historian, Valley Forge National Historical Park; and Gretchen Worden, Assistant to the Curator, Mütter Museum, The College of Physicians of Philadelphia.

For typing the manuscript with enthusiasm amid a multitude of office duties, I am deeply obligated to Brenda Peake,

Preface

Secretary, History Department, State University College at Brockport.

To my wife, Irene, and my son, Richard Jr., whose interest and encouragement are essential to my work, I am especially grateful.

Richard L. Blanco
Lancet Way
Brockport, New York
April 1979

I.
An Apprenticeship in Philadelphia

Jonathan Potts was an eighteenth-century American physician who had the finest education and training available to the medical profession in the North American colonies. One of the first medical graduates of the College of Philadelphia, Potts practiced in rural Pennsylvania, where he encountered diseases that plagued agrarian communities. A cultured gentleman, a leader in country politics, a friend of Benjamin Rush and Anthony Wayne, Potts was an ardent patriot who joined Committees of Safety and who, in 1775, enlisted in a rifle battalion that marched to the siege of Boston. Determined to aid his country during the Revolutionary War, Potts was sent in 1776 by the Continental Congress to a military hospital in upper New York, organized for the Canadian campaign of the Continental army. Later that year Potts supervised infirmaries established in Philadelphia for the casualties of General George Washington's army retreating from the Hudson to the Delaware. Potts again volunteered to serve under Washington in December 1776, and participated in the decisive victory at Princeton. In 1777 Potts directed hospital services at Fort Ticonderoga, and that autumn he won the praise of General Horatio Gates for his skillful handling of casualties at the battle of Saratoga. Appointed in 1778 as Purveyor for army hospitals at Valley Forge, Potts acquired a reputation as a humane and conscientious medical administrator.

Because of physicians such as Potts, a gradual improvement in medical care for the Continental army occurred by 1780—in hospital organization, in the control of contagious diseases, and in the enforcement of sanitary standards for the rank and file. A study of Potts's career reveals the obstacles that confronted army doctors on bloody battlefields and in pestilential hospital wards, and it indicates that the protection of the soldier's health was a vital factor in the successful conduct of military operations. Jonathan Potts epitomizes the accomplishments of American doctors in military medicine during the Revolutionary War.

Jonathan Potts was born on April 11, 1745, at Popodickon, Colebrookdale, in the future Berks County, Pennsylvania.[1] John Potts, his Quaker father, was a wealthy ironmaster. Ruth Savage Potts, his Quaker mother, was also a member of an iron-making family. John Potts had inherited a flourishing frontier enterprise of mines, forges, farms, furnaces, and a vast wilderness acreage, which he successfully enlarged to become a leading entrepreneur of the colony. The iron industry in colonial America resembled large-scale agricultural activity. Furnaces dotted the countryside, where ore, wood, limestone, and waterpower were available. The typical "iron plantation" was relatively self-sufficient, remotely situated, employed scores of workers, and required thousands of forested tracts to feed its hungry furnaces. Pig iron produced in the Potts furnaces was converted to bar iron at local forges, from where it was shipped eastward for further processing in Philadelphia.[2]

In 1752 John Potts moved his large family to Pottsgrove Manor, their new home. The spacious three-storied house at the junction of the Manatawny Creek and the Schuylkill River was an architectural masterpiece for rural Pennsylvania. The edifice had a sandstone exterior, walls two feet thick, and an impressive Georgian interior featured by corner cupboards, cushioned window seats, and a large central hallway. The mansion was tastefully furnished with imported carpets, intricate wood panelings, Philadelphia Chippendale furniture, an eight-day clock, and an array of china and silver that dazzled envious visitors.[3]

John Potts was a Justice of the Peace, a contributor to the Pennsylvania Hospital, an original member of the Library Company founded by Benjamin Franklin, and a supporter of Franklin's political party in the Assembly. A man of power and influence, Potts symbolized an English country squire who furnished his domicile with an elegance that matched Philadelphia's stately mansions. With slaves and indentured servants toiling on his estates, John Potts surveyed his domain from his imposing home on the hill overlooking the Great Road leading thirty-six miles to the Delaware. In addition to his extensive mining and forging interests, Potts owned sawmills, gristmills, breweries, and huge stretches of timber. As the merchant, banker, and real estate broker for the area, he virtually dominated the economy of the Manatawny region. The village of Pottsgrove (the future Pottstown) was a "company town" with a store, a tavern, churches, and nearby farms, livestock, and orchards. In such an environment Jonathan, his four sisters, and eight brothers were raised in comfortable circumstances and were destined for prominence in American society.

The shrewd John Potts realized that his community would remain small and isolated unless he attracted more settlers. The Penns, the proprietors of the colony, had demonstrated the commercial success of their new towns, such as Easton, Carlisle, and especially Reading. In order to capitalize on the lucrative trade of the expanding farmlands, other ambitious developers were founding new communities away from Philadelphia's economic orbit. Potts hoped that his hamlet could become a prosperous trading center and a convenient stopover for travelers. To encourage newcomers, he had sites surveyed in the standard gridiron fashion that shaped Pennsylvanian towns into squares, and he staked out a wide main street flanked by rows of lots of potential householders. Leasing plots to his relatives, to his workers, and to immigrants, Potts organized the first town in the future

Montgomery County. Under his terms, leasees were required to build houses within two years, or they would forfeit their property rights. Like the typical townbuilder, Potts kept a few lots for himself and collected rents from others; he also donated some land for the welfare of the community.[4]

To promote his project, he deeded property in 1753 to the Society of Friends. A decade later he donated another plot to German settlers in the area who sought to build their own church. Reverend Henry Melchior Muhlenberg, the patriarch of Lutheranism in America, visited Pottsgrove in August 1764 to confer with the ironmaster about this parish. "Since there is an exceedingly large number of German Protestants who live within a circle of several miles of the place," Muhlenberg noted, "it is true that a very large congregation could be gathered here."[5] By 1769 Pottsgrove had another place of worhsip for members of the German Reformed Church. Potts also built an inn, a schoolhouse, and a general store; he even provided a ferry for passengers crossing the river. Regardless of Potts's energy and his village's advantageous location, Pottsgrove grew slowly. Only nine houses were contructed by 1764, and only fifteen by 1768; by 1775 Pottsgrove had only twenty houses, and a population of about two hundred. It was Reading, sixteen miles to the west, and not Pottsgrove, that became a thriving town for Pennsylvania's back country.

Only a broad outline of Jonathan's rearing at Pottsgrove is known, and school records of his boyhood are not available. The settlement had meager educational resources; Jonathan's parents apparently had few intellectual interests; no church-related or community school existed in the immediate vicinity during his youth; and it was difficult to attract capable schoolmasters to remote areas. Quaker John Potts would have wanted his children literate in order to comprehend the Bible and his sons capable of managing aspects of his burgeoning enterprises. In 1745 he began to hire tutors for his brood. In that year one Thomas Pulter received £25 yearly for his task; in 1747–1748 other schoolmasters taught some of the young Pottses. By 1757 John Potts entered his sons David and Joseph in a boarding school, but details about such arrangements for some of the other sons do not exist.[6] Fortunately for Jonathan, a level of schooling obviously superior to the instruction of itinerant schoomasters was available at Ephrata, twenty-seven miles to the west of Pottsgrove.

Founded in 1732 by German exiles from the Rhenish Palatinate, the Seventh Day Baptists at Ephrata Cloister practiced an ascetic, communal way of life, and like Quakers they were pacifists and were opposed to judicial oaths. Flourishing in William Penn's "Holy Experiment," this virtually self-sufficient community of three hundred inhabitants stressed ideals of asceticism and religious contemplation. Ephrata had high intellectual attainments. In 1738 a remarkable book of German hymns was printed at the Cloister, and in 1743 the Brethren produced the Great German Bible, the first non-English Bible published in North America. Thereafter the press produced a stream of hymnals, religious tracts, and a series of illuminated manuscripts, the Cloister's most remarkable artistic accomplishment. Ephrata had several schools—for adults, for children of the congregation, for poor younsters of the area—and a Classical Academy for older students. Perhaps Jonathan learned his alphabet in schoolmaster Ludwig Hocker's primary school and from the Cloister's own *Christian ABC Book,* designed to inculcate religious principles in youths. Jonathan may have even attended the Academy, a secondary-level boarding school that attracted pupils from Baltimore, Germantown, and Philadelphia, and which offered Latin and mathematics in the curriculum.[7] Proud of the Teutonic background from his father's Anglo-German heritage and his own schooling, Jonathan Potts would one day address his German patients in Pennsylvania, declaring: 'I am German by birth and education."[8]

Luckily for Jonathan and his brothers, their father had the vision and the means to send them (for indeterminable periods) to the prestigious Academy in Philadelphia, where Quaker grandees enrolled their sons. Started in 1751 under Franklin's inspiration, the nonsectarian Academy soon had

150 students in its Charity School, its English School—where practical subjects were offered for business careers—and in its Latin School—where the classics were taught in preparation for the professions. Under Provost William Smith, the classical curriculum dominated. Jonathan probably obtained instruction in rhetoric, history, politics, literature, natural philosophy (physics), mathematics, and French. Because of Smith's dedication to science, the Academy stressed such courses in the three-year curriculum far more than any comparable institution of learning in America. Unquestionably, John Morgan (1735–1789), a member of the first graduating class of the College of Philadelphia, acquired sound instruction in botany, biology, and chemistry, which prepared him for the vigorous training at the University of Edinburgh.

Why Jonathan decided to study medicine is conjectural. Five of his six surviving brothers joined their father's business or entered mercantile firms in Philadelphia; only John Potts, Jr., followed the professional career of a lawyer, and Jonathan that of a doctor. Jonathan could have been inclined to study medicine due to many factors; one influence may have been the family physician, Dr. Phineas Bond (1717–1773). One of Philadelphia's leading doctors and the younger brother of the more famous Dr. Thomas Bond, Phineas, an ex-Quaker from Maryland, had studied medicine in five European cities, and in 1743 joined his brother in partnership. The Bonds had a thriving practice, and they were active in civic affairs. In public health matters, for example, they examined shiploads of immigrants from Europe for cases of "Palatine fever," isolating them if necessary at the pesthouse on Fisher's Island in the Delaware.[9] The busy brothers were involved in numerous philanthropic activities. Phineas was a staff member of the Pennsylvania Hospital, a trustee of the Academy, and a founder of the American Philosophical Society. Typical of the broad interests of Philadelphia's leading doctors, he contributed to a medical library, belonged to an immigrant-aid society, and was a stockholder in Benjamin Franklin's Hand-in-Hand Fire Insurance Company.[10] The Bonds had a lucrative practice, and many city notables were among their patients—Franklin, Joseph Galloway, Benjamin Chew, Samuel Wharton, Samuel Rhoads, and Francis Richardson.[11] Apparently Phineas was a very affable man, who lived in the shadow of his renowned brother. As Dr. Casper Wistar wrote about Phineas Bond in 1818, "No medical man in Pennsylvania ever left behind him a higher character for professional assistance and amiable qualities of the heart."[12] Perhaps it was during visits to Dr. Bond's office that Jonathan decided to study medicine under this kindly gentleman.

Superior master-doctors who would supervise young men in medical instruction were rare in the colonies, and parents paid high fees to secure the admission of their sons as apprentices to a physician's household. Jonathan probably began his five-year apprenticeship with Bond in 1761, at the age of sixteen. The agreement between a preceptor and his pupil was a business arrangment similar to apprenticeship agreements in printing, carpentry, or blacksmithing. For about £100, the preceptor agreed to teach his pupil the art and mystery of his craft. Along with medical instruction, the master provided his assistant with bed, board, and clothing. As the typical indenture for an apprentice specified: "He shall not commit Fornication, nor contract matrimony, within the said Term. At Cards, Dice, or any unlawful Game he shall not play, . . . He shall not absent himself Day or Night from his said Master's Service. . ., nor Haunt ale-Houses or Play-Houses."[13]

The typical medical apprentice performed numerous menial tasks from dawn through candlelight. He was required to cut wood, build fires, run errands, collect fees, deliver medicine, brush his master's coat, tend his horse and carriage, sweep the consulting room, cultivate the herb garden, and carry the lantern on night calls. Jonathan also cared for Bond's surgical instruments and his apothecary equipment. Much of his time was spent as a druggist's assistant at the Bond's apothecary shop on Second Street at the Sign of the Golden Mortar.[14] Jonathan worked there with pestle and mortar to pulverize drugs and to prepare them as pills or powders. As part of his apothecary's training, he crushed dried herbs, roots, and bark; he spread plaster, boiled syrup, and prepared lotions, salves, and ointments. Jonathan was also required to cut splints, to make bandages out of old sheets, and to cleanse vials, bottles, sieves, and sponges. And if the doctor's wife insisted, he also served as butler for his master's social affairs.

Jonathan listened to his master prescribe in the office; and after he acquired the rudiments of medical lore, he probably accompanied Dr. Bond as an orderly to assist in minor surgery, in lancing abscesses, in reducing fractures, and in assisting in the bleeding of patients. Later he could be entrusted to pull teeth, to dress wounds, and to assist in complicated surgical operations. If Jonathan were fortunate, his master may have had a skeleton or an anatomical chart in his office for young Potts to study; perhaps he even witnessed the occasional dissection of a cadaver.

Somehow during this toil an apprentice found time to read the medical classics, to improve his knowledge of Latin, to pore over lecture notes taken by his preceptor at a university, and to copy letters—written by his master in his consultations with colleagues—into an elementary clinical case book.[15] Near the end of his training, he would be entrusted with more responsibilities—handling the account book, visiting patients at home and in the hospital, and performing minor surgery without immediate supervision. Such training was both grueling and exhilarating to Benjamin Rush, a distant cousin of Jonathan's. Rush, a graduate of the College of New Jersey (Princeton) and an apprentice of Dr. John Redman, commented that during his apprenticeship:

> I was absent from his business but eleven days, and never spent more than three evenings out of his house.... In addition to preparing and compounding medicines, visiting the sick, and performing many little services of a nurse to them, I took exclusive charge of his books and accounts.... I read in the intervals of my business and at late and early hours, all the books on medicine that were put into my hand by my master or that I could borrow from other students of medicine in the city.... I kept a commonplace book in

An Apprenticeship in Philadelphia

which I recorded every thing I thought curious or valuable in my reading in my master's practice.[16]

At the conclusion of a successful apprenticeship, the preceptor provided his helper with a small medical library, a pocket set of instruments, and a statement of service and proficiency. This certificate was registered in a court of record to attest that the apprentice was qualified to practice medicine and pharmacy. Yet defects in such training were inevitable, because standards of apprenticeships varied considerably. If the preceptor had been well instructed himself, if he possessed a university degree, and if he had a sincere interest in improving health services, then the results of the apprenticeship may have been beneficial to the public. But inasmuch as many preceptors were poorly educated products of the same system, most apprenticeship training was erratic and haphazard. Few apprentices read the basic medical literature. Very few studied specimens or anatomical plates, and many had never even witnessed a dissection. Even if the preceptor had a genuine concern for upgrading standards, his efforts were invariably thwarted by limitations on his time, the sparseness of his library, the lack of equipment to teach anatomy and physiology, and the fact that he rarely possessed the broad theoretical and practical exposure to medicine provided by a university faculty. Many preceptors regarded their apprentices less as a means of improving the level of medical care than as a means of additional income and as a source of cheap labor.

Yet Potts was not the typical apprentice; he had been trained under a university-bred physician, and he was fortunate to be in Philadelphia, a city which offered ample cultural and educational opportunities for aspiring doctors. Inhabited by diverse ethnic, religious, and nationality groups, Philadelphia was becoming the third largest city in the British empire; and as the fastest growing city in North America, it was already the financial and commercial leader of the colonies. The main harbor on the seacoast for boatloads of Irish, Scotch-Irish, and Germans pouring into the land, the metropolis not

9

only dominated the Delaware Valley, but also embraced eastern Pennsylvania, western New Jersey, northern Maryland, and much of Delaware, which together comprised one of the richest agricultural areas in the Atlantic world. Philadelphia was the busiest port on the coast, and its two miles of wharves jutting out into the river accommodated hundreds of ships that plied the waters of America, the Caribbean, and the North Atlantic. Philadelphia's hegemony in maritime trade was based on its propinquity to fertile farm country spreading in all directions which provided its merchants with ore, furs, flour, meat, grain for export and for provincial distribution. A boom was under way in the 1760s (3,000 houses were counted in 1760; 4,500 in 1769; 5,400 in 1775) as the City of Brotherly Love became the throbbing center for the processing of farm, mineral, and forest products through an industrial base of sawmills, paper mills, breweries, iron foundries, and tanning, hardware, furniture, and cooperage establishments.

Because of its size, location, economic advantages, and ethnic diversity, the Quaker City was also the cultural leader of the colonies. In the arts, the sciences, and humanitarian causes, Philadelphia had a lively cosmopolitan life; it supported lending libraries, literary clubs, and scientific societies. Mirroring the intellectual excitement of the European Enlightenment, Philadelphia's elite were familiar with names such as Bacon, Newton, and Harvey. They could boast that their own city had men of letters who were part of the international scientific community. The aged John Kearsley was a physicist, an astronomer, and a botanist, who contributed scholarly articles to learned European journals. John Morgan was a member of the Royal Society of London and the London College of Physicians. Benjamin Franklin had been awarded honorary degrees from Oxford, Yale, and Harvard for his achievements in electricity. John Bartram, the famed botanist, was renowned for his encyclopedic knowledge of American natural history; and David Rittenhouse was famous for his contributions in physics and astronomy. Philadelphia was foremost on the continent in advanced technical skills—printing, engraving, clockmaking—and in the manu-

An Apprenticeship in Philadelphia

facture of precision instruments. Philadelphia was a city increasingly more receptive to the secular, rational, scientific approach to knowledge, and it was an exciting place for ambitious and inquisitive youth.

In medicine, Philadelphia's accomplishments were impressive. Out of thirty known city practitioners in the 1760s, at least eight had European training, and twelve made significant contributions to their fields. From 1753 to 1777, over thirty publications on medical subjects (articles, reprints of English medical works, newspaper essays, dissertations) appeared in local presses. Although most of the works concerned the treatment of smallpox, Philadelphia physicians commented about malaria, scrofula, hives, throat distemper, lead poisoning, and the use of electricity in therapeutics. Philadelphia was proud of its medical men. Boasting a fine hospital, a medical society, a medical library, and an expanding list of publications, doctors in Philadelphia were developing a sense of pride as they strove to raise standards of their occupation. On the eve of the Revolution, medicine in the metropolis was acquiring the dignity of a profession.[17] Although it is difficult to determine how much Potts assimilated from this intellectual ferment, additional opportunities to learn about medicine were available in private anatomical classes, unique for the colonies, and in the first voluntary hospital in America, the Pennsylvania Hospital.

Potts was probably among the twelve students who attended anatomical lectures that began November 1762 in the chambers of Dr. William Shippen, Jr. (1738–1808).[18] A graduate of Edinburgh, with additional surgical and obstetrical training in London, Shippen had just returned from Europe, married the socially prominent Alice Lee of Virginia, and opened his practice in Philadelphia. During his course of instruction he dissected the corpses of suicides and executed criminals, and he utilized "visual aids" sent from London—a skeleton, specimens, and illustrations—to amplify his lectures. The notebook of Jonathan Elmer, a member of that class, demonstrates that Shippen offered a systematic description of the human body and of the functioning of its organs. In the first lecture, devoted to definitions, the student-apprentices were informed that the human body was "a complex hydraulic machine," that without a knowledge of anatomy, "physicians and surgeons cannot do justice to the world in their profession," and that a study of anatomy would protect them from atheism. In the second lecture, Shippen explained the chemical properties of the blood. The final part of the sixty-lecture series concerned amputations. Shippen declared that "an amputation is sometimes necessary, but not, nearly so often as has been thought, though all agree that it is necessary in a Mortification...."[19]

In January 1765 the versatile Shippen advertised a new course of twenty lectures on obstetrics and prenatal care. His instruction, the first in North America on this subject, prepared medical men to replace midwives in the management of complicated cases. Regardless of the popular abhorrence of dissections, suspicions by the citizenry that graves were being robbed for human material, and the novelty of classroom lectures about pregnancy, Shippen's private school was a success. His courses constituted the first regularly organized teaching of medical subjects in the American colonies. John Adams, the observant Bostonian, visited Philadelphia in 1774 and remarked that Shippen invited him to his chambers. "Here was a great variety of views of the human body, whole and in parts," remarked Adams. "The Dr. entertained us with a very clear, concise and comprehensive lecture upon all the Parts of the human frame."[20] Shippen proceeded even further in his pioneering work; he contemplated organizing a faculty for bedside teaching in the Pennsylvania Hospital such as he had witnessed in London hospitals. But it is unclear if he planned to link medical teaching with the College of Philadelphia into a medical school with formal university connections. Although Shippen was quite capable of imaginative work, he was not a skillful organizer, and he may have been waiting for John Morgan, his more energetic and flamboyant colleague, to return from Europe.

Shippen and Morgan had pursued the same training in Britain only a few years apart, and in Scotland they had con-

An Apprenticeship in Philadelphia

sidered the possibilities of establishing a medical school in the Quaker City. Dr. John Fothergill of London, a Quaker deeply interested in the progress of the colony, discussed the matter with Shippen in 1758 and with Morgan in 1760. The time was ripe for such an undertaking, Fothergill suggested in 1762 to James Pemberton, a prominent Philadelphian. While Shippen was developing his lectures at home, Morgan completed his studies in Europe. After making the grand tour of the Continent, holding discussions with illustrious scientists, and winning the acclaim of his colleagues abroad, Morgan returned home in May 1765.[21] Soon thereafter he offered private instruction to twelve students on the theory and practice of medicine. John Archer, Morgan's busy apprentice, was in this class and wrote to his wife: "I am daily at Dr. Morgan's shop and Monday, Wednesday, and Friday attend his lectures—the course is four Pistoles [£3, 8 shillings], and a dollar. Tuesday, Thursday, and Saturday at Dr. Shippen's— the course, six, Pistoles."[22] Archer recorded that Morgan stated in his lectures that "Nature is the Physician and we only her Assistants waiting with diligence to embrace her Indications, to strengthen her when weak, to correct her when too violent and even to shew her the most salutary way . . ., that Death may be disappointed pro tempore, and the Sick restored to health and Vigor again." During his instruction on the diagnoses of diseases, Morgan stated that diseases were as numerous "as Men and Beasts which are not, nor never will be full known." In his lecture on the pathogenesis of fever, Morgan again stressed nature's powers and the limited scope of medical knowledge. "When we consider the various Mechanisms of the human body, as far as the Researches of the most able and imaginative Physiologists can penetrate, there still remain wonders to him unknown." Scientists knew very little about bodily functions, he admitted, "for there is a World of Contemplative Mysteries in it, that are beyond the reach of human Understanding. Nature is mysterious, tho' her Laws are regular: she is most rational altho' we do not understand her."[23]

While teaching, Morgan promoted his plans for a medical

school to be formally linked to the College of Philadelphia. Snubbing Shippen in the sponsorship, Morgan won the support of Thomas Penn, the colony's proprietor, and of the Trustees of the College. On May 3, 1765, he was appointed professor of the theory and practice of medicine, and on May 30–31 he read his lengthy discourse on the proposed medical school. He urged the appointment of a qualified faculty, affiliation with a university, sound academic preparation by applicants for the training, a planned and graded curriculum, close cooperation with a teaching hospital, high standards for graduation, and chairs of anatomy, chemistry, materia medica, and the theory and practice of medicine. In his speech he did not mention the need for a dissecting room or for a chemical laboratory. Nor did he advocate academic positions in surgery, midwifery, or pharmacy, indicating, thereby, the lingering inferiority that surgery was held in Europe and that the apothecary's trade could be learned through a mere apprenticeship. Although deeply hurt by Morgan's failure to consult him about the grand project, Shippen applied to the trustees for a teaching post in the new institution, a request that was soon granted. But in the process he antagonized Morgan. As Morgan explained the situation about the appointments:

> I was already elected Professor of the Theory and Practice of Physic, and recommended Dr. Shippen to the Trustees to the Professorship of Anatomy, and he was choosen to fill that place. Depending upon the influence he supposed he had among the Trustees, to degrade me from my rank as eldest professor which he attempted to claim, and to usurp a precedence over me, he made the attempt but was foiled in it ... Nothing but his envy then produced a contest for preeminence, which he called a misunderstanding.[24]

Thus the new medical school was under way in December 1765 with its two proud and contentious professors. The dispute by Morgan and Shippen over the academic appointments

An Apprenticeship in Philadelphia

left a bitter legacy, as the two doctors became intense rivals for prestige.

The first session of formal instruction began with ten students. Shippen lectured on anatomy and surgery; Morgan on materia medica and pharmacology. Morgan's second year of lectures covered chemistry and the theory of practice of medicine. For two years Morgan and Shippen comprised the entire faculty of the embryonic medical school. Although the curriculum was inferior in scope to that of prestigious European universities which offered medical training, it was a definite improvement over the typical education for apprentices in America.

The classroom lectures of these two men were supplemented by the hospital teaching of Dr. Thomas Bond, whose course in clinical medicine became an integral part of the program of medical education at the college. Bond was one of the foremost physicians of the day and, with Franklin, was one of the prime founders of the Pennsylvania Hospital.[25] In 1752 he accomplished the first amputation in the hospital by removing the leg of Susannah Bromholt, and in 1756 he performed the first recorded lithotomy in the colonies. Bond believed that the typical medical lectures were insufficient preparation for potential doctors, so he initiated special instruction for students by permitting them to accompany him through the wards as he examined patients, and he thereby offered the first clinical instruction in North America. Morgan and Shippen appreciated the value of Bond's methods and persuaded the trustees to include his instruction as part of the students' practical training. By December 1766 Bond's course was incorporated into the curriculum. Describing the importance of bedside teaching, Bond declared in a famous speech that "Infirmaries [were] the Grand Theaters of Medical knowledge. There the Clinical Person comes into the Aid of Speculation and demonstrates the Truth of Theory by Facts . . ." Bond stated that he informed students of his diagnosis and prognosis of a case, and the medical authorities upon which he relied for information. But "if the Disease baffles the power of Art," he admitted, and the patient died, then Bond demonstrated what he termed his "error," by "exposing all the Morbid parts to view, . . . and by what means it produced death . . ."[26]

Before Bond's course formally became part of the curriculum of the college, Potts was attending the Pennsylvania Hospital as a student apprentice. The hospital was the best example in the colonies of a civic undertaking financed partly by appropriations from the Assembly and partly by private contributions. Heretofore, hospitals in America had multiple functions as workhouses, as houses of correction, and as places to cure the poor sick; but the Pennsylvania Hospital was the first permanent public general hospital on the continent. Opening in 1752 in a coverted house, by 1756 the institution was located in a new brick structure at 8th and Pine Streets. An east wing and a center hall—part of a larger complex eventually completed by 1804—were available in Potts's day. Originally intended for the insane, for paupers, and for sick strangers, private patients could be treated in private rooms by any surgeon or physician they selected. Male patients were quartered on the first floor; women on the second; and lunatics in the basement. The 130-bed hospital was an impressive institution. The building had the best bathing, heating, sanitary, and ventilating facilities of any edifice in North America; it also contained a museum, an apothecary shop, and by 1768 a laboratory.[27]

The hospital may have educated the local public in hygienic matters, and it may have undermined the popular reliance on quacks and faith healers. For doctors, the great advantage of the institution was that for the first time in North America they could discern, under one roof, varieties of the same disease. With ample human material available (some 6,600 medical and surgical cases were treated by 1775),[28] physicians could watch the progress of a disease from its inception to death, and they could inspect corpses for lesions. This opportunity for unsurpassed clinical observation signified that medical training was more complex than the

An Apprenticeship in Philadelphia

mere memorization of authoritative texts, and that physicians could experiment by varying the treatments.

How effective was this model hospital in curing patients? As a conscious imitation of the British voluntary hospital of the eighteenth century, it was designed to treat the sick-poor suffering from curable, noncontagious diseases. Occasional criticisms of the hospital administration occurred, but because of the paucity of evidence, the relative efficiency of the institution is difficult to determine. For example, it did not admit terminal cases or patients with infectious diseases. Impressed with the hospital's elegant exterior, Dr. Robert Honyman, a Scot visiting the colony, nevertheless remarked on March 7, 1775, that the wards were very crowded and that a stench pervaded the corridors "that renders it insuperable even to me, who had been pretty much used to such places."[29] Adams had toured the hospital the previous year and remarked:

> We saw, in the lower Room under Ground, the Cells of Lunatics, a Number of them, some furious, some merry, some Melancholy, ... We then went into the Sick Rooms which are very long, large Walks with rows of Beds on each side, and the lame and sick upon them—a dreadful Scene of human Wretchedness. The Weakness and Languor, the Distress and Misery, of these Objects is truly Woefull Sight.[30]

One clue to the deplorable conditions is the mortality rate in the hospital. From 1753 to 1772, about 12 percent of the patients died, a figure that can be very roughly compared to the rate of 6 percent to 13 percent of admitted patients in British hospitals for that era.[31] Thus, in the best hospital in North America, with rigid restrictions on the types of patients admitted, a large proportion of them perished.

For a fee of £8.2s. (used to purchase library books) and with a preceptor's letter of recommendation, some students were permitted to attend the hospital. In late December 1765 Potts, Rush, and three other students were authorized by the

Board of Managers to accompany staff physicians on their rounds.³² Hospital students sometimes acted as "dressers," but normally they observed the therapy and bedside manner of their preceptor and his colleagues. Rush mentioned that he was privileged to watch six physicians at work while in hospital training. Few occasions for postmortems occurred, and when students had an opportunity to examine a cadaver, they seized it. On April 22, 1766, one of Dr. Thomas Bond's patients died in the hospital, and young Archer remarked that after Bond's prognosis, "a Desire of Improvement excited the attending students, to have the body opened, which was accordingly done . . ."³³ Sometimes, students amused themselves with corpses in the dissecting room. Hence, a stern warning came from the managers, sensitive to public criticism, that "as the indecent conduct of some young Surgeons upon dissecting dead bodies, occasioned a general uneasiness and fear in the minds of all human people, the Managers desire the concurrence of the Physicians in remedying this evil . . ."³⁴

During his hospital training, Jonathan Potts witnessed the treatment of maladies on a far wider scale than he had in Phineas Bond's office or on house calls with his master. Over 450 patients were treated at the hospital in 1766 for numerous afflictions—cancer, gallstones, ruptures, eye infections, palsy, lunacy, "scorbutic ulcers," venereal diseases, "drunken madness," and other sicknesses. Forty-two of this number died, eight "escaped," 113 remained at the year's end, and the rest were discharged.³⁵

By the summer of 1766 Potts had acquired a grounding in the liberal arts and preparation in the essentials of medicine. The lectures he attended and the textbooks he mastered provided him with a broad philosophical approach to medicine. The time spent in the wards and at the hospital demonstrations provided him with clinical and surgical experience. Without the possibility of anesthetic control and without a knowledge of antiseptics, no physician dared to probe body cavities. But Potts had ample opportunities to assist in ampu-

An Apprenticeship in Philadelphia

tations, in repairing hernias, in cutting for stone, and in removing external tumors.

Potts could have terminated his medical training when his apprenticeship was completed; his professional education was far superior to that of most American practitioners. Many so-called "doctors" had little formal education; they had not attended medical lectures, nor did they have clinical experience. In an era when licensing of health services was not required, when North American colleges had yet to confer medical degrees, when little regulatory legislation in medicine existed, it was easy for quacks, the ill-trained, and especially for crude former apprentices to advertise themselves as qualified to a gullible public anxious for cures. Potts and Rush, the recipients of the best medical training available in America, were adventuresome youths, and they desired advanced training, additional scientific background, and other cultural opportunities not available at the fledgling medical school in Philadelphia. They sought a European university that offered a regular course of study in medicine, and one that would grant the diploma of M.D. to certify to their professional talents. Potts and Rush looked across the Atlantic to Edinburgh University.

II.

A Term in Edinburgh

The path over the Atlantic to Europe for medical students had been charted by Morgan, Shippen, Redman, the Bonds, and other Philadelphia physicians who had received their advanced training at Paris, Rheims, Leyden, or Edinburgh. Dr. William Shippen, Sr., remarked that William Shippen, Jr., his son, had an American college degree, that William, Jr., had studied medicine under his own supervision, and that the youth had frequently witnessed the work of eminent colleagues. "But for want of that variety of operations and those frequent dissections which are common in older countries," the elder Shippen explained, "I must send him to Europe. His scheme is to gain all the knowledge he can in anatomy, physiology, and surgery."[1]

For traditional classroom instruction, Edinburgh had the greatest attraction for American medical students. Since 1730 its medical curriculum had been revised by a famous faculty trained in Leyden by Herman Boerhaave (1668–1738), the greatest teacher of medicine of the century. Edinburgh, the "Athens of the North," was a lively cosmopolitan center, and medicine was taught there at a level higher than that at any other European institution. The study of medicine was virtually stagnant at Oxford and at Cambridge, where students began their study of physic only after completing seven expensive years of a classical curriculum. Because of a common citizenship for British colonials, no language difficulties, and the preeminence of the northern capital as a fountainhead of ideas, Americans tended to matriculate at Edinburgh. In 1749 John Moultrie of South Carolina earned his diploma there; by 1800 over one hundred Americans graduated from Edinburgh with the medical degree, and perhaps another one hundred studied there for brief periods. By 1771, of the thirty-three Americans who held the prized Edinburgh degree, nine were Pennsylvanians. For a Quaker such as Potts (Rush was a Presbyterian), Edinburgh offered an additional advantage, because the Test Act, which barred dissenters from matriculating at English colleges, was not enforced in Scotland. With a medical degree from the Scot university, which required three years of study and a thesis written in Latin, Potts and Rush realized that they would possess an enviable academic distinction that would guarantee their professional success.[2]

The theoretical study in Edinburgh's lecture halls was usually concluded with, or proceeded by, shorter periods of practical work in London, where at the four hospitals of the metropolis students could "walk the wards" with a physician or surgeon. Thomas Ruston, a Philadelphian, paid his fee in 1763 for the privilege of observing in St. Thomas's Hospital, "where I have an opportunity of seeing a great variety of cases treated by the different physicians, and many operations in surgery."[3] Along with these teaching hospitals were the private schools of anatomy, surgery, and midwifery, at which students attended clinical lectures and where they learned technical procedures relatively unknown in America. While in London the budding physicians usually observed the demonstrations of William Hunter, the foremost anatomist of the day, at his chambers at Covent Garden, or they studied the obstetrical techniques of Dr. Colin McKenzie, the famed man midwife at his "lying-in" hospital on Crucifix Lane. Like Morgan and Shippen, they might be invited to hear the renowned Sir John Pringle, who would expound on principles of military hygiene he had acquired during the Seven Years War. To cap off their experiences in Britain, affluent Ameri-

A Term in Edinburgh

cans made the grand tour of the Continent to call on luminaries of the Enlightenment such as Voltaire and Morgagni, who would stimulate their impressionable minds. Their education and European travel completed, the young colonials then returned home as polished, sophisticated physicians eager to open lucrative urban practices.

With recommendations from their preceptors, professors, and other influential countrymen, Potts and Rush prepared for the great adventure. Just before he departed for England in the summer of 1766, Potts made a decision that significantly altered his career. Now twenty-one years old, Potts became engaged to Grace Richardson (born February 6, 1745), a daughter of Francis and Mary Richardson. She was a Quaker from Chester, a granddaughter of George Fitzpatrick, the famous Pennsylvania preacher, and the niece of Joseph Richardson, Philadelphia's noted goldsmith.[4] Grace promised to wait for her fiancé until he returned from overseas with the coveted medical degree.

Their farewells made and their trunks packed, Potts and Rush sailed for Liverpool on August 31 aboard the *Friendship*.[5] As Potts described the momentous event on the first page of his small journal: "I was accompanied by a great number of my Friends. We purchased our stock at Reedy Island [twelve miles below Wilmington] and left the [Delaware] Capes that evening."[6] While contemplating the splendid undertaking before them, the young men were naturally apprehensive about the dangerous Atlantic crossing. One ship on which a Philadelphia student was sailing had been captured by pirates, and he spent a prolonged captivity on Hispaniola before he could resume his trip to Europe. On a vessel to Portsmouth, another medical student was captured off Cornwall by French privateers, and he was held at Bayonne for months before being released. Young Shippen's storm-wracked frigate nearly ran out of food at sea; its passengers and crew survived on water and salted meat before eventually docking at Belfast. For Potts and Rush the worry was not pirates or provisions, but the fear of seasickness. Writing to a friend on September 2 from Cape Henlopen, where letters were dropped to a pilot boat, Rush commented "The Bay is rough, and the bellows swell considerably but have as yet produced no seasickness in my stomach. But oh! I dread tomorrow!"[7] Early on the voyage, Potts became very ill. Explaining that his malady was caused "by motion of the Intestines occasioned by the motion of the ship," he added that "I was excessively sick but was treated with the greatest compassion and tenderness by my good friend . . . Mr. Benjamin Rush."[8]

The vessel encountered such violent storms on the Atlantic that the youths were terrified. On September 19 Rush remarked that "the seas raged and roared in a most terrible manner . . . Nothing would equal ye terror [that] was impressed upon my mind. All the idea I have ever formed of a storm at sea were far short of what my Eyes now beheld."[9] And in a graphic passage Potts also decribed the sheer panic that he experienced: "The Gales were so violent and we could not carry a Rag or Sail but lay too [sic] under our bear [sic] Poles expecting every moment would be our last as the Sea broke all over."[10] As huge waves inundated the frail craft, Potts recorded that "we cried out to ye Lord in our distress and he delivered us out of our trouble." In a letter written to his brother Joseph after the voyage, Jonathan pondered his "wonderful deliverance," and believed that a Divine hand had saved him. "It is to Him alone," he declared with a new-found religious fervor that "I look for succor."[11]

After a perilous sailing along the treacherous Irish shoreline and a near shipwreck at Holyhead off the coast of Wales, the battered *Friendship* arrived at Liverpool on October 21. After fifty-one days on storm-tossed seas, a companion on the voyage, James Cummins, a young Scot merchant from the West Indies, was so ill that he died from the ordeal. But Potts and Rush soon recuperated. The two spent a busy week touring the bustling port; they visited the dockyards, the infirmary, the charity school, the salt works, the glass and china factories. Liverpool's notorious slave ships anchored in the harbor symbolized for Rush an "inhuman practice."[12]

A Term in Edinburgh

Needing an entree into local society, Potts, like American Quakers before him in England, ingratiated himself into a local Meeting that was part of the trans-Atlantic network of the Society of Friends that stretched over the ocean. Friends usually took a certificate from their home Meeting to present to Quaker circles in Britain; thus Quaker Charles Moore, who journeyed to Scotland from Philadelphia in 1748, was said to be "Religiously disposed . . . a diligent Attender of our Meetings for Worship . . ."[13] With a certificate from John Pemberton, the Clerk of the Philadelphia Yearly Meeting, Potts called upon John Scott, a Quaker merchant in Liverpool. The Englishman accompanied Potts to nearby Warrington in order to meet Samuel Fothergill, one of the most distinguished preachers of the era. On his trip through America in the 1750s, Fothergill had visited far-flung Quaker communities from Georgia to Massachusetts, and had many admirers in Pennsylvania. Widely acclaimed for his evangelical oratory, Fothergill was a major link in the hierarchy of Quakerdom. Potts attended the Meeting in Warrington, and stated that Fothergill "was very glad to see me and kindly promised to mention me to his Brother the Doctor. He preached a most Excellent Sermon upon the abuse of the Divine Manifestation of the will of God in ye Hearts of Men."[14] Anxious to assist the young colonial, Fothergill gave Potts a note to his brother in London, the famed Dr. John Fothergill, a well-known internist and botanist and the chief correspondent of the London Friends Yearly Meeting to the Philadelphia Yearly Meeting. Samuel Fothergill also provided Potts with another important contact—William Miller, a Scot businessman and the so-called "King of the Quakers" in Edinburgh.

Anxious to begin their studies, Potts and Rush left Liverpool by coach on October 31 for the trip northward. The companions traveled through Lancashire, Westmorland, and Cumberland without mishap, and they commented in their journals about quaint towns, grim castles, pleasant taverns, and the kindness of strangers. Potts was dismayed with his first impression of Scotland. After passing through a dreary area near Selkirk on November 4, he lamented that the countryside was "perhaps the most dismal in all the world, being nothing but Mountains and Rock in which the inhabitants are a kind of centaurs as Men and Brute live together."[15] At one isolated place on their journey, the young men spent the night in a dirty cottage. To avoid being pestered by insects, Rush remarked that they kept on their coats in bed. "But our precautions did not avail," Rush chuckled, "for poor Mr. Potts the next day enjoyed much the Royal pleasure of scratching himself."[16] Rush's statement probably accounts for Potts's notation that he had spent a sleepless night, and that he repented "ever entering the House at all."[17]

Arriving in Edinburgh on November 6, too late for the introductory lectures, Potts and Rush found lodgings together and presented themselves to prominent physicians of the city—Sir Alexander Dick, President of the Royal College of Physicians; William Cullen, the great medical oracle of Scotland, who inspired generations of students; David Clerk and Colin Drummond, physicians at the Royal Infirmary. Potts gave Dr. Dick a letter from John Morgan which stated that he had advised the young men to study at Edinburgh. Potts ("my particular friend") and Rush, stated Morgan, "did me the pleasure of attending my Lectures with an assiduity that marks out the progress they will undoubtedly make in Physic under the Tuition of some of the ablest Instructors in the World, the Professors at Edinburgh."[18]

To facilitate their way into the ranks of Edinburgh's intellectual elite, Potts and Rush had solicited influential Pennsylvanians to write on their behalf to Benjamin Franklin in London, where he had resided since 1764 as Agent for the Pennsylvania Assembly. Franklin had assisted so many of his young countrymen in Europe with loans, advice, and counsel that they were termed his "American children." Prominent Philadelphians, such as Samuel Wharton, the land magnate, Joseph Galloway, the Speaker of the Assembly and Franklin's close political adviser, and Charles Thomson, a former Latin master of the Academy and now a prosperous merchant, all communicated with Franklin to praise the talents of the two youths. But Franklin's all-important letters of introduction to his contacts in Edinburgh were delayed, and the young men became impatient. In late October Potts and Rush had written from Liverpool to request Franklin for assistance and to remind him, tactfully, how important his letters were to Americans in Europe.[19] By December 10 Franklin's messages had still not arrived, so Potts again wrote to the busy savant, stating "that as I am somewhat apprehensive you have not received these letters [from Philadelphia] I have taken the liberty to repeat my request, as I find since my arrival here that letters from you in our favour will be of infinite service to us."[20] But the wise Franklin, always solicitous about promising young Americans overseas, had already corresponded in December with Alexander Dick, William Cullen, and William Robertson, the noted historian and Principal of the University.[21] Moreover, Franklin offered some advice to his new protégés. Study hard, he urged, and "refrain from all idle, useless amusements, . . ." Explaining to the young Philadelphians that they were fortunate to study with such illustrious men, Franklin advised them:

> Be circumspect and regular in your behaviour at Edinburgh (where the People are very shrewd and observing) that you bring from thence as good a Character as you carry thither, and in that respect not be inferior to any American that has been there before you. You have great Advantages in going there to study at this Time, where there happens to be collected a Set of truely great men, . . . I recommend one thing particularly to you, that, besides the Study of Medicine, you endeavour to attain a thorough knowledge of Natural Philosophy in general . . . I mention this, because I have observed that a number of Physicians here [in Britain] as well as in America, are miserably prepared in it.[22]

Heeding Franklin's advice, the young men had already started their work. Although classes had commenced in late October, they were able to purchase tickets of admission. Their professors were Joseph Black in chemistry, John Hope in materia medica, Alexander Monro II in surgery and anatomy, and William Cullen in institutes of medicine (physiology and pathology).[23] These were the professors who had inspired hundreds of students at Edinburgh; these were the authors of books that became medical classics. Walter Jones, a Virginian, wrote home enthusiastically in November 1766 that Black, Cullen, and James Gregory (who taught the practice of medicine) "exceed each other in their several Departments, the great expectations the Public had formed of them."[24]

The social and institutional life of the 250 medical students was highly organized. The Americans spent their mornings listening to lectures (many delivered in Latin and at a rapid pace), and their afternoons and evenings devoted to revising their classroom notes. Classes began at eight in the morning and continued until seven in the evening, with an hour for lunch between three and four. Although not all students attended all classes, the typical workload was heavy. One student reported seven hours of lectures daily, and another claimed that he toiled eighteen hours every day. Although hospital training was not part of the formal instruction at the university, Potts and Rush attended clinical demonstrations at the Infirmary, and watched surgical operations in the hospital theater.

Potts and Rush were eager to bring luster to their homeland. As Arthur Lee of Virginia wrote in 1761, his countrymen were "in general well esteemed for their close application to their studies."[25] Perhaps more conscientious than the supposedly carefree Irishmen, and more gracious than some impoverished Scots, the Americans, as colonials, were somewhat self-conscious; and they felt obliged to excel and to prove their abilities. Whatever their nationality, however, Walter Jones categorized his classmates as the "fine gentlemen" with private incomes who rarely studied, a second group characterized by some breeding but who usually lacked funds for fees and books, and the "vulgar" who were "entirely devoid of everything polite." As the Virginian explained to his brother, struggling on his tidewater plantation at home to

A Term in Edinburgh

support him, the study of medicine was very expensive. Jones realized that he could not live like "the Fine Gentlemen . . . of Independent Fortune . . .," but with his brother's aid he hoped "to live genteely . . ." When he arrived in Edinburgh in August 1766, Jones claimed that to maintain that station in life he needed £100 yearly, but by May 1767, to his dismay, his actual expenses totaled over £140.[26] Regardless of their incomes, ambitious students tirelessly copied entire volumes of notes and reviewed the latest medical literature. In their quarters they dissected animals, and in the weekly meeting of the Virginia Club and the Medical Society they debated philosophical concepts, practiced their Latin, prepared for exams, and acquired poise and self-discipline.

Life was exciting for the Philadelphians. Writing to a Princeton classmate, Rush described the intellectual fascination of Edinburgh where "the theory of physic is like our dress always changing." Proclaiming that a revolution was under way in medicine, Rush exclaimed: "The old doctrines of the blood, nerves, etc. are now exploded, and much more rational ones are substituted in their room."[27] Likewise glorying in the exciting milieu of the northern capital, Potts wrote home in January 1767:

> I have been constantly employed in attending the college, where I daily receive new improvements in Medical knowledge, and hope to return to my native land to answer the expectations of all my Friends, with the character of a good physician, and what I prefer to everything else, the character of a good man.[28]

Along with his studies Potts discovered other aspects of Edinburgh life. If Potts appreciated the picturesque views of the walled city—the somber castle on its rocky heights, Arthur's Seat, Salisbury Crag—he neglected to mention them. Living in Edinburgh, a city with a population of 80,000 but with only one-third the area of Philadelphia, had its problems. The city was congested, its lanes were filthy, and sanitary arrangements were crude. Edinburgh had only two main thoroughfares, High Street and Cowgate, which connected with innumerable lanes, paths, and courts. To add to the usual dirt and stench of a congested metropolis, dwellers of high-storied tenements heaved out their nightly refuse to the streets below for the morning trash collection. Rush slyly remarked that unwary visitors walking at night sometimes gained the dubious distinction of being "naturalized" by the garbage heaped upon them. "As yet I have escaped . . ., but my unfortunate friend Potts has gained the honor before me."[29] Regardless of the filth and congestion of the lively city, Potts found Edinburgh a thrilling experience and stated that "the want of beauty and loveliness . . . is well compensated for by the great kindness of the inhabitants."[30]

The medical students lived with private families and generally participated in community activities. Potts's social life in the city revolved around the Edinburgh Meeting of Friends. The group, consisting of some twenty members, was led by William Miller for the men, and Mollison Strettle, Miller's mother-in-law, for the women. Miller was a horticulturist with a profitable nursery business. His home was the center of the Friends biweekly gatherings, which were devoted to long periods of intense meditation undisturbed by any preaching. Typical of the deep introspection that characterized the stern moral exercise of these Quakers, Potts remarked that during his three months at this gathering of merchants and artisans, he had not heard "a word externally . . . [but] it has been quite otherward inwardly, where the never failing teacher is ready and willing to teach all those who diligently and faithfully attend to his word." Contrasting these quiet devotional periods with the more formal assemblies of Quakers in Philadelphia, Potts declared that "I really believe that there is more life and heartfelt religion in the silent meeting at Edinburgh than in the Meetings of the highly favored-people of Philadelphia. . . ." So fervent was this religious enthusiasm since his terrifying ship-board experience with the awesome powers of nature, that Potts refrained from attending plays, dances, and concerts. "I have taken off my ruffles, and untied my hair, and am not ashamed to use the plain language [Thee and Thou] to the greatest Man in Edinburgh . . ."[31]

Absorbed in his medical studies and in his religious obligations, Potts still thought constantly of the girl he left behind. "My dear Gracey, . . . the partner of all my pleasures as well as sorrows. Tell her, my love for her is stronger than ever," he requested his brother, "and that I never knew the value of her good company until I was deprived of it."[32] Then suddenly Potts's activities in Edinburgh were interrupted by dramatic news from home about his fiancée. On February 1, 1767, Rush recorded that he had just bid farewell to Jonathan, who had left hurriedly for London. "His sudden and unexpected departure," Rush noted, "was owing to some letters which he received from his Friends desiring him immediately to return to a young lady to whom he was engaged who was greatly indisposed upon his Accnt . . ."[33]

No indication of Potts's mental turmoil is apparent in his commonplace description of the countryside that he observed on his coach journey southward. Yet one clue to the psychological strain he endured is apparent when Potts considered the opportunities he had forfeited at Edinburgh. As Jonathan admitted, "I prefer [Grace's] welfare and peace to all the vain pleasures and satisfactions I expected to receive from my Education at Edinburgh where I must confess I had every advantage possible from study under so great Masters as the Professors in the College." Writing in his journal in early February at the Pennsylvania Coffee House near Fleet Street in London, Potts reminded himself that when he returned home, "I am to act submissively to my parents . . ., but they are by no means to reproach me much less my ever Dearly———." Although Potts actually believed that he had lost "all prospects of rising in life," as he scribbled, yet he was comforted by the thought that he had not lost his father's "patronage."[34]

Unable to catch the *Pennsylvania Packet* from London, Potts had to wait another three weeks for a vessel bound for the Delaware. In the meantime he received a certificate from the Edinburgh Friends addressed to Philadelphia Friends.

Noting that Jonathan had faithfully attended their meetings for three months, the seventeen signatories to the letter attested that "his Deportment ... was conspicuous and admirable ... and his whole conduct was truely sober and circumspect ..." Regretting his sudden departure, the Scot Quakers hoped that "it may please Providence to carry him safe back to his native land."[35] Delighted with the certificate, Potts responded to his Edinburgh Friends by hoping that an "outward Preacher" would emerge from their ranks to guide them. "I firmly believe," Potts stated, "the Lord will in his own due and appointed time, raise up among you as He shall think most properly qualified for that high and noble office."[36]

In order to purchase books, his passage home, and articles for his new household, Jonathan borrowed £70 from Franklin.[37] Potts bought a Bible, surgical instruments, a *London Pharmacopoeia,* and medical tracts written by Monro, Pringle, Linneus, Robert Whytt, and Thomas Syndenham. In preparation for his forthcoming domestic life, he acquired a number of items, including a tankard, a punch ladle, tableware, kitchen utensils, and "a Drinking Cup with two handles." He also took home a garnet necklace, "a cup to warm children victuals ... [and] a Sewing Case for my wife."[38]

On March 5, Potts sailed from England on a voyage that ordinarily lasted seven or eight weeks. Exactly when Potts landed at Philadelphia is uncertain, but he certainly arrived too late for the birth of Mary Francis, his daughter, on April 4, 1767. Jonathan and Grace probably encountered obstacles in their efforts to be married within a Meeting. Instead of holding the marriage at a Friends Meeting House, the procedure was that the couple be joined in an unofficial but recognized Quaker gathering in the home of a Friend.[39] On May 5, 1767, such a marriage for Jonathan Potts and Grace Richardson was performed in the residence of Thomas Rutter, Jonathan's brother-in-law and a Justice of the Peace for Berks County. Ten of the twelve witnesses to the event were members of the Potts family, Martha Rutter was the eleventh, and one Anne D——, was the twelfth. As the marriage certificate stated in part: "He the said Jonathan Potts standing up and in solemn manner takeing [sic] the aforesaid Grace Richardson to be my wife and promise with the Lords assistance to be unto her a faithful and loving husband until Death part us . . ."[40]

The Quaker celebration of a marriage was either quite simple or rather lavish. After a wedding the bride and groom normally spent about two weeks at the home of the bride's father, where visitors called on the couple and shared tea, wine, and cakes with them. At the end of this period the newlyweds usually moved to their own home and were expected to return the visits. Grace, a birthright Friend, had married out of Meeting, and she sought to rectify her mistake. At the Philadelphia Monthly Meeting on October 30, 1767, at which memberships were vested, marriages announced, and written confessions of errors considered, Grace Potts underwent humiliation by publicly admitting her so-called guilt in a procedure known as the "acknowledgement." As the document reads:

> The Women Friends in a paper signed by Grace Potts, late Richardson, with which she attended the Meeting condemn her Unchastity before marriage, and the Women Friends having Grounds to hope she is sincere in her profession to sorrow, Benedict Dorsey is desired to read the paper at a Public Meeting as usual.[41]

Thus the paper condemned her error before marriage; the Friends, believing in her sincerity, accepted her appeal; and Grace was thereby not disowned. When Grace was later in Philadelphia, she received a certificate (January 26, 1774) that was sent to the Exeter Monthly Meeting (the parent unit in Berks County), so she remained in good standing with the Friends.

As for Jonathan's link to Quakerism from this point, the record is obscure. He is mentioned in records for attending a Meeting in Berks on his wedding day. But, oddly enough, in the meticulously maintained accounts of the Exeter Monthly

Meeting and in the Philadelphia Monthly Meeting, Potts is not again cited.[42] But the omission from Friends' records concerning Jonathan does not signify that he lost his Quaker faith. Yet no further mention about his membership or about possible disownment by the pacifist Quakers during the Revolutionary War of "Fighting Quakers" is available. Regardless of his precise affiliation to Quakerism, Potts remained a deeply religious man, and references to the Divine abound in his letters.

Potts had a happy married life with a large family; Grace bore him six more children. Writing in July 1768 from Edinburgh, where he had just earned his medical degree, Rush confided to a friend about Jonathan's second child, named Benjamin Rush Potts:

> My friend Jonathan Potts tells me in his last letter that his wife was safely delivered of a son on the 18th of last May which he says he intends to call Benjamin after me but I rather suppose it is after Dr. Franklin. I cannot help smiling every time I think of Jonathan being so early the father of two children. May he enjoy happiness in them.[43]

At the age of twenty-one Jonathan had ended his promising career in Edinburgh to marry the woman he loved. Without the coveted medical degree and with a family to support, he faced an uncertain future as a mere practitioner. Yet he had some advantages—a fine apprenticeship, a classical education, a term at Edinburgh, connections with influential Philadelphians, and a determination to ascend the pinnacle of his profession. Furthermore, he would be helped by a substantial family inheritance and by opportunities for advancement offered by the College of Philadelphia, which was preparing to graduate its first class of medical doctors.

III.
The Medical World of Jonathan Potts

The medical practice of Jonathan Potts typified the state of the healing art in Pennsylvania. Data about his work as a country practitioner—the diseases he treated, the surgery he performed, the fees he charged, and the drugs he dispensed—provide information about the state of the profession. A glimpse of Potts's professional activities from 1767 to 1774 offers a microcosm of medicine in late colonial America.

Potts practiced in an era when few advances occurred in the theory or practice of medicine. A scientific explanation of disease was unknown. No doctor considered a germ theory, pondered the cellular structure of the human body, or viewed insects as vectors of pestilence. The extent of chemical knowledge was limited; the level of microscopy was rudimentary; subjects such as neurology, pathology, and physiology were in their inception; and bacteriology, that would bring an awareness of bacteria and microbiological agents, was a century in the future. Opportunities for investigating human cadavers were rare; the training of medical personnel was disorganized; not a single medical journal was published in the colonies; and no scientific society in North America consciously pursued medical research. In public health matters, political authorities functioned within a narrow legislative framework, and few administrative arrangements had been devised to protect communities from epidemics.

Doctors were handicapped by additional restraints. Owing to the speculative pathology of the era, they were limited in their ability to heal because of their ignorance about the causes and treatment of illness. Medical thought during the Enlightenment was still based on the so-called harmony of the human body. The ancient Greeks, and the medieval scholastics who refined the thought, claimed that health was a state of bodily balance and that illness was one of imbalance. Disease was reputed to be caused by a change in one of the four bodily humors. Such changes—an excess of a humor, a disturbance of a humor, or the putrefaction of a humor—resulted, it was believed, from an improper diet, a malignant environment, or an unhealthy mode of living. The essence of this humoral, or Galenical, theory was the restoration of the proper balance by aiding nature through diet, rest, bathing, and by purging the body through chemical and mechanical means.

During the eighteenth century this inhibiting concept was challenged by major developments. New data about the environment, numerous achievements in science, the emergence of learned societies, the philosophic empiricism of the age, the increased dissemination of information, and the demand for evidence created a climate of opinion favorable to novel ideas. Medical authorities had to assimilate many discoveries replacing or modifying traditional beliefs—the circulation of the blood, the organisms revealed by the microscope, the anatomical knowledge gained from dissections, and the principles of Newtonian physics that established principles of classical mechanics.

As a result of the impressive breakthrough in the physical sciences, medical philosophers such as Boerhaave sought a similar grand Newtonian synthesis which would impose order upon the chaotic state of pathology and physiology. Boerhaave gathered empirical evidence about blood, other bodily fluids, and the glands that produced them. He fused the old metaphysical doctrines with the new scientific data into a well-organized medical "system" by blending fact and theory. Boerhaave taught that the human body had two basic components, the fluids and the solids. Health, he believed, was the proper interworking of solids and fluids; disease was the faulty interaction of these elements. Thomas Syndenham (1624–1689) adapted Boerhaave's anatomical principles and physiological observations, and applied these concepts to febrile diseases. Leading bedside medicine back to the Hippocratic tradition, he provided a modified humoral theory by claiming that particles of morbific matter from the air entered the body to produce putrefaction of the humors. The Boerhaavian explanation of disease was also reinforced by William Cullen (1710–1790) who concentrated on the supposed "tensions" in the nervous and vascular systems. He believed that some inexplicable conditions in the atmosphere, termed effluvia, caused pestilence. This morbific matter was either contagious (emanating from diseased humans) or miasmatic (arising from swamps and marshes). To remove the "spasms" of the arteries caused by this action, he recommended depletion remedies to remove the obnoxious humors, and stimulants to restore the healthy condition of the body.[1]

The ironic aspect of these efforts to modernize the traditional humoral theory is that the new concepts merely rationalized the standard practices of bleeding and blistering the body, and reinforced the conventional pharmacology of centuries past, which was often useless in therapy and sometimes harmful to patients. The speculative pathology that flourished in Potts's time not only inhibited progress in therapy, but also blocked developments in major surgery. If illness was ascribed to impure bodily fluids, then the surgeon's functions were necessarily limited to superficial operations on bodily surfaces and its extremities.

This unscientific generalization by the systematists of medicine and their efforts to classify diseases into hundreds of categories, like the flora and fauna of the planet, led to such confusion that medicine remained a backward science. Without an understanding of the bodily changes produced by disease, or an appreciation of the chemical, structural, and functional alterations resulting from sickness, the physician was unable to visualize what was transpiring to his patient.

Diagnosis of common ailments—spots, rashes, fevers, sore throats, and so on—provided the profession with surface clues, but doctors generally remained perplexed about the pathogenesis of a disease. James Tilton, one of Potts's classmates, indicated this confusion by stating that "the ordinary endemics of our country proceed from vicious qualities in the air we breathe . . . [and] the noxious quality proceeds from chemical combinations in the atmosphere that are poisonous to the human body."[2] Within such an intellectual framework, the famous Shippen bled pregnant women because menstruation had not occurred in nine months. Rush bled copiously for fever because a "bounding pulse" was considered dangerous. As he explained: "The effect of bloodletting is as immediate and natural in removing fever as the abstraction of a particle of sand is to cure an infection of the eye."[3]

Beyond the restraints in the theory of medicine which impeded therapeutical success, practitioners labored under many technical handicaps. Potts and his colleagues were poorly equipped with diagnostic tools to aid the senses. They lacked the stethoscope, the clinical thermometer, and the hypodermic syringe. No device to measure blood pressure was available; nothing was known about tissue cultures, urine analysis, and except for gross changes, little data were extracted from blood examinations.

Regardless of the level of a practitioner's education, the treatment for most diseases was similar—depletion remedies and stimulants. Doctors bled their patients with a spring lancet for colic, jaundice, pleurisy, rheumatism, and dog bites. Usually, ten ounces of blood were removed for rheumatism, and twelve for pleurisy; if a patient showed little improvement within a day, he was subjected to a second bleeding. As Dr. William Buchan, a contemporary Scot medical oracle, advised:

> Bleeding is proper at the beginning of all inflammatory fevers, as pleurisies, peripnemonies, etc. It is likewise proper in all typical inflammations as those of the intestines, womb, bladder, stomach, kidnies, throat, etc., also in the asthmas,

sciatic pains, coughs, head-aches, rheumatism, the apopolexy, and bloody flux. After fits, blows, bruises, or any violent hurt received, either externally or internally, bleeding is necessary. In a word, whenever the vital motions have been suddenly stopt, from any cause whatever, . . ., it is proper to open a vein.[4]

Doctors also cupped, blistered, scarified their patients, applied setons, and gave enemas, sometimes even for common colds. Some of these measures may have provided relief to the exhausted patient. But these rigorous body-wracking techniques may have weakened the sickly more than these measures strengthened them. Though information about the processes of life increased in Potts's era, though the boundaries of pathology expanded (due to the experiments of Morgagni), and though some occult aspects of therapy were eliminated, little progress occurred in medicine. Doctors were unable to utilize the data derived from biology, physics, or chemistry. Undoubtedly medical practice in colonial America, as well as in Europe, rested on dubious empirical foundations.

Inasmuch as few specific diseases were then identified, we are uncertain about what types of illness Potts encountered. Few records of disease patterns exist, many outbreaks of pestilence were not recorded, and diagnosis was confusing and inaccurate. Furthermore, a major difficulty in differentiating diseases based on contemporary descriptions is due to the bewildering medical nomenclature of the period, to the regional variations in the terminology of a disease, and to the fact that a description such as "asthma" or "consumption" may actually mean another distinct entity. Yet sufficient evidence has been compiled to demonstrate that doctors treated many infectious, communicable, and degenerative diseases. Few bills of mortality are available for rural America in the eighteenth century, but a standard generalization about health conditions is that the death rate was high and that life expectancy at birth was low. Populations were exposed to numerous afflictions due to many environmental factors—

ignorance about bodily nutritional requirements; crowded, poorly constructed, and inadequately ventilated homes; primitive attitudes about sanitation; carelessness about water and sewage; enervating conditions of manual toil; and the frequent exposure to the elements. The route of contagion was generally unsuspected, and the concept of contagion itself was usually not acknowledged. Doctors were unaware of the distinctions between cardiac and pulmonary disorders, and they knew little about opthalmology and mental illness. The profession was ignorant about micosis, leukemia, tuberculosis, and viral hepatitis. Data about dietary and glandular diseases were not available until the twentieth century. The vaccines and antibiotics now used against many diseases were not available. Colonial Americans lived under environmental conditions comparable to the most backward nations of the modern world.[5]

The colonists were plagued by many insidious diseases. Malaria, a deadly killer, was a frequent and dreaded visitor to North American ports. The subject of Potts's particular interest, "ague," or "intermittant fever," as it was termed, is an infection produced in man by a protozoan parasite transmitted through the bite of the female anopheline mosquito. Another devastating disease was "bloody flux"—a term used to describe various enteric complaints ranging from simple diarrhea, to bacillary dysentery, to typhoid fever. Dysentery and typhoid—both labeled "long fever" or "nervous fever"— could cut through the ranks of men assembled for colonial warfare and could paralyze military operations. Common to jails and army camps, dysentery was caused either by bacteria or by protozoa commonly transmitted by house flies to human food. Typhoid is an acute infectious disease caused by a bacterium carried in an unhygienic water supply, and sometimes by house flies that settle on human food. As typhoid resembled typhus and dysentery in its epidemiological features, it puzzled physicians, and not until 1837 was it differentiated.

Smallpox, exceedingly contagious and often fatal, was the most feared malady. Readily identified and intensely studied, the "King of Terrors" was a hideous disease that killed, maimed, and crippled its victims. Another destructive enemy was yellow fever, a sinister import from the Caribbean. Its cause was unknown, and the relationship of mosquitoes to the spread of the fever was unsuspected. However, few serious outbreaks of yellow fever occurred in the northern colonies after 1761, and not until 1793 did it reappear in Philadelphia. A high incidence of respiratory disorders flourished every winter—influenza, pleurisy, pneumonia, severe colds and coughs, and other diseases of the upper and lower respiratory tracts. Though not as dramatic as the famous outbreaks of pestilence of the era, such diseases were a more significant factor in colonial mortality.

Another common disease was typhus, a feared pestilence that, along with malaria and bubonic plague, is one of the three insect-borne diseases that have had a decisive impact on the course of history. Often called "putrid fever," typhus is an acute infection that occurs when humans are confined and crowded together under unsanitary conditions and when body lice, infected by ingesting rickettsiae from the blood of an infected rat, are their close companions. Man is infected when the dry feces of the insect, packed with the deadly parasite, is rubbed into the skin, falls on the conjunctiva, or is perhaps inhaled into the lungs. The saliva of the louse carries an irritant, and a person becomes infected by crushing the insect and rubbing the content of the insect's gut into his skin and into the puncture made by the louse. Typhus flared on immigrant ships coming to America, and it erupted frequently in army camps during the Revolution.

With respect to the long-suffering females of the family, apparently few women lived to menopause. Many died prematurely from illnesses of the household and from the dangers of bearing an average of seven children. Women frequently succumbed to toxemia, hemorrhaging, malpresentation, and sheer maternal exhaustion. Last in the category of common diseases were dietary diseases. Scurvy, pellegra, and beriberi were present, but because of the variety of foodstuffs in the colonies, these maladies were not severe in North

America. Though dietary diseases rarely killed, they opened the path to a host of fatal and debilitating infections.

In Potts's account books are numerous citations for children. Youngsters were particularly susceptible to disease, and childhood mortality was high. The art of pediatrics was in the future, and a doctor's obstetrical work was normally limited to the delivery of difficult cases, because midwives usually supervised regular births. No control over milk or water supplies existed. Diphtheria, scarlet fever, summer diarrhea, tonsillitis, tuberculosis, mastoiditis struck down infants with fearsome regularity. Such diseases, along with mumps, measles, chicken pox, and whooping cough, took a toll of one-half the childhood population before the age of five.

To treat this awesome array of diseases, physicians were almost helpless. Remedies were available only in the treatment of scurvy, malaria, and smallpox. The value of citrus fruit to ward off scurvy was familiar maritime lore to generations of seamen, but until James Lind, a Royal naval surgeon, experimented with limes and lemons (along with cider, raw onions, and sauerkraut) to supplement the sailor's fare, no scientific proof of the efficacy of this remedy existed. A century and a half before the antiscorbutic properties of vitamin C were known, Lind recommended fruit and vegetables to supplement the dried and salted rations on shipboard. As a result, by the 1790s scurvy significantly declined in the services. In the treatment of malaria the use of Jesuit's bark (cinchona or Peruvian bark) was the great breakthrough of the era. Along with the standard depletion therapy, feverish patients—not only those suffering from malaria—were often given a dose of pulverized bark diluted with wine and rhubarb. Although chemically unrecognized, the effective element in the bark was quinine. But bark was unpalatable, its potency varied, and it was often ineffective. Medical authorities disagreed about its use, and not until 1854 was bark acknowledged as a prophylactic against malaria.

The first victory over a contagious disease occurred in treating smallpox. The disease is characterized by fever, vomiting, headaches, severe pains in the back, and eruptions appearing on the forehead and hair roots and spreading over the body in dark spots. Decades before Edward Jenner's vaccination technique was adopted in Britain (1795), inoculation, or variolation, was tried in Boston (1721). The treatment consisted of placing pus from a blister of an infected person directly into the bloodstream of a healthy person by an incision in the skin. This action caused a mild form of the disease, and it thereby prevented an inoculated person from again being infected. The resulting infection was usually mild, and the chances of survival were far better than in cases of ordinary contagion, or "the natural way" as colonials such as George Washington, whose face bore scars of the disease, phrased it.[6]

Although inoculation usually provided immunity for the inoculated, it invariably aroused community opposition, because the procedure was dangerous. Unless inoculation was carefully supervised and performed by skillful inoculators, it could spark an epidemic. Severe penalties were enacted to punish unauthorized inoculators, and much public suspicion about the treatment remained by 1775. Yet the fear of the loathsome disease forced many individuals to undergo the danger and the illness of inoculation in order to ward off the horror of the naturally acquired contagion. Patients were isolated, and immune persons cared for them; others were confined to remote buildings and provided with food and fuel; some cities had pesthouses, and some doctors had private sanatoria where mass inoculations were administered. By the 1770s the tendency was to regulate inoculation rather than to prohibit it; laws were revised to specify inoculation conditions and to set a minimum quarantine period. Long before the germ theory of disease was proven, smallpox was the one infectious disease which doctors could successfully combat.

In contrast to the British and Continental distinction between physicians and surgeons, American physicians usually practiced surgery. As surgeons, they limited their treatment to the surface of the body and its extremities. Surgery consisted basically of treating cuts, bruises, sprains, burns; lancing boils; removing abseses; setting fractured bones; treating septic conditions; fixing dislocated joints; and repairing gunshot wounds. More adventuresome surgeons could operate on a hairlip, perform tonsillectomies, attempt paracentesis (a surgical puncture of a cavity for aspiration of a fluid), and operate on the gall bladder for removal of stone. They could perform only two capital operations, trepanning and amputations. Trepanning was an operation for head concussion, performed by making an incision in the scalp and removing some bone from the skull in order to remove the pressure from the brain. Amputations of limbs were extremely dangerous. One estimate is that 50 percent of all amputated cases were fatal. Without a means of protecting his patient from infection or a method to relieve him from the painful probing, sawing, cutting, and stitching of the operation, a surgeon's chances of success were quite limited. He knew nothing about the nature of infection or about the danger of shock. He expected a flow of "laudable pus," a white inodorous excretion, as essential for healing. He could not operate safely on the bodily cavities; anatomical explorations of the thorax and abdomen were still in the future.[7]

Not only was a physician-surgeon intellectually limited in the scope of his operations, but he was also technically impeded by his crude surgical equipment. Potts's instruments consisted of only some twenty-three items such as lancets, scalpels, needles, amputation saws, amputating knives, surgical knives, a bone-cutting scissors, a tissue retractor, surgical scissors, a trepine, a bullet extractor, various forceps, a cautery, and a molar extractor. For cuts, bruises, and bleeding, a surgeon had salves, ointments, and astringents. In his bag a surgeon also carried tow, lint, pins, tape, compresses, bandages, plaster, thread, candles, and a container of wine or spirits. No effective anesthetic existed, so he used opium, liquor, or oil of cloves to deaden the pain and to dull the senses. Sometimes a patient undergoing an amputation, held down to the table by four strong men, was given a musket bullet on which to clamp his teeth during the agony; hence the term "to bite the bullet."

With only this equipment, Potts had to repair the damage to human frames common in agricultural societies, where accidents were frequent—from working with wood and metals, handling farm implements, riding horses, repairing wagons, and hunting-trapping activities. Without adequate heat or light, doctors operated in an environment that moderns would consider filthy. Modern antiseptics were not introduced until later, and not until the 1860s were asepsis (providing sterile conditions) and antiseptics (combating infection) introduced into surgery. Surgery was at a low point in the eighteenth century, and it seemed remote from contemporary discoveries in pathology and physiology. Even knowledge about the circulation of the blood led to no major significant results on the operating table.

Potts's practice in Pottsgrove, as revealed in his ledgers and account books, demonstrated this level of medicine. Why Potts returned to this hamlet—after sampling the excitement of three cities—remains a puzzle. Since April 1767 John Potts, Sr., had been continually ill, and he may have required constant attention. Other factors such as a low rent, no competition, and the guarantee of regular patients may have been factors in Potts's decision to open his office there on May 28, 1767, three weeks after his marriage. Potts treated Thomas Rutter, his relative and first patient, by bleeding him and making him vomit. He gave a stomach plaster to Arch McCall and a carthartic to James Hochley, two local inhabitants. Thomas Dewees, the innkeeper, bought drugs for his family. Potts's first recorded surgery in Pottsgrove was to dress a blister for a nephew and to bandage the finger of Rutter's slave. In addition to Potts's father, his three brothers, Dewees, and Rutter, some other patients can be identified—Adam Clecknor, the mason, Israel Potts (no relation), the potter, and Nathaniel Chestnut, the plantation brewer.[8]

The number of his patients was small. In August Potts treated only twelve patients; by autumn the average monthly number was thirty. Potts presumably spent most of his professional time on house calls, and may have carried his drugs and surgical instruments in his saddlebags or in a bag on the floor of his gig. His office may have consisted of a room in his home. A cupboard served as a medical cabinet, a wooden table as his examination platform, and some chairs and a desk completed the furniture. In such modest circumstances the rural practitioner served not only villagers, but also farmers and artisans for miles around, as well as itinerant settlers, peddlers, and traders.

To improve his status in the profession, Potts returned in December 1767 to Philadelphia to prepare for his degree. He also continued to practice. New names appear in his ledgers—Susannah Morris, Thomas Yorke, Clement Biddle, Francis Richardson, along with David, Joseph, and Thomas Potts. In Philadelphia, Potts had more opportunities for consultations with colleagues, and notations in his account book attest to discussions with Morgan, Redman, and Thomas Bond. Potts was probably preoccupied with preparation for his examinations, and he may have restricted his practice in order to study. Only thirty patients are listed in early 1768, nine in June, and only four in October, his last month in the city.[9]

The medical school that opened in 1765 had undergone major changes since Potts's departure for Edinburgh. It offered degrees and had a larger faculty and a broader curriculum. On May 12 the Trustees of the College declared their intention to grant the bachelor of medicine degree. High academic standards prevailed. A candidate had to present a certificate of proficiency from his preceptor, to demonstrate his ability in pharmacy, and to possess a statement attesting to hospital attendance for one year. Applicants with a college degree were admitted automatically to the program; those without a degree had to prove their knowledge of Latin, physics, and mathematics. To further encourage talented men, the trustees also announced the availability of the doctor's degree in physic. For this distinction, a candidate had to be twenty-four years old, to have had his bachelor's degree three years, and to write a thesis. By late 1768 the faculty was rounded out. Adam Kuhn, who had returned with his Edinburgh degree after studying with Linneus in Stockholm, was appointed professor of botany and materia medica.[10] Rush, who had specialized in chemistry with Black in Edinburgh, was named professor of chemistry. Philadelphia now had a four-man faculty compared to Edinburgh's seven. Although the College of Philadelphia could not rival Edinburgh, the future of its medical department seemed promising.

By early 1768 Potts was close to his degree, and in the spring he and the other students took their examinations. The ten candidates—five from Pennsylvania, two from New Jersey, three from Delaware—passed their examinations, and on June 21, 1768, the graduation ceremonies were held. After various addresses by dignitaries, the degrees were conferred. Potts delivered the valedictory speech on "The advantages derived in the study of physic from a liberal education in the other sciences." The new bachelors of medicine listened to concluding remarks by Shippen, who urged them to provide "charity to the poor, humanity to all." In an impressive moment in American history, Potts and his classmates were the first graduates of a medical school in North America. Appreciating the significance of the ceremony, the trustees proclaimed: "This day may be considered the Birthday of Medical Honors in America." The members of this proud class indeed represented a new era for the medical profession in the colonies.[11]

Before Potts returned to his practice in Pottsgrove, his father died (June 6, 1768). The financial consequences of the death of John Potts, Sr., to his children were important. The ironmaster was a very wealthy man, and the complicated legal arrangements of his holdings took years to settle. By 1774 the proceeds from his real estate amounted to £19,000. Although the largest portion of his income and property was left to his wife, John Potts, Sr., provided ample shares of his estate to his sons and daughters. His initial bequest to them was divided into three categories. The smallest shares went to his daughers, the largest portions to his sons who were engaged in business. In the third category were the two professionals in the family—Jonathan the doctor, and John, Jr., the lawyer. "I have given my sons more than my daughers," the ailing Potts had stated, "being of opinion *that as sons* they are entitled to more." Smaller bequests were alloted to sons

Jonathan and John because "of the extraordinary expense I have been put to for their educations . . ." Jonathan received about £440 in 1768, a comparatively large sum when the average yearly profit of a Pennsylvania farmer was only £16 to £30. In 1770 each child of John Potts, Sr., received another £1,000, and in 1779 another £835. Jonathan thus resumed his career with a degree and with a substantial inheritance to augment his meager earnings.[12]

The practice that Potts resumed at home in July 1769 remained small. In August he had only eight patients, and in September, fifteen. Some new names appear regularly on his ledger. Most of his patients had English names, or names perhaps anglicized from German. By the end of 1769 he had earned £50 for five months' work. The following year Potts's list of patients grew slowly, averaging about thirty a month, and more visits to outlying settlements such as Yellow Springs were recorded. German names, such as Jacob Grub and Jacob Hoover, appear more frequently, along with citations about Clement Biddle the clockmaker, Derek Pennypacker the miller, Jedah Boone the farmer, Morgan Conner the surveyor, Thomas Dundas the merchant, and Edward Biddle the Reading lawyer. In 1770 Potts earned £150 in fees, and in 1771, his last year in Pottsgrove, he earned £183.

Potts's fees appear typical of the era. He charged 1s. to 7s. for visits, depending upon the distance, and an additional 5s. for "rising in the night." His fee for bleeding was 1s. 6d., lancing a boil 1s., an enema 1s. 6d., an emetic 1–2s., extracting a tooth 2s. 6d., treating blisters 3s. 6d., and inoculating a child 5s. He charged 15s. to fix a broken finger, £1 to treat a dislocated elbow, £1. 5s. for a fractured elbow, and £2 for a fractured thigh. His drug charges varied from 1s. for cream of tartar, 2s. 6d. for camphor, 9s. for laudanum, and 2s. 5d. for the popular Godfrey's Cordial.[13]

His fees can be compared with other contemporary fee tables. One is the account book of Hugh Mercer of Fredericksburg, Virginia, whose apothecary shop was often visited by Washington. Mercer charged 1s. for a vomit, 2s. 6d. for bleeding, 3s. 6d. for blistering, and a flexible scale for visits.

John Archer of Delaware charged amounts almost identical to those of Potts. In their fashionable Philadelphia practice, the Bond brothers were more expensive—2s. 6d. for an emetic, £3 for inoculation, and £10 for trepanning.[14]

A broader comparison of fees can be made with those of New Jersey practitioners. For the first time in colonial North America, a group of medical men printed a list of charges for their services. On July 23, 1766, in New Brunswick the New Jersey Medical Society published a list of rates for visits, operations, and consultations. The Jersey doctors stated that their fees were not derived "by law or custom, and that many inconveniences arise from such defect . . ." and that they expected "a just and equitable reward for their services." (For the Table of Fees and Rates, see Appendix 1.) The society promised to adhere to these rates "'till the Legislature shall interpose, or some happier method be devised for determining a matter so interesting to both the public and the profession."[15]

While engaged in practice, Potts prepared his dissertation on malaria. The disease had established a strong foothold in North America, and it was a major cause of morbidity and mortality among the colonists. The distinctive and recurring pattern of fever and chills, marked by clearly defined remissions, made the disease relatively easy to identify, but classification of fevers was very imprecise, and no orderly or systematic analysis existed. The relationship between the disease and swampy areas had long been suspected; yet the relationship of the mosquito as the vector of human malaria and the protozoan parasite that it transmitted was not understood until the twentieth century. After citing some authorities on the subject (Galen, Boerhaave, Syndenham), Potts stated that he encountered intermittent fever "almost every day." He discussed the pathogenesis of the disease by noting its seasonal character and the difficulty in differentiating it from other diseases and by stating that the fever impeded the circulation of the blood so that "the heart was not sufficiently activated." What triggered the pestilence? Potts explained that "all such things as suddenly start perspiration within the bodily fibers were responsible." Such causative factors, he hypothesized, were climatic changes, weather variations, careless eating and drinking habits, as well as "widespread affluvia ... or the damp, unhealthy air, or vapour arising from marshes ... which activates the fever." The therapy he recommended was to place the patient in a well-ventilated room out of the sun, to provide him with cooling drinks and with frequent clothing changes. For medication he prescribed cathartics, sudorifics, purgatives, and frequent doses of bark, "the only drug on which we confidently rely as a help against danger." Admitting that the disease baffled him, Potts hoped for the sympathy of his examiners. "The more learned they are," he concluded, "the fairer they will show themselves to this endeavor."[16]

Potts's thesis was not very original. He relied heavily on authority, and he revealed obscurity and uncertainty about anatomical details. Potts offered no empirical evidence, no comparison of cases, nor any record of experiments or dissections to reinforce his speculation. Typical of the contemporary medical treatise, Potts utilized monistic pathological concepts to explain a disease on the basis of unproven but, supposedly, universal principles. Yet his work was a useful synthesis of information about malaria, and he modestly admitted his bewilderment about it. And in fairness to Potts, very few dissertations in his era, either in America or in Britian, became landmarks in medical thought.

Following the Edinburgh tradition, after his dissertation was submitted, Potts and three other candidates took their written and oral examinations. Their professors tested them on the entire field of medicine, including an explanation of a Hippocratic aphorism and the diagnosis and therapy of two cases. No problems were posed, no experiments cited, and no hypothetical questions were asked. The examinations were devised to probe a candidate's memorization ability rather than his reasoning powers.[17] At the graduation ceremonies on June 18, 1771, the audience listened to Provost Smith summarize the accomplishments of the college since its inception, and to the candidates defend their theses. After Morgan spoke about the professional responsibilities of doctors, the degrees were conferred. Potts again participated in another significant moment in American medical history; he was one of the college's first M.D.'s. Benjamin Franklin wrote to Thomas Bond that he was delighted "to see our school of physic being able to make a figure. I do not know why," he continued, "it should not soon be equal to that in Edinburgh."[18]

His prestige enhanced by his new degree, Potts prepared to leave Pottsgrove for a location that provided a more lucrative practice. He selected Reading, a town with a future. Founded in 1748, the village expanded rapidly to a population of 1,000 by 1752 and to 2,000 by 1774. Reading attracted many German settlers to the area. Commenting in 1783 on the settlement "where only thirty-six years ago, was a mere wilderness," Dr. Johann David Schoepf, a Brunswicker, remarked that "the inhabitants are principally German, and almost all are in good circumstances . . .," each family owning about two hundred acres of land.[19] The center of the Tulpehocken and upper Schuylkill Valleys and the economic hub for the northwest back country, Reading was a bustling town. Its commercial links stretched westward to villages such as York, Sunbury, Carlisle, and Northumberland. At Reading, farmers sold their rye, flax, wheat, hides, and dried peaches, and purchased salt, sugar, and textiles. From Reading, boatmen plied their flat-bottomed craft down the river to Philadelphia with heavy cargoes of furs, hides, and grain, returning with manufactured goods from the seaboard. The yearly fabrication of 40,000 felt hats gave Reading an industrial base, strengthened by milling, weaving, coopering, and brick-making enterprises. Farmers, traders, rivermen, and adventurers thronged its streets. Gambling at nightly cock fights attracted appreciative audiences, and thirty taverns in the little town provided thirsty farmers and travelers with the means to relax.

At the center of Reading, the seat of Berks County, was the courthouse that symbolized law, and the political link to the province. Reading, stated Schoepf, "has four principal streets which run exactly parallel with the four points of the compass, and where they cross stands a handsome courthouse."[20] By 1764 Reading had a library, and by 1773 a fire company and three churches. Reading's men of substance managed the town, controlled the courts, supervised the legislative affairs of the county, and promoted real estate ventures. Edward Shippen served in Reading as the Crown prosecutor; Edward Biddle represented the county in the Assembly. Colonel John Paton and his stepson, Mark Bird, had extensive forging interests. Edward Burd, Peter Scull, and James Wilson, the future political theorist, argued cases in the Court of Common Pleas. Others active in the town were Henry Haller the innkeeper, Edward Scull the surveyor, George Nagle the miller and sheriff, Morgan Conner the surveyor, and Thomas Dundas the merchant. Opportunities for ambitious men were abundant in Reading, where Potts opened his practice on April 26, 1772.

Reading needed Potts. On his first day of practice he had eight patients, including Paton, Biddle, and Mordecai Lincoln the farmer. His business expanded rapidly, and by May he daily handled fifteen to eighteen callers. On June 16 he bandaged the hand of Daniel Brodhead, the famed Indian fighter. Nagle, Haller, and Dundas often visited his office, as well as the Burd family, the Boones, the Conners, and the Lincolns. Some of these names can be identified, and the Boones and Lincolns had distinguished descendents. But who were "Widow Rhees," "George the tailor," "the carpenter at the furnace," and "Samuel Potts's Dutchman"? Potts's practice continued to expand; he treated about 240 patients in 1772, about 300 in 1773, and 330 in 1774.[21]

The income from his work significantly increased. For his first three months in Reading, he earned £60; by the end of 1772 (the only year for which his Reading earning are available) he earned £300. In the Middle Colonies, agrarian laborers earned from £25 to £45 yearly, depending upon food and lodging arrangements; artisans earned from £20 to £25 a year. The salaries of clergy varied from £70 to £100. The income of doctors, generally below that of lawyers, fluctuated considerably, depending upon their ability to collect fees, and whether they were paid in such items as poultry, firewood, or farm produce. In general, doctors ranked behind lawyers and were close to the income level of preachers. The majority of doctors earned enough to place them in that amorphous group categorized as the middle class, but many doctors found it difficult to earn a living because of competition, since the field was easily accessible to the untutored. From an estimate of the earnings of colonial physicians, it appears that Potts's income of £300 in 1772 ranked him about halfway up the ladder of pecuniary success for his profession.[22]

Perhaps 80 percent of a doctor's income came from the sale of drugs. Because no formal distinction existed between medicine and pharmacy, Potts purchased quantities of raw drugs and patent medicine from wholesalers, and as a function of his practice he retailed them in Reading. His drug suppliers in Philadelphia were Jacob Hoff, William Smith, Patton and Williams, and Christopher Marshall, Sr., the most famous druggist in the colonies. To increase his earnings, Potts opened his apothecary shop in Reading. As the *Pennsylvania Gazette* noted on September 28, 1772: "An apothecary shop is just opened by Doctor Jonathan Potts, at the house where Mr. Dundas lately kept store . . ., where Drugs and Medicine of the Best Quality are disposed of, on as reasonable terms as they may be purchased in Philadelphia."[23] Potts sold paints and brushes in his drugstore, and like the typical apothecary of the day he may have stocked oils, putty, varnish, window glass, garden seeds, figs, prunes, and raisins. As no pharmaceuticals were manufactured in the colonies, Potts's main source of drugs was Europe—to be mixed and compounded in his store—and herbals gathered from his garden, his greenhouse, and the surrounding forests. Over the entrance of his shop, an apothecary hung a sign decorated with a painting of a golden ball, a mortar and pestle, an ointment pot, or the figure of a dove, deer, or a dragon.

Potts probably utilized two rooms for his drug trade, a salesroom to display his wares and a laboratory to prepare medicine for customers. To show his goods an apothecary often placed a large sheet of glass, consisting of twenty-four panes, at the store front behind which stood bottles of drugs in solution macerating in the sun. In the front room Potts probably had "patent" medicines arranged on shelves, bulk medicines and crude drugs stored in drawers, and a prescription counter on which stood a brass scale with its balancing pans. The shelves were also filled with drug containers such as Delft-ware jars, ornately decorated in bright colors. Crude drugs, powders, pills, ointments were also kept in colored gallipots, or in earthenware jars painted red, white, or brown to indicate their chemical content, as well as in flint glassware, stoneware jugs, pottery jars, and green-glass containers. In the rear room an assistant toiled with mortar and pestle to pulverize, grind, and mix the drugs. Here in the back was the apothecary's main equipment—a piece of shining tile on which to manipulate the pill mass with a spatula, a bolus knife for rolling the pills, a graduated pill divider, an additional weight scale, the distillation apparatus, and an array of sieves, funnels, retorts, and other glass vessels. On the hearth a kettle simmered, exuding exotic odors of spices, aromatics and the fumes of volatile drugs. At Potts's, customers hoped to find the oils, pills, balms, tonics, powders, extracts, salves, elixirs, ointments, decoctions, and linaments to cure their ills.

The demand for drugs depended upon the physician's prescription and the patient's self-diagnosis. For culinary and medical purposes the woman of a household often had her own herb garden, where she grew such plants as catnip, bloodroot, angelica, peppermint, and perhaps some species not indigenous to the area. A housewife usually had recipe books containing formulas for tanning, preserving, and soap making, along with cures for men and animals that had been handed down from generation to generation. In addition to teas and extracts from her garden, she could purchase crude drugs from an apothecary shop to prepare medicines at home—mustard, jalap, saltpeter, pink root, castor oil, sarsaparilla, and mercurial ointments. She could also buy at Potts's such items as Daffy's Elixir, Anderson's Pills, Bateman's Pectoral Drops, James's Fever Powder, Godfrey's Cordial, and Hooper's Female Pills.

Basic to Potts's pharmacopoeia were the expensive imported drugs or "capital" medicines. Among the many items listed in his ledgers are the following: opium, olive oil, Spanish fly, wormwood, tartar emetic, camphor, Epsom salts, Glauber's salts, and balsamic preparations. He used opium and laudanum to relieve pain, prescribed calomel as a hearty purgative and as an emetic for diphtheria and scarlet fever. If one purgative did not work, he tried jalap, ginseng, or castor oil. Epsom salts and Glauber's salts were used for mild pukes and emetics. For fever, bark and tartar emetic were standard. A mixture of bark and rhubarb was usually given for malaria. A famous aid to digestion was gentian root. Olive oil was used for internal lubrication. To alleviate the respiratory tract, doctors prescribed balsams, gun ammonias, and turpentine resins. Cloves was a stimulant and cinnamon a carminative to expel stomach gas; "tar water" (a mixture of water and evergreen resin) was prescribed as a panacea for many illnesses.

In the surrounding flora, Potts had an assistant scour the woods for local herbals. A number of native drugs were extracted from sumac, bayberries, tamarind, black cherry, licorice, mallows, sassafras, wintergreen, witch hazel, slippery elm, and dogwood bark. Jimson weed was smoked in a pipe to cure asthma. Pokeberries were dried in the sun and used in a plaster for cancer. Catmint tea was prescribed for fever; sassafras root and alderbuds to purify the blood; sour dock root to cure the "itch"; grape wine for hair tonic; boneset for consumption; yellow dock root and rattlesnake root for pleurisy; and goldenrod, elderberry, and dogwood bark were reputed cures for dysentery. Mandrake and bloodroot had many uses. While the efficacy of many of these imported and native drugs as remedies is dubious, a careful physician could alleviate some discomfort from malaria, syphilis, dysentery, and respiratory ailments.[24]

Thus Potts was not only a physician and surgeon, but also

a pharmacist. Although we know something about his fees, his patients, and his therapy, we know little, except for one incident, about the problems he encountered. In an era when only 400 out of an estimated 3,500 practitioners in the colonies had medical degrees, he had to compete with a variety of unqualified personnel who offered medical services to a gullible public—midwives, quacks, bone setters, faith healers, folk practitioners, itinerant lithotomists, and preacher-physicians, in addition to a motley group of former weavers, butchers, and shoemakers. He also had to contend with the inevitable tendency of the ill to rely on self-medication. The household recipe book contained remedies for common ailments derived from folk medicine and Indian lore, as well as gleanings from medical authorities. Advice about therapy was also available in almanacs, in newspapers, and in such domestic medical books, or dispensatories, as William Buchan's *Domestic Medicine,* John Tennants's *Every Man His Own Physician,* and, the most famous work in this category, John Wesley's aptly titled *Primitive Physick,* of which thirty-two editions were printed by 1828. Because of the availability of such materials and the natural reluctance of people to incur the expense of a doctor, Potts presumably was not summoned to a bedside until the illness was very serious, all household remedies were exhausted, and other human efforts had failed. At times, fears, superstitions, and religious attitudes of a community, as well as the lack of public health regulations, inhibited a doctor's effectiveness. In many rural areas, diseases and other ailments were commonly attributed to occult forces, heavenly punishment, or the purgation of sin.

Such an event occurred near Reading in Potts's time. Although impressive gains had been made in Pennsylvania since the 1750s in acquainting the public about the value of inoculation for smallpox, some German immigrants resisted the treatment. In September 1768 the *Pennsylvania Chronicle* noted that sixty children had died near Reading in two months from smallpox. "The German inhabitants," the newspaper complained, "cannot be dissuaded from the Pernicious Method of Keeping the sick in hot-stove rooms, under a hot

Regimen, to which doubtless, so great a mortality is especially to be attributed. 'Tis much to be lamented that the Prejudice ... against Inoculation are not removed."[25] In 1771 smallpox again erupted in Reading, where 318 cases occurred and fifty children died. Potts made a commendable effort to halt the ravages of the disease by appealing to his patients in a letter that may have been the basis of a speech. Potts assured his German audience in Berks that inoculation procedures had been well tested with excellent results. He noted that the last time smallpox struck the area, one-third of the chilren with the disease had died, but that "of those who were inoculated there only died one child, and that child was in an unsound state at the time of its being inoculated." He went on to state:

> It is a well known fact that of one hundred persons born in this part of the world there are at least ninety who have the small pox in some part of their lives, of these twenty are known to die in the most favorable times [sic] and twenty more wear very disagreeable marks of this cruel disorder the remainder of their Days, one loses an eye, another perhaps both eyes, and others are so reduced and weakened that they never after enjoy a good state of health....
>
> Why then my countrymen should we be the last in adopting this most happy method? have we not the same regard and tenderness for our children that other people have? or do we set a less value on our lives, or are our German Women less anxious about the preservation of their beauty?

Attempting to dispel the notion that inoculation was displeasing to God, Potts asked why his patients even bothered to call a doctor for any sickness. "Why not rely only upon Providence," he asked, "while without, making use of any natural means whatever?"[26] Though it is difficult to determine how effective this message was in overcoming local opposition, at least in Reading, Potts inoculated frequently that year.

Within this framework of a seemingly static state of the profession, it is apparent that improvements were under way in education, licensure, and the dissemination of ideas. A decade before Shippen and Morgan held classes in Philadelphia, Thomas Wood in New Brunswick (1752) and William Hunter in Newport (1754) held lectures on anatomy. In New York, Dr. John Bard and Dr. Peter Middleton dissected human bodies in the 1750s to enlighten their students. Samuel Bard, the son of John Bard, aspired to initiate formal academic medical training in New York. He and six other graduates of European universities constituted the projected staff of the medical school of King's College. Founded in November 1767, with a faculty perhaps superior to that of the College of Philadelphia, King's, on May 3, 1769, graduated the first M.D. in North America. Bard also took the leadership in acquiring a charter for a New York hospital, built in 1773.[27] With Philadelphia and New York leading the way, could Boston be far behind? In fact, not until November 1781, when Dr. John Warren won the backing of the Boston Medical Society, did a proposal for a medical school gain support. Soon after, the Members of the Harvard Corporation authorized a medical school consisting of two professors, and classes began in the autumn of 1783.[28] Meanwhile, by 1775 King's and the College of Philadelphia had conferred fifty-one medical degrees. On the eve of the American Revolution, advanced medical education in America was firmly rooted.

Licensure regulations were devised. In 1736 the Virginia Legislature enacted a fee bill for doctor's charges, but the law soon lapsed. New York City in 1738 tried to establish control over midwives, but the regulations were difficult to implement. In 1760 the Provincial Assembly of New York passed a medical licensure law, the first in the colonies, which provided for the examination of physicians by government officials. But the legislation was not enforced, and semi-illiterates continued to practice medicine without legal restraints. In 1772 the New Jersey Medical Society petitioned the Assembly to require practitioners to undergo an examination before receiving provincial sanction to practice, and such a law, embodying the prototype of state examination boards, was established. However, little evidence exists to demonstrate that the New Jersey measure was heeded. Granted that these attempts to regulate medical personnel were ineffective, yet such efforts would be revived during the Revolutionary War to improve the quality of regimental surgeons. The final authority to license that emerged from the colonial experience would be the future states, rather than voluntary or federal agencies.[29]

In the intellectual realm, gains were made in medical knowledge by the wider distribution of books and journals from Europe, by a greater knowledge of the botanical world, and by a better understanding of epidemic disease. In two cities at least, medical training was becoming more exact, and some stability in the profession occurred, with father-and-son teams such as the Shippens, the Bards, and the Bonds. More Americans were attending universities overseas, and their European experience was highly instrumental in elevating education and training standards at home. The influence of the clergy was still strong in the profession (six of the thirty-eight members of the New Jersey Medical Society were ministers), but their influence as healers was diminishing due to complaints about fees from their parishioners, the growing secularization of society, and the improved educational demands of medicine which made a sharper distinction between the divines and the doctors. More autopsies were performed, information about the solid structure of morbid anatomy was enlarged, and because of Shippen and Moultrie, obstetrics gained a degree of specialization. Americans were contributing learned essays to European periodicals on smallpox, diphtheria, yellow fever, scarlet fever, and lead poisoning. Even the duties of a physician were defined by Samuel Bard in his discourse on professional ethics. Thus, while no dramatic developments occurred in American medicine by 1775, yet in numbers, in training, and in sophistication, the profession was improving. The Revolutionary War would provide further impetus to professionalizing medical practice.

Potts typified the "new breed" of doctors emerging by the 1770s. Educated and cultivated men like him were invariably admired by their communities, were known to several generations of families, and were called on for advice in local affairs. In times of trouble they offered leadership to their countrymen. Scores of these doctors served on Committees of Correspondence on the county and provincial level, and many helped to provide the ground swell of support for the Revolutionary movement. Twenty-one doctors were members of the First Provincial Congress of Massachusetts, 5 physicians were signers of the Declaration of Independence, 16 delegates with medical training served in the Continental Congress, and 1,400 medical men volunteered for the Continental army and navy. Jonathan Potts was such a man. He became an active participant in the great political crisis between America and Britain in 1774 which threatened to erupt into war.

IV.
The Doctor as a Patriot

On the eve of the Revolution, Potts was a respected community leader. After the passage of the Boston Port Acts in March 1774, he supported political protests about British oppression, and he voiced the radical rhetoric of the Revolution. Potts served on Committees of Safety, represented Berks County at provincial conventions, and helped to establish emergency controls for the colony. When fighting erupted at Lexington and Concord on April 19, 1775, Potts was already a dedicated patriot, determined to fight for American liberty.

Potts bitterly opposed the Boston Port Acts, or "Intolerable Acts," enacted by the British Pariament in early 1774 to punish Massachusetts for its Tea Party. The Crown did not curb seditious Massachusetts with this repressive legislation, nor did it intimidate other colonies. Boston's Committee of Correspondence appealed to other provinces to assist the Bay Colony in the crisis, to cooperate in a boycott of British goods, and to present a united front of opposition to the Ministry at an intercolonial congress. Radicals along the entire seaboard formed organizations to arouse the public, to protest against the hated laws, and to pledge assistance to beleaguered Boston. The response in New England, in the Middle Colonies, and in the South varied as regional leaders pondered the consequences of an embargo on British trade and of their participation in an unauthorized assembly.

Richard L. Blanco

When Paul Revere rode into Philadelphia on May 19, 1774, with Boston's plea for assistance in his saddlebags, Pennsylvania was unprepared to assist her northern neighbor. Pennsylvania was still "the Peaceable Kingdom." Regardless of some discontent with imperial policies, most Pennsylvanians in 1774 disdained treasonous activity and remained loyal to the mother country. No "Boston Massacre" had bloodied Philadelphia's streets, and instead of a scandalous Tea Party, the Quaker City sent back to England the East India Company tea ship, unladen and unharmed, that docked at its wharves.

Pennsylvania was cautious about talk of independence. The politically dominant Quakers in the Assembly, allied with German sectarians, disdained violence and war. They knew that Anglican influence in the colony was slight and that the hand of British rule was mild. Only one-half the population was of English extraction, and this group was influenced by Friends' doctrines of "inner light" and was not sensitive to concepts about political rights. The Germans, Scot-Irish, and other nationalities had been attracted to the colony by its religious toleration and by its generous land policies. For most inhabitants, Crown rule was not oppressive. Wide stretches of fertile farmland made Pennsylvania into a veritable cornucopia, and the colony's prosperity helped to muffle discontent. Most Pennsylvanians were farmers; many were unfamiliar with the English language and were unconcerned with complicated constitutional issues. Problems about crops, the weather, and livestock were far more urgent than obscure political grievances against the British.

Yet complaints had mounted in Pennsylvania against the Crown. The Proclamation of 1763, which prohibited settlement west of the mountains, angered the restless Scot-Irish. The Stamp Act of 1765 antagonized Philadelphia merchants and artisans and led to a temporary boycott of British goods. The Townshend Acts, which imposed new duties, reformed the customs service, and placed Crown officials beyond colonial control, infuriated more of the citizenry. Although the Townshend Acts were repealed in 1772, serious damage had occurred in imperial relations. Then came the Tea Act of 1773, which led to Boston's tumultuous Tea Party. The resulting Intolerable Acts in 1774, which revoked the Massachusetts Charter, closed the Boston port, and impinged on basic judicial rights, caused political shock waves in Pennsylvania. To men like Potts, a conspiracy, under way since 1765, had been designed by evil British Ministries to deprive Americans of their freedom. The punitive legislation against Boston was so vindictive that colonial leaders realized that self-protective action was essential. It was this plea for provincial cooperation that Revere carried into Philadelphia.

The response of the Quaker City was a town meeting held at City Tavern on May 20, 1774. The participants in the boisterous affair petitioned Governor John Penn to convene the Assembly in order to seek a redress of grievances from the Crown. From the City Tavern conclave emerged a radical leadership that condemned the Intolerable Acts and recommended the summoning of a Continental Congress and the creation of a Committee of Correspondence. To pressure the Governor and the Assembly to appoint delegates to the Congress, and to arouse support in the outlying counties, the Committee of Correspondence in Philadelphia dispatched circular letters to acquaintances in the back country, who formed a convenient network for political action.

The counties reacted quickly. Although Pennsylvania politics pivoted around events in Philadelphia, the intense discussions had ramifications far beyond the port, and towns in the interior were drawn into the controversy. To execute the general will of the community, local Committees of Correspondence were formed. These committees assumed control of the counties by voting funds for the Associators (as the militia were called), by denouncing the British Ministry, and by articulating the polemic which justified resistance to imperial legislation.

On July 2, 1774, the courthouse bell in Reading clanged the summons to a town meeting. The citizenry denounced Parliament's claim to total sovereignty, condemned the Intolerable Acts, pledged support to Massachusetts, and elected its own delegates. The participants at the Berks County meeting declared: "This assembly do [sic] unanimously resolve ... that the power claimed and now attempted to be put into execution by the British Parlaiment are [sic] fundamentally wrong, and cannot be admitted without the destruction of the liberties of America."[1] They elected Potts and five others to the Committee of Correspondence for Berks, with instructions to send provisions to Boston, to maintain contacts with committees of other counties, and to inform the public of current developments. The popular Potts was also designated as one of the seven delegates from Berks to the provincial convention to be held in Philadelphia.

At the convention held in late July the representatives sought conciliation with England; they refrained from defiant proclamations of rebellion and called for an amelioration of the tense Crown-colony relationships. Yet Potts and his fellow delegates indicated that unless their complaints were satisfied, they would urge a boycott of British imports.[2] Meanwhile the Assembly had convened, and it appointed delegates to the First Continental Congress, which met from September 5 to October 26 in Philadelphia. Aware that their countrymen desired peace, the Congressional delegates proceeded cautiously. As Congress debated, Revere again rode into the city; this time he presented Boston's fiery Suffolk County Resolves. These declarations denounced the Intolerable Acts, called for an embargo on British trade, and urged the formation of a provincial army. Rejecting Loyalist pleas for moderation, Congress on September 18 endorsed the resolves. As John Adams correctly predicted: "America will support Massachusetts or perish with her."[3] Congress also promulgated the terms of the Continental Association, which committed the colonies to commercial retaliation against Britain. The association provided for price regulation, the encouragement of domestic manufactures, and the formation of provincial organizations to enforce these agreements. To amplify the constitutional duel, Congress issued the Declaration of Rights and Grievances, called on the provinces to ratify its decisions by conventions, and recommended that a Second Congress meet in 1775 to solidify policies.

Potts played only a minor role in these developments. But because of his familiarity with numerous German families in the Pennsylvania Dutch counties, he endeavored to win their sympathy for Congress. In January 1775 Potts wrote a political essay that supported the editorial policy of the *Pennsylvania Staatbote*. Published by the influential John Heinrich Miller, the *Staatbote* had a circulation of 6,500, which linked German communities from New York to the Carolinas.[4] Since 1765 the militant Miller had lectured his readers about major political issues. Even so, the Stamp Act was repealed, and the Townshend Acts had only a minimum impact on the farming settlements of the interior. Concerned mainly with local matters, until 1774 the Germans remained relatively passive about broader colonial matters. No Teutonic Sam Adams or German-speaking Sons of Liberty emerged from their ranks. To overcome that indifference, Philadelphia revolutionaries toured the back country. As part of this effort to arouse the German constituency, Miller reported that the Crown was trampling on its fundamental rights.

Potts contributed to this political enlightenment with his carefully reasoned, but apparently unpublished, analysis of the crisis. He explained that the basic issue was "Whether we should submit to the arbitrary and unconstitutional claims of a British Parliament—or enter into an opposition which might involve her in a dangerous and bloody war." Denouncing Loyalist doctrines of traditional loyalties and passive resistance, the fiery doctor labeled the policies of George III as "cruel and tyrannical." Potts urged his correspondents to support Congress in the crisis and to prepare for war. Indignant with colonists who shunned a fight, Potts exclaimed that "a wretch" who could not even appreciate the consequences of the repressive legislation on his own welfare "does not deserve to breathe the free air of America." Neither "British fleets or armies shall tear us from our privileges ...," he trumpeted. "I will oppose any submission."[5] Long before the vast majority of his countrymen were willing to proclaim such drastic views, Potts had argued that resistance to British tyranny was justified.

These efforts to awaken the German community were linked to the policy of commercial warfare. On December 5, 1774, another public meeting was held in Reading, at which Potts, Burd, Nagle, and Biddle were elected to the Committee of Observation. At still another assembly in busy Reading on January 4, 1775, Potts and six other delegates were appointed to represent Berks at the Second Provincial Convention in Philadelphia. This convention was called to renew the vigor of the faithful, to implement the terms of the Continental Association, and to ratify the proceedings of Congress. The convention declared its determination to resist despotism and to defend American liberties. In a series of economic measures to demonstrate the colony's self-sufficiency, it recommended the local production of wool; the cultivation of hemp, flax, and barley; and the manufacture of salt, gunpowder, tinplate, glass, nails, copper, and printers' type. The convention also urged that weapons be stockpiled, that farmers avoid slaughtering sheep for market, and that the Associators enforce the boycott, check profiteering, and report on suspicious Loyalist activities. As Potts wrote to Edward Burd at the close of the meeting on January 25: "The Convention had carried the point unanimously, in approving the proceedings in every part of the Continental Congress and private committees are appointed to bring in resolutions to encourage manufactures . . ."[6]

On January 16, 1775, Potts, as Secretary for the Committee of Observation for Berks, urged his neighbors to cooperate with these measures. He advised that they should "exercise every public virtue, and act as became men in the solemn cause of liberty." Potts explained that the committee hoped that storekeepers would cooperate on prices, and that farmers would raise flax and hemp and would refrain from killing lambs. "The preservation of wool being an object of the greatest consequence," he observed, "the Committee flatters

The Doctor as a Patriot

themselves that the farmers will cheerfully observe their recommendations."[7]

The radical zeal in Philadelphia for war with Britain came to fruition on April 24 with the astounding news about the bloody clashes between Massachusetts militia and British regulars at Lexington and Concord. The city began to raise money for war, to crush dissent, and to form military units. The reaction to General Thomas Gage's raid on New England villages spread rapidly through the Pennsylvania countryside. Thomas Mifflin, one of the colony's leading revolutionaries, wrote Potts on April 27 that the Philadelphia citizenry was arming. "The whole town is filled with companies exercising," he exclaimed. "We have armed our people to a military frenzy." Exaggerating the danger of a British attack on the colony, Mifflin warned Potts and his committee to "hold yourself ready to assist us at an hour's warning."[8] When the Second Continental Congress met in Philadelphia on May 10, blood had been spilled in Massachusetts, and patriots in upper New York had captured Fort Ticonderoga. Proposals for moderation were shelved as Congress prepared for the struggle.

In Berks the call to arms was rapid, and the surge of support for Massachusetts was impressive. Scores of sympathizers for the rebel casualties wore pieces of black ribbon on their garments, and volunteers flocked to join the associators. On June 30 the Assembly named ranking officers for battalions and recommended that counties organize the militia into companies. Congress appointed George Washington as Commander in Chief of the provincial forces at Cambridge, and it requested that twelve battalions of riflemen—two battalions each from Maryland and Virginia and eight from Pennsylvania—join Washington's army of New Englanders, who had the enemy besieged in Boston. By early July one company under Captain George Nagle, the son of a German immigrant, was formed in Reading, and soon after, another Berks company was organized.[9] In Nagle's company G were Potts's friends, Morgan Connor and Edward Burd; Potts himself joined as company surgeon, one of Pennsylvania's first doctors to go to war.

Colonel William Thompson was the commander of the Second Continental battalion composed of men from York, Berks, and Lancaster Counties. Writing from Carlisle on June 27, Thompson appointed John Biddle to gather wagons and provisions for the battalion, and he designated Reading as "the place of rendevous . . ., and the eighth of July the time of meeting there."[10] A supply center for General Edward Braddock's army during the French and Indian War, Reading was a major military magazine during the Revolution, providing flour, flints, blankets, wagons, and muskets for Continental troops. By July 20 seven companies had assembled there for the march to Massachusetts, and three more hastened to the bustling town. The riflemen set off not in a full battalion but in separate companies. The zeal to arrive at Cambridge first led to a brisk race through four colonies for the honor of being Pennsylvania's "First Defenders." Legend has it that Nagle's company, leaving Reading on July 7, won the contest. The Berks men tramped through Bethlehem, New Windsor on the Hudson, Litchfield, Hartford, and Framingham, arriving at Cambridge on July 25 after a 450-mile trek.[11] The enthusiasm was so great to have a shot at the "lobsters," as the redcoats were called, that other riflemen hastened to the siege. By late August, Thompson's battalion of 600 troops, encamped on Prospect Hill, was ready for action.

After the carnage on Bunker Hill on June 17, little action occurred for the rest of the summer. As Private George Morison of Pennsylvania observed, the enemy "did not seem disposed to disturb our camp as long as we do not attempt to assail their encampment."[12] Because of their reputed marksmanship, the riflemen were exempt from camp duty. On August 16 Morgan Connor wrote to Samuel Potts that the frontiersman's buckskin jacket and leggings worn by the Pennsylvanians impressed the New Englanders. "A hunting frock is like a full suit at St. James's, it may pass anywhere."[13] Edward Burd wrote home that his comrades had crept close to British lines, "and as soon as a head appears they pop away at him."[14] Yet except for sniping, the Pennsylvanians, whose avowed sharpshooting was overrated, made little impact on the progress of the siege. Owing to their refusal to perform fatigue duty and to dig entrenchments, the riflemen made a poor impression on the officer corps. Colonel Edward Hand from Lancaster remarked that he was actually ashamed of their wretched discipline.[15] The unruly companies wasted so much powder and lead that General Charles Lee, their divisional commander, prohibited them from firing over 150 yards. Washington was so dismayed by these careless troops that he ordered them to stop wasting ammunition. The only significant skirmish in which some riflemen participated was in late August at Ploughed Hill, an American outpost near Bunker Hill. Thereafter the riflemen were required to perform camp duty, like the New Englanders, and the contest settled down to a long, monotonous investment of Boston.

Where was Potts during this baptism of fire for his townsmen? Unfortunately no evidence exists to indicate if he actually was at Boston. He may have marched to Cambridge and may have remained there a brief period, but whether he served on the line cannot be determined. On July 27 he signed a promissory note in Reading in favor of Edward Biddle, and on August 24 he treated a patient at home. Then a long gap in the pages of his account book until September 16 suggests that his absence was due either to sickness or to committee assignments. Probably, Potts did not serve at Boston.[16]

Potts may have experienced some of the difficulties encountered by battalion or regimental surgeons during the campaign. Even if he served only briefly in 1775, during the constant mustering of troops at Reading, Potts probably noted the problems of health services for the Continental army—preventive medicine for the rank and file, the establishment of sanitary standards, the formation of military hospitals, and the procurement of drugs and equipment.

As troops from six colonies were quartered in their autumn cantonments around Boston, their regimental surgeons contended with several difficulties. The 140 surgeons and their mates who participated in the campaign were relatively young and inexperienced, and they represented communities that expected them to guard the health of their own fellow provincials.[17] The concept of a medical corps for a national army was beyond the colonists' comprehension. Nor did the generals and the politicians appreciate the difficulties of providing medical care for thousands of men massed in unhygienic conditions. From their British opponents and from their own limited experience, the Americans had to learn the rudiments of military medicine.

Some American doctors had served with the redcoats during the French and Indian War. Morgan, Hand, Mercer, James Craik, Isaac Foster, John Jones, Samuel Stringer, among others, were familiar with the organization of the British army medical department. The Medical Board for the British army consisted of a Physician General, a Surgeon General, and an Inspector of Infirmaries. The Physician General placed physicians in general hospitals and on the staff of field commanders. He and the Surgeon General inspected drugs and equipment supplied by the Apothecary General. The Surgeon General designated staff surgeons and apothecaries for main hospitals, but regimental colonels appointed their own surgeons and mates. With the Inspector of Infirmaries, the Surgeon General shared in the supervision of medical officers, in the preparation of sick returns, and in the control of hospital personnel. The Surgeon General also supervised the Purveyor, who performed the commissary duties of purchasing straw, linen, bedding, and provisions for the sick.

The army medical administration provided the staff maintained in Britain for garrison troops and for disabled veterans. During a war, general hospitals were established behind combat zones in large towns. Closer to the fighting were the field hospitals, or "flying hospitals," utilized during the spring-to-fall campaigning, which functioned as intermediate stations between the line and the general hospitals. Near the battlefield were the regimental hospitals, which were merely collections of sick and wounded troops under a surgeon's care. Few of these hospitals—general, field, regimental—had trained nurses or orderlies. Only when rear-line hospitals became crammed with patients did the military designate some misfits from the enlisted men to serve in the supposedly degrading ward duty. The wounded were removed to safety by comrades ignorant of rudimentary first-aid procedures. During the tide of battle, casualties could remain for hours on a field littered with corpses; sometimes days passed before they received attention. Not until the Napoleonic Wars was human ingenuity applied to the problem of providing prompt treatment by trained personnel near the line and by quick transportation by horse-drawn ambulances to sanctuary. Until then, as at Bunker Hill, casualties were dragged off by their friends, carried on canvas, sailcloth, blankets, and wooden frames, or were hauled off to safety in carts or in wheelbarrows.

No formal training in military medicine existed, and regimental surgeons were often unfamiliar with the essentials of wound surgery and preventive medicine. Yet astute American surgeons could learn from their British colleagues about treating battlefield injuries, and about checking the appalling sickness rates that typified the traditional European campaign. During spring mobilization, about 3 percent of the troops usually were sick; by midsummer, even without any fighting, 6 percent of an army was normally unfit for duty; and by autumn, even with little combat and maneuvering, the rate of soldiers incapacitated by disease often soared to 12 percent.[18]

British publications in operative surgery were useful to the patriots. Numerous books contained information about wounds, fractures, amputations, powder burns, cauterization, and the pathology of inflammation. During the Enlightenment, little progress had occurred in wound treatment—a grim, bloody, and unscientific affair. Operations performed on wounded troops now appear incredibly crude and gruesome, although the level of surgery for civilians was similar. Chemical anesthesia was not available until 1846, and antiseptic techniques in military hospitals were not attempted until

1871. Intense pain and hemorrhaging were inevitable, and operations were performed with little concern for hygienic matters. If the patient were not killed by the shock and the bleeding, then his chances of developing septicemia, or gangrene, were quite high. The surgeon could provide very limited relief to men who had been hacked, burned, pierced, punctured, fractured, twisted, or smashed during a battle.

The majority of wounds was classified as gunshot wounds from the musket, rifle, or pistol, and from cannon, which fired heavy missiles that could sever or crush a man's body and limbs. The musket propelled a round, jagged ball that, when fired within a hundred yards, caused enormous damage to the human frame. The soft lead ball fired at a low velocity had a tendency to flatten on contact; it usually lodged in the tissue, made a larger wound, and often caused infection by forcing bits of skin and clothing into the wound. Another category of wounds was that of incised and puncture wounds caused by swords, cutlasses, knives, and bayonets. In close combat the sword and bayonet were deadly weapons, and penetrations of the chest and the abdomen were often fatal. The difficulties of saving severely wounded men were compounded by the inevitable neglect, exposure, and crude handling of casualties. Chances of healing complicated injuries were so remote that surgeons, toiling among scores of mutilated bodies, could not waste time on dangerous surgery. Hence they divided their patients into three categories—men who needed only first aid, those who could be saved by prompt surgery, and those who were so badly smashed that they were practically impossible to salvage.

Among the British army and naval surgeons who wrote about wound treatment, the most famous was John Ranby. As Rush commented: "In gun-shot wounds of the joints, Mr. Ranby's advice of amputation was followed with success."[19] When little hope of saving a limb existed, Ranby urged immediate amputation to save a life. "The neglecting ... of taking off a limb frequently reduces the patient to so low a state," he warned, "as must unavoidably render the practice of subsequent operations if not entirely unsuccessful, at least very dubious."[20] Ranby assumed that infection could be prevented by the removal of blood from the injured area, and hence copious bleeding before and after the operation was usually prescribed. After the battle of Dettingen during the War of the Austrian Succession, Ranby explained, he removed fifteen ounces of blood from a wounded man, had him transported fifteen miles, and bled him again, and then again the following morning. "Repeated bleedings in the beginning draw after them many advantages. They prevent a good deal of pain and inflammation, lessen any feverish assaults, forward the digestion, and seldom fail to obviate ... a long train of complicated symptoms that ... interrupt the cure, miserably harrass the poor patient, and too often endanger his life." Ranby was unclear about the nature of shock, which remained a mystery for decades, nor could he clarify the baffling question about precisely when a surgeon should operate. Whatever the timing of the amputation, an operator had to be fast, strong, and forceful as he cut and slashed, relatively immune to the screams of his patient. A surgeon had to remain stoical, Ranby advised: "You should in all aspects act as if you were entirely unaffected by their groans and complaints."

The first surgical textbook published in America was by John Jones of King's College. His *Plain Concise Practical Remarks on the Treatment of Wounds and Fractures* (1775) was a timely compilation of material written by Europeans, and reflected Jones's experience in the French and Indian War.[21] He provided instruction about treating fractures and wounds, and he specified how surgical assistants should grip a patient, where to make incisions, and how to probe for a ball. The informed surgeon had books to guide him, but such information was often overlooked in the frenzy of battle. The lack of time, the flow of casualties, the surgeon's own stamina, and the shortage of drugs and surgical instruments presented innumerable problems not envisioned in the textbooks.

Some useful works by British doctors on preventive medicine were also available. Richard Brocklesby's *Oeconom-*

ical and Medical Observations (1764) provided practical advice about diet, housing, ventilation, location of campsites, and the treatment of fifteen diseases incident to military service.[22] His major contributions were to recommend stricter standards for the selection of army surgeons, to urge that surgeons "attempt the practice of physick," and to stress how vital to the success of a campaign was the enforcement of hygienic rules by combat officers. Donald Monro, of the Scot medical dynasty, described his experience during the Seven Years War in *An Account of the Diseases which were most frequent in the British Military Hospitals in Germany* (1764), a handbook replete with data about health matters in garrisons, on shipboard, and on overseas expeditions.[23] Noting a causative relationship between disease and the natural environment, Monro perceived that the hazards of soldiering exposed the men to unique occupational diseases. He outlined the treatment for twenty ailments, provided three diet tables, and listed the drugs necessary for a field chest. His comments about regimental hospitals were particularly sensible. Monro emphasized the need for numerous small hospitals close to the line; he warned against crowding the general hospitals; and he urged strict attention to the drainage, cleansing, and fumigation of these sites.

Sir John Pringle was the most influential writer on military medicine during the eighteenth century. In his *Observations on Diseases of the Army in Camp and Garrison* (1752), he classified diseases typical of military service, and he suggested means to cure them. His classic work on military hygiene related how disease decimated the British army in northern Europe during the Seven Years War to such a point that troop losses from combat were relatively small compared to losses from disease. Actually, only 1,500 British troops were killed in battlefield injuries during the struggle, but 154,000 perished from sickness. To ward off pestilence that was triggered, Pringle thought, by temperature changes, "putrid air," improper diet, insufficient sleep, and so on, he suggested that the troops benefited from frequent clothing changes, ample rest periods, daily cleaning and ventilation of

The Doctor as a Patriot

quarters, and plentiful supplies of fresh fruit and vegetables. Pringle stressed that "putrid fever" invariably resulted from packing slovenly troops into barracks, transports, and hospitals without sufficient air and space. He contended that army hospitals, because of their unsanitary conditions, ironically were the greatest slayers of troops. To avoid typhus, prevalent in hospitals, Pringle urged that instead of cramming the sick in damp, grimy, large buildings, they be scattered among small regimental hospitals. "The want of pure air [in general hospitals] cannot be compensated by diet or medicine; . . ." Airy and spacious rooms were necessary, he stated, to house casualties. "For this reason not only barns, stables and graneries . . . but also churches make the best hospitals . . . [and] the less danger there will be of breeding contagious distemper."[24] Regarded as "the father of military medicine," Pringle influenced hygienic practices in the British army, but not until the 1790s. His advice was usually overlooked by both the British and the American military during the Revolutionary War.

The Americans could thus overcome their relative inexperience in military medicine by relying on the British practice with large armies. James Tilton of Maryland, one of Potts's classmates, noted that Monro, Pringle, and Brocklesby were the only English essayists on the subject. "It is remarkable," he concluded, "that none of the military writers have paid much attention to . . . military hospitals."[25] Not only did the patriots learn about wound surgery, preventive medicine, and pharmacy from the British, but the enemy also had the army medical organization that they could emulate.

The organization of American military medicine began early in 1775 when the Massachusetts Provincial Congress procured medical supplies for its battalions. Although thirteen medical men participated in the actions at Lexington and Concord, and the provisional government used homes and churches in Cambridge as hospitals, no formal medical department was created. As volunteers from other New England colonies poured into the seige of Boston, a more permanent medical service was required.

Richard L. Blanco

In June 1775 standardized rations of food and drink for the troops were devised, and the procurement of tents, blankets, and clothing was under way. By July, as Congress assumed control of the army, delegates in Philadelphia considered medical matters. Because of careless food preparation, the casual handling of waste, and the pollution of watersheds, the danger of "camp disease," or dysentery, was apparent. Washington ordered officers to enforce sanitary standards and to control the disposal of offal and garbage. The success of these directives is difficult to determine, because recruits were unaccustomed to public-health regulations and because the inspection system in many regiments may have been ignored. Linked to the hygienic problem was that of possible epidemics. Smallpox had lurked in Boston since 1774. Many troops were from small villages; probably they had not been exposed to the disease, and consequently they represented a reservoir of immunes quite susceptible to the pestilence. Surgeons inspected men for signs of the disease, soldiers with indications of the contagion were isolated, and smallpox hospitals were provided. Fortunately smallpox did not erupt on a large scale, and inoculation measures, which may have been resisted by the soldiery and which would have weakened the long lines around Boston, were not attempted.

One problem was the shortage of drugs. But the rebels overcame this difficulty, for they controlled most of New England, their privateers captured enemy ships carrying medicine, Massachusetts doctors donated medicines, and quantities of drugs were confiscated from Loyalist physicians and apothecaries. When a critical need for medicine developed in June 1775, the Massachusetts Council of Safety appointed Andrew Craigie as apothecary with the task of stocking drugs. Another difficulty was the recruitment of hospital personnel. In May, the Massachusetts authorities appointed some Boston doctors to staff the general hospital at Cambridge; to weed out incompetents from the ranks of regimental surgeons, the doctors instituted what was probably the first medical examination of candidates on an interprovincial level. As James Thacher, a regimental mate, remembered;

"Six of our number [sixteen] were privately rejected as being unqualified ..."[26] Massachusetts authorities also devised procedures for "sick call" and disciplinary codes for hospital patients, and acquired the nonprofessional personnel (nurses, stewards, orderlies) for the hospitals. By the summer of 1775 Massachusetts had created the nucleus of the future medical department of the Continental army.

The crisis in medical services came when the slaughter on Bunker Hill demonstrated the need for a more centralized hospital department to be superimposed on the provincial forces. Soon after assuming command, Washington realized the inadequacies of medical care and commented to Congress: "I have made inquiry into the establishment of the hospital, and find it a very unsettled condition ... I could wish it was immediately taken into consideration, as the Lives and Health of both Officers and Men so much depend on a due Regulation of this Department."[27]

Congress studied the matter, and on July 27 it approved the Hospital Bill. This legislation for a "hospital" (meaning medical department) established a general hospital staff managed by a Director General, who supervised four surgeons, twenty mates, an apothecary, and other personnel. The staff duties were adequately defined, but the scope of the director's authority over the bickering regimental surgeons was not clarified; he was assigned innumerable purchasing and commissary duties in addition to his medical functions. Yet, considering the magnitude of pressing domestic and diplomatic problems confronting the busy delegates in Philadelphia, the Hospital Bill was a solid legislative achievement.

During the siege some regiments suffered severely from the lack of food, fuel, clothing, shelter, and from diseases such as diarrhea, jaundice, arthritis, and respiratory ailments. Despite strenuous efforts to shelter and provision the men by autumn, many units were poorly supplied. Some private homes were used to house the men, and many wooden huts were constructed; yet some regiments were still shivering in tents in January 1776. It is remarkable, however, that a new army, with units of men from different provinces and crowded together under unfavorable conditions did not have a higher incidence of disease. Perhaps because of the absence of sustained combat and long marches, and the generally healthy condition of these hardy provincials, the army did not succumb to pestilence.

A difficult matter for the medical men at Boston was the state of their morale. The regimental surgeons bitterly resented Dr. Benjamin Church, a respected Boston physician, who on July 27 was appointed Director General. With enough time and support, Church may have shaped his department into an efficient organization. Unfortunately Church feuded with the regimental surgeons, who opposed his supervision. Contrary to orders, they retained their sick in regimental hospitals, they refused to supply Church with sick returns, and yet they demanded that he supply them with drugs and equipment. However, Church was soon dismissed. Since early 1775 he had been suspected of being a spy, and for months he had been under observation for treasonous activities. Removed from his post on October 5, Church was tried, convicted, and exiled for treason. The administration of the medical department thus began the war with acrimony.

To replace Church, Congress selected John Morgan. Arriving at Cambridge on November 29, Morgan was challenged by the task of reforming the department; he inherited the problems of meager supplies, low morale, and little authority to supervise the regimental personnel. A haughty man, Morgan complicated his task by antagonizing generals, politicians, and the regimental surgeons with his temperamental outbursts. To his credit he instituted the policy of appealing to the public for surgical dressings, he acquired quantities of drugs, and he renewed the system of examining candidates for surgeoncies. But his directorship at Boston was characterized by incessant quarreling with his subordinates, a factor that resulted in an unsavory reputation for the department.

With the arrival in late February of heavy cannon dragged through the snow from Ticonderoga, Washington prepared to terminate the long siege. He had powerful batteries placed on Lechmere Point and on Dorchester Heights, so the city and British shipping were within range of the American guns. Anticipating an attack by General Sir William Howe on these fortifications, Morgan made extensive preparations for the fighting by recruiting nurses, preparing teams of stretcher bearers, stocking hospital stores at Harvard College, and instructing his surgeons about wound treatment. Owing to a storm, Howe's pending attack planned for early March on the American lines was aborted, and on March 17 the British evacuated Boston and sailed for Nova Scotia.

Fearful of entering a city rumored to be ridden with smallpox, Washington had one regiment immunized before it entered Boston. Fortunately the port was virtually free of the contagion, and by March 20 the Continental army entered Boston. Before the mass inoculation of the army was attempted, most of the troops were marching to New York. But the secret use of inoculation by the remaining soldiery at Boston, who intermingled with the citizenry, kept the virus flourishing through the spring and summer. With the permission of the Massachusetts Legislature, the troops stationed at Boston and the local inhabitants underwent inoculation. Thacher related that out of 500 men in his regiment, only one man died from inoculation.[28] By late 1776, in the most successful demonstration of large-scale inoculation in the colonies, five thousand people in Boston had been inoculated, and only two died. Part of this success was due to Morgan, who wrote an introduction to Thomas Dimsdale's work on the subject, in order to assure the public of the efficacy of the new method. In the older technique a physician made two deep incisions in the flesh, inserted a thread seeped with the pus from a ripened pustule into the cut, and covered the wound with a bandage or plaster. An improved, but secret technique had been devised by Dr. Benjamin Sutton. Dimsdale learned the Suttonian procedure and refined it. He advocated a two-week period of preparation of special diet, ample rest, and cathartics. Then he inoculated patients by a shallow puncture, inserted a small amount of serum from an unripened pustule, and left the wound uncovered. The final step was recuperation by a bland diet, moderate exercise, and various medications. The use of the safer Dimsdale method, as popularized by Morgan, may explain the success of the program at Boston, which offered a model for the future mass inoculation of the entire Continental army.

The army doctors at Boston had acquired some experience in military medicine, and they had managed to keep the ratio of sick men during the ten-month siege to an average of 12 percent.[29] They learned that the fear of illness could inhibit enlistments, that the incidence of disease increased with the size of the army, and that the troops could be kept healthy by the maintenance of certain living conditions. The medical department had functioned under relatively favorable conditions. Contagious diseases were not widespread, and few combat casualties occurred. With some notorious exceptions the troops were adequately provisioned and sheltered, many New England doctors volunteered their services, the local public was overwhelmingly sympathetic, drug supplies were sufficient, and the campaign was conducted along static lines near populated market and supply centers. A significant factor, too, was Washington's personal interest in hygienic matters, reflected throughout the war in his general orders, which testify to his concern for the welfare of his troops. But whether the medical department could function effectively in less fortunate circumstances had yet to be determined.

Meanwhile Potts remained in Pennsylvania involved with his public duties. In November 1775 he was in Philadelphia informing the Committee of Safety about gunpowder production in Berks County; in December he studied the output of muskets in local armories. His responsibilities increased in 1776. By early February he had the task of caring for prisoners of war (men, women, children) captured on Lake Champlain who were confined in Reading (as well as in York and Lancaster). Reading continued as a supply center for the army, and new battalions assembled there. As a Congressional entry of March 23 indicates, Potts made health inspections of the Second and Fourth Regiments of Arthur St. Clair and Anthony Wayne, and again in April Potts was cited for providing medicines to other Pennsylvania regiments.[30] Clearly Potts was active in supporting the patriot cause.

Potts sought a more important role in the Revolution, and he desired an appointment in the medical department. At first he hoped to be named the regional director of the department in the Middle Colonies, but because of administrative changes, he requested an appointment to supervise a hospital in Canada. An American invasion of Canada had begun in October 1775, and by the spring of 1776 the Americans expected that Quebec would topple. Anticipating an American victory on the St. Lawrence, Potts petitioned Congress on April 29 for a post:

> that upon application made . . ., to be appointed Director of the Hospital for the Army in the middle Department, Your Petitioner was encouraged by many Members of your Honourable House to hope for such an appointment. . . . That by the movement of the Army since that time it appears the Hospital under the Direction of Doctor Morgan will be placed in the Middle Department, and your Petitioner is informed it will be necessary to establish one in Canada.
>
> He therefore prays he may be appointed Director of the Hospital there and hopes by a constant and faithful discharge of the Trust reposed in him, he will merit the approbation of this Honourable House and he will pray.[31]

Potts's credentials were impressive, and on May 10 Congress resolved that he be named to a high position in the Northern Department (upper New York and Canada) under the jursidiction of General Philip Schuyler, but without a specific title. As the resolution read: "that Potts . . . be employed in the Canada Department as the General shall think fit."[32] Owing to the fluid nature of the Canadian campaign and to the fact that Schuyler had already named Dr. Samuel Stringer (1734–1817), his protégé and personal physician, as Director of the hospital in the Northern Department, Potts's official status was unclear until June 6, when he was designated "a Physician and Surgeon in the Canada Department" under the supervision of Stringer.[33] Potts did not receive the high position that he coveted, but he agreeably acquiesced to being second in command. After corresponding on the matter with John Hancock, the President of Congress, Washington assigned Potts to the hospital on Lake George. In late June Potts probably called upon Washington at his Manhattan headquarters. Although no record of the visit exists, Joseph Reed of Pennsylvania, Washington's adjutant, wrote a letter of introduction on June 24 to General John Sullivan, commanding the Northern army on the St. Lawrence. Reed described Potts as "a Gentleman of Character in every respect and most indisputable zeal in the publick Cause."[34] Potts sailed up the Hudson that month to assume his new duties. At Lake George and Lake Champlain, he would need all his skill and talents. The Northern army, its ranks crippled by smallpox, was in full retreat to Ticonderoga, pursued by a triumphant British army.

V.
The Canadian Campaign and Fort Ticonderoga

In late June 1776 Potts sailed up the Hudson to Albany with General Horatio Gates, the new field commander for the Northern army, to assume his post. Their ship, the *Polly*, carried medicine and provisions for the hospital at Fort George.[1] The doctor and the general knew that the American army at Quebec had been routed in May and that it had retreated up the St. Lawrence. Potts and Gates also learned that the patriot force was ravaged by smallpox, but the reports about the disasters that had trickled to the seaboard seemed exaggerated. Few could have envisioned the catastrophes that struck the command which had nearly captured Quebec. The American invasion of Canada illustrates many instances of daring and heroism. For medical history the episode is significant because it illustrates that the prevalence of contagious disease was a major factor in the campaign. Potts barely arrived at Fort George in July when he encountered the most severe challenge of his career—hundreds of troops suffering from smallpox were entrusted to his care, the pitiful remains of an army that had almost conquered Canada.

In September 1775, when British power had virtually been driven off the continent, the prospects of capturing Canada were alluring. One wing of an invading American army, assembled in Maine, would tramp through the unmapped wilderness to the St. Lawrence to pounce upon Quebec.

Another wing, mobilized in New York, would journey up Lake George and Lake Champlain and then along the rivers flowing northward to the St. Lawrence, from where it would capture Montreal. Since the Americans expected to ascend these routes quickly and since only 1,100 redcoats guarded the province, the opportunity to make Canada into "the Fourteenth Colony" seemed excellent. Yet the planners of this adventure overlooked the difficulties of marching through trackless forests, of coordinating two widely separated commands, and of preventing epidemics in an area where smallpox was endemic.

In late September Colonal Benedict Arnold assembled 1,150 men at Fort Washington (Augusta) for the march to Quebec, supposedly a three-week trek of 180 miles. Arnold expected to mount the Kennebec and Dead Rivers, portage over the Height of the Land, and then descend the Chaudiere River to the St. Lawrence. Isaac Senter, a recent apprentice, and three mates comprised the medical team. Fortunately two officers with medical training also joined the expedition, and Arnold had been an apothecary. Traveling up the Kennebec in heavily laden boats, the troops had to tug and haul their craft past miles of foaming rapids and churning cascades. By October 9, they reached Norridgenock Falls, which marked one-third the distance, and entered what Senter termed "a howling wilderness." Scores of men began to drop out along the trail, worn out from toil, diarrhea, and dysentery. After a back-breaking portage to the Dead River by October 16, another hundred men, exhausted and drenched, quit the expedition. "The army was much fatigued," Senter recalled, "being obliged to carry the batteaux, barrels of provisions, warlike stores, etc., on their backs through a most terrible piece of woods conceivable."[2]

Beyond the Dead River Arnold's men struggled through bogs, swamps, gorges, and rock-strewn rivers. Pelted by incessant rain and early snows, they camped without shelter on frozen ground. Although the men occasionally supplemented their dwindling rations of rancid pork and damp flour with nuts, berries, fish, and game, some men were so famished that they consumed pieces of soap, mocassins, and moosehide jackets. By October 21 only 700 men remained for the fearsome portage over the Height of the Land. The starving troops barely reached Lake Megantic, from where, after feasting on game, they managed to stagger to the Chaudiere. An advance party there provided them with provisions acquired at a French settlement. The next sixty miles of the journey were comparatively easy, and by November 8 the Americans reached the St. Lawrence. Arnold rested his troops, and then ordered them over the river to capture Quebec. The city was well defended, and it seemed impregnable to men who lacked cannon. Confident that the bastion would topple to a siege, Arnold withdrew up the river to await reinforcements from New York. The expedition actually required 45 days and 350 miles. The near success of this epic achievement may be explained by Arnold's dynamic leadership, by the intense motivation of his men, and by their remarkable physical stamina.

The expedition under Schuyler's supervision from upper New York was delayed due to supply problems and to a determined British defense of a fortress. Schuyler, a quartermaster in the French and Indian War, had 2,800 troops stationed at Albany, the upper Hudson, the Mohawk Valley, Skenesboro (Whitehall), Fort George, Crown Point, and Ticonderoga. To prepare for the invasion, Schuyler had to contend with numerous manpower and logistical problems. Relatively isolated from seaboard commercial and manufacturing areas, Schuyler had to organize supply lines from lower New York and from western New England to provision his remote posts. He acquired food and equipment for his men and established supply depots on trails running north. His soldiers cleared roads, built wharves, bridges, and stockades, and cut timber for oars, boats, and barracks. Schuyler organized teamsters into wagon trains, had sawmills and powder mills erected, and gathered carpenters, oar makers, sail makers, and blacksmiths to assemble a fleet at Skenesboro.

Inasmuch as Congress neglected to provide his command with a hospital staff, Schuyler had to recruit his own medical personnel. When Schuyler arrived on July 18 at Ticonderoga, the base for the expedition, he was shocked at the wretched condition of his troops. He complained to Congress that they had neither tents, blankets, nor provisions, and that a fifth of them were already sick. To Governor Jonathan Trumbull of Connecticut, Schuyler commented on July 31, "the troops here sicken fast, for want of proper hospital, we are under the necessity of leaving the sick with the well."[3] As Congress had not authorized a hospital for the Northern Department, Schuyler stated that he had asked Dr. Samuel Stringer to be director for his command. Stringer, who served as a mate with General James Abercromby at Ticonderoga in 1768 and was considered the foremost doctor in the Albany area, reluctantly accepted the position. As Schuyler informed Gouverneur Morris, a prominent New York politician, Stringer originally refused the request, but "at length he was prevailed not only to give up an extensive and beneficial practice . . ., but brought along with him a large Stock of his own medicine."[4]

Stringer collected drugs and equipment, and he recruited surgeons and mates. He acquired vacant homes in Albany for his general Hospital, and at Fort George he utilized some barracks as his field hospital. By early October the busy Stringer was on Lake George supervising the construction of quarters for 300 sick. His correspondence abounds with references to masons, bricklayers, carpenters, and woodcutters. Stringer also drafted women attached to Ticonderoga regiments as nurses, forwarded medical stores to the garrisons, organized transportation for the sick from Ticonderoga to Albany, and set up an apothecary shop at Fort George.[5] Unfortunately for Stringer, Congress, intent on the siege of Boston, failed to appreciate the difficulties of providing medical care in the wilderness. Anticipating a swift and glorious campaign in Canada with few casualties, Congress tardily authorized only two surgeons and two mates for Stringer, a staff which, he warned, was inadequate for the army. Then Stringer encountered another problem. Congress had appointed Stringer as "Director of the Hospital, chief physician and surgeon to the army in the Northern Department," but it neglected to define

The Canadian Campaign and Fort Ticonderoga

Stringer's relationship to Morgan, the Director General. The priority of Stringer's appointment before Morgan's, the virtual autonomy of Schuyler's army, and the lack of a Congressional resolution clarifying Morgan's authority over regional hospitals provided fuel for a heated controversy between the two doctors. Furthermore, although medical arrangements for the lake posts were adequate, only regimental surgeons and mates accompanied the troops into Canada; no provision was made for establishing general hospitals along the St. Lawrence or for inoculating troops, except for arrangements that a military commander could devise.

Meanwhile the expedition for Montreal was under way. In late August Schuyler ordered General Richard Montgomery to sail up Lake Champlain with 900 troops into Canadian territory. Joining Montgomery in early September at Isle aux Noix with another 800 men, Schuyler led the force thirty miles up the Richelieu to attack the small settlement at St. Jean's. Though heavily outnumbered, the British garrison successfully repulsed the assaults, and the Americans had to cope with a difficult investment. Ill with scurvy and rheumatism, Schuyler relinquished the field command to Montgomery and returned to Ticonderoga. The siege of St. Jean's continued under very unfavorable conditions. The Continental encampment was on low swampy ground, the men were poorly provisioned, and they were constantly soaked by heavy rains. On September 21 Benjamin Trumbull, a chaplain, remarked that "our men have been wet near twenty days."[6] Commenting on the difficulties, Montgomery reported to Schuyler that "we have become like half-drowned rats crawling through a swamp."[7] The American effort was close to collapsing in early October when another 700 troops arrived with tents, provisions, and artillery. On October 18 Chambly, a small British outpost up the Richelieu, fell to the Americans, and on October 25 St. Jean's finally surrendered. Only one hundred Americans were combat casualties, but a few hundred were removed from the line due to chronic sickness. Furthermore the defense at St. Jean's had delayed the invasion for seven weeks. Some two thousand troops remained, Trumble reported, "and I believe [they] will go forward with good spirits notwithstanding the Season is so far advanced."[8]

Montgomery encountered little resistance up the Richelieu. By November 11 he held Sorel, and by November 13 his troops were poised near Montreal. Unable to defend the city, General Sir Guy Carleton, the Governor General of Canada, scurried off to Quebec. Montreal fell easily to the Americans on November 13, and soon thereafter, with the capture of Three Rivers, the entire St. Lawrence was opened to the invaders. Yet because of sickness, desertions, and the expiration of enlistments, Montgomery had only 500 men. Leaving General David Wooster in Montreal with 200 soldiers, Montgomery hastened to join Arnold at Quebec. Standing boldly and defiantly, Quebec could withstand a siege until the spring of 1776, when transports from Britain, sailing up the St. Lawrence, could bring redcoats to drive off the rebels. Still without artillery or entrenching tools, Arnold and Montgomery wondered how their small force could capture the bastion in the winter.

A hospital under Senter's care was established by Arnold in a convent at St. Roque's Gate near the St. Charles River. The poorly clad American troops on the line were chilled by the bitter cold, and men with pneumonia and other respiratory complaints began to crowd the wards. A more fearsome enemy appeared before Christmas when five patients, diagnosed for smallpox, were removed to an isolation center. Caleb Haskell, a Rhode Island fifer, remembered that he and his sick companions who were stricken by smallpox "were carried three miles out in the country out of camp."[9] No American physicians were present at Quebec, apparently no Canadian doctor volunteered to help, and evidently no ranking officer removed from duty men who displayed early signs of the disease. Although one could fault the commanders for not establishing a rigid medical inspection system, it was actually the inexperienced medical men who erred. Senter displayed his own ignorance of the danger by noting on December 17: "From this day to the 3rd, nothing occurred of consequence except that smallpox broke out and on the 18th five men were brought into the hospital."[10] Because of no official inoculation policy, many troops sought out local quacks in the suburbs, or they inoculated themselves. In late December, remembered John Henry, a Pennsylvania soldier, "Great numbers of the soldiers inoculated themselves . . ., by lacerations under the finger nails by means of pins and needles, either to obtain an avoidance of duty, or to get over the horrible disease in an easy and speedy way."[11] By early January the contagion was spreading rapidly. James Melvin, a Massachusetts private, noted in alarm: "Some more taken with the smallpox, and we expect it will be a general disorder, for we are very thick, nasty, and lousy."[12]

A more critical problem was the assault on Quebec. During a howling snowstorm on December 31 the Americans gambled on a surprise attack. Although the Continentals penetrated the city and fought for hours, the defenders maintained control of the streets and repulsed the raid. The battle was a disaster for the patriots—82 Americans were casualties, 372 were captured, Montgomery was killed, and Arnold was crippled with a wound. Even with this defeat the Americans, who had nearly captured Canada in one night, clung to their posts through the winter, hoping that Washington and Schuyler would reinforce them.

Under Wooster's direction the siege continued as a trickle of fresh troops arrived. Smallpox continued to spread. "Numbers of soldiers inoculated themselves, . . .," Senter observed. "Scarce any of the New England troops had ever had the disorder . . ."[13] By early February 1776 fifty men were hospitalized with the disease, and within two weeks another fifty crammed the wards. In contrast to the success of the medical staff at Boston, the surgeons at Quebec were unable to enforce a quarantine. With the exception of Arnold, who could hobble on crutches by March, most officers seemed indifferent to the danger. By early April about seven hundred men, or nearly one-half the force, was struck with the pestilence. Pleading with Congress on April 27 for medical assistance, Wooster lamented the shortage of drugs and surgeons and the spread of the contagion. Reinforcements who marched into the encampment, he explained, "took the smallpox as they arrived, either by inoculation, or the natural way."[14]

Dissatisfied with the progress of the siege, compared to the success at Boston, Congress on April 15 ordered Arnold to Montreal and replaced him with Wooster; then on May 1 Congress dismissed Wooster for General John Thomas, a Massachusetts physician. When Thomas appeared, he had 1,900 troops on paper, but 800 were ill with various ailments. About 500 were actually fit for combat, he noted, "the rest were invalids, chiefly with the smallpox."[15] Men deserted, enlistments expired, provisions dwindled, and the anticipated French-Canadian support for the *Bostonnais,* as the Americans were called, never materialized. The hopes of capturing Quebec seemed more remote. Nathan Rice, a former law clerk of John Adams, remarked that the army had only nine small cannon and that the powder and shot were nearly expended. "Add to this the smallpox raging and destroying and no medicines for the sick."[16] By early May, even though Schuyler had sent supplies on the long trail northward, Thomas had provisions for only a week. Finding his position at Quebec untenable, Thomas decided to retire up the St. Lawrence to await supplies and reinforcements. While the Americans were preparing to decamp on May 6, troops from Britain led by General John Burgoyne landed near Quebec. As the Americans evacuated, Carleton saw his opportunity, and with a force from the city he smashed the American lines and terminated the siege.

The Continental army was so scattered and so demoralized that it panicked and ran. Gunners left their cannon, soldiers dropped their muskets, surgeons abandoned hospital stores, and invalids scattered to the river, hoping to escape. Some troops were captured while crossing the St. Lawrence; some were trapped in the forests; others wandered for weeks before finding sanctuary. About two hundred sick were left behind, stated Lewis Beebe, a surgeon's mate from Massachusetts,[17] but most of the smallpox patients reached safety, with disastrous consequences for the healthy. The

The Canadian Campaign and Fort Ticonderoga

army that had nearly won Canada became a mob of filthy, hungry, terrorized men fleeing from the relentless British advance.

Forty miles up the river at Deschaumbault, Thomas tried to regroup his battered army, but he had to continue the retreat another forty miles to Sorel. "The escaping army . . . carried the smallpox among them . . .," remarked Lieutenant Charles Cushing of Massachusetts, "and boatloads of sick with it were landed among us, so that there was no possibility of escaping it, and it was contrary to [Thomas's] orders to be inoculated."[18] In Montreal, where some regiments had fled, Arnold sought to alleviate the danger of an epidemic by using the East India Company warehouse for mass inoculation. But Thomas, his superior, prohibited the treatment and threatened stern punishment for violation of his orders. Then a Congressional Committee on the scene (Benjamin Franklin, Samuel Chase, Charles Carroll) overruled Thomas, noting that three-fourths of the troops had not been inoculated and that the treatment was necessary to preserve the army.[19] But before mass treatment could begin, the army was retreating down the Richelieu. Ironically, Thomas, a medical doctor, died on the way, blind and delirious from smallpox.

American reinforcements hurried to rescue the stricken army. Hastening to ward off Carleton's attack were 5,500 new troops under Generals John Sullivan and William Thompson. With this force came a flow of weapons and provisions, so that a summer's reconquest of the St. Lawrence seemed feasible. But Sullivan underestimated the size of Burgoyne's army, and, prematurely, he ordered his men into battle. At Three Rivers on June 8, where only 500 redcoats were expected, Thompson's 2,000 Americans blundered into 6,000 British regulars, who shattered Sullivan's offensive. More than 7,000 Americans were scattered over Canada, but after the defeat only 3,500 could be counted as effectives. Unable to hold Montreal or the upper St. Lawrence and fearful of being trapped on the Richelieu, Sullivan had to retire south. "Everything is in the utmost confusion," he wrote Schuyler, "a dispirited army filled with horror at the thought of seeing their enemy . . . Smallpox, famine, and disorder has rendered them almost lifeless."[20] Even the dauntless Arnold, evacuating Montreal, acknowledged that the invasion was over.

The retreat up the Richelieu continued to Chambly, where Beebe was stunned to find large barns overflowing with smallpox cases. From dawn to dusk, "in the dirty stinking place," he heard the plaintive cry of 'Doctor, Doctor,' from every side."[21] The soldiers went on to St. Jean's, where boats were assembled for the passage down Lake Champlain as Burgoyne pressed closer. The army was so battered by defeat and sickness, Arnold explained, that "if the enemy comes we shall not be able to oppose him, sick, ragged, undisciplined, and unofficered as we are."[22] Stringer arrived at St. Jean's and informed Schuyler on June 7 that conditions were so hopeless that "it [is] impossible for one to be of any service to the army in these parts . . . I must say that if I had seen the irregularity of our affairs, I would not have entered the service . . ." Indignant that the quarrelsome Sullivan had accused him of selling medicines to sick men, Stringer swore "that I am determined to quit the service. You must be sensible that the Hospital appointments are little attended to, as to render my Office very disagreeable, and now reduced as I am, here to the business of a Storekeeper, . . ."[23]

On June 18 Sullivan's men prepared to disembark from St. Jean's. They struck their tents, gathered their provisions, and hurried to salvage equipment. Some men with smallpox staggered to the boats, looking like ghoulish creatures from the grave. The able-bodied placed them in the bows and sterns of the bateaux and transported them up the river to Lake Champlain. The sick lay lifeless, exposed to the broiling sun and to hordes of black flies and mosquitoes that crawled over their helpless bodies. As the craft moved over the water, a sickening odor arose from this floating hell—the stench of smallpox. To the moans of pain and anguish, the oarsmen rowed twelve miles to the Isle aux Noix, the last chunk of Canadian soil held by the Americans.[24]

On that flat desolate island, ten miles from the boundary of New York, the army disembarked. About 2,000 had smallpox, perhaps 2,000 had dysentery or malaria, and perhaps 3,000 were still fit for duty. The island was small, firewood was scarce, hostile Indians roamed the nearby shores, the days were torrid and the nights damp. From over the soggy encampment came the incessant wailing of the sick pleading for relief. Shocked by the horror, Beebe wrote that he was "struck with amazement . . . to see the misery of the poor distressed creatrues . . . No mortal will believe what they suffered . . ."[25] On this purgatory, daily burial parties heaved swollen human carcasses of the dead into huge pits at the tip of the island.

Since this ragged horde was incapable of fighting, Sullivan ordered another retreat—to Crown Point, ten miles above Ticonderoga. "One fortnight longer in this place," he informed Washington on June 19, "will not leave us enough men to carry off the sick."[26] To save Sullivan's army, every available craft on the Lakes—canoes, bateaux, longboats, whaleboats—were hurried north. The tortured sick were again crammed into open craft, and were exposed to pelting rain for the five-day voyage of 100 miles. On July 2, 3,000 men were hauled ashore at Crown Point. Witnessing the scene was Colonel John Trumbull, Gates's aide, who left a graphic commentary:

> It is difficult to conceive a state of much deeper misery. The boats were leaky, and without awnings; the sick being laid upon the bottom without straw, were soon drenched in the filthy water of that peculiarly stagnant muddy lake, exposed to the burning sun of the month of July, with no sustenance but raw salt pork, which was often rancid, and hard biscuit, or unbaked flour; no drink but the vile water of the lake, . . ., and scarce any medicine.[27]

The clothes of the sick had been unchanged in weeks and hung in rags; their skins were so swollen that the slightest movement seared their flesh. Some were blind from the swelling on their faces; their tongues and lips were caked dry like scorched leather. No drugs, nurses or adequate shelters were available for them.

After visiting the dilapidated fortress crammed with sick, John Adams wrote his wife: "Our misfortune in Canada is enough to melt a heart of stone. The Smallpox is ten times more terrible than the British, Canadians, and Indians together. The Smallpox, the smallpox, what shall we do with it!"[28] The sick had still another horrible journey ahead. On July 7 at Crown Point the generals decided to move the healthy to Ticonderoga. Sullivan had been recalled in disgrace, to be replaced by Gates, who would defend Ticonderoga. Schuyler would return to Albany to supervise reinforcements, and Arnold would direct the building of the fleet at Skenesboro. The sick would be shipped to Fort George, Schuyler informed Washington, where timber cut at the mill on Wood Creek was available for shelters, and "where 2 houses are ready for 350."[29]

Thus ended the most disastrous American campaign of the Revolutionary War, with casualties estimated at 40 percent.[30] On June 25 Arnold reported from Crown Point that one-half the army was incapacitated.[31] From Ticonderoga on July 27 Nathan Rice remarked that 6,000 troops were in the area, and that 3,800 were sick.[32] Commenting upon the losses, Governor Trumbull noted that "about three thousand were sick, another 3,000 were well. This leaves us about five thousand men to be accounted for; of these the enemy have cost perhaps one thousand, sickness another three thousand; which leaves three thousand; in what manner they are disposed of is unknown."[33] The campaign demonstrated that experienced medical personnel supported by energetic military leadership were necessary to protect the health of the army and that, more than the bullets and bayonets of the enemy, disease had wrecked the invasion. Over 5,000 men had perished, were captured, or were rendered unfit for service in ten weeks, and Canada was irretrievably lost.

Potts arrived at his post in early July, just before the sick were landed. Fort George was a small stone fortress for 400 troops on a slight slope at the southern end of Lake George that encompassed a wharf, a barracks, and an incompleted hospital that sheltered about 300 patients. As boatloads of

The Canadian Campaign and Fort Ticonderoga

sick arrived on July 13, Potts must have been stunned to confront such human wretchedness that crowded out of the craft, a virtual armada of misery. Stringer at Ticonderoga notified Potts that hundreds of patients were being sent down the lake, and he directed Potts to finish the construction of a kitchen, the apothecary shop, and the hospital wards. Aware that Potts lacked adequate shelter for this pathetic horde, Stringer advised: "Have the sheds on the lake shore fitted up with cribs or berths for their reception." As mattresses were not available, Stringer laconically suggested that "a quantity of hemlock trees, if procured will make not bad bedding...."[34] How Potts, on his first assignment with the Continental army, was to accomplish all these tasks was not specified. Fortunately some help was on the way. On July 13 Gates ordered that more women from the Pennsylvania regiments at Ticonderoga be dispatched to Fort George to serve as nurses. Stringer arrived soon thereafter and complained bitterly to Gates that he could not possibly handle so many patients. The hospital was inundated with sick, he lamented, and the medical stores promised months ago had not arrived. "In the name of God," pleaded Stringer, "What shall we do with [the patients], my dear General?"[35]

The exact number of sick at Fort George that summer cannot be precisely documented but there are some clues. An unsigned return from Fort George for July 12–26 shows that 1,497 men were admitted, 439 discharged, 51 died, 3 deserted, and 1,004 remained.[36] In late July Potts declared that 1,500 had been admitted and that 300 had been discharged.[37] Potts was so overworked that he admitted his inability to keep correct figures. Apologizing to Gates on August 8 for his tardy returns, Potts explained:

> I hope you will not attribute its late appearance at this time to any neglect on my part as I can with truth assure your Honor nothing is left undone in my power to reduce every matter relative to the hospital in order. The number of sick being great, they employ all our time, and having but one clerk who is to enter the names of every person admitted, discharged, died, or deserted as well as to superintend the

issuance of provisions, makes it almost impossible to comply with your order as punctually as I could wish.[38]

Neither Potts, nor Stringer, nor anyone else at the time could have realized that they were administering what would be the largest military hospital of the Revolutionary War.

Overwhelmed with toil, Potts wrote to Morgan at Manhattan, beseeching him for aid. In a letter written August 1 Potts described the emergency at Fort George:

> Without clothing, without comforts, or a shelter sufficient to screen them from the weather, I assume your known humanity will be effected when I tell you upwards of one thousand sick ... labour under the various disorders of dysentery, bilious putrid fever, and the effects of confluent smallpox; to attend the large number we have four seniors and four mates.

Even his drug supply was exhausted, Potts explained:

> And our little shop does not afford a grain of jalap, ipecca, bark, salts, opium, and sundry other capital items and nothing to be had in this quarter; in this dilemma our efforts are exhausted for solution, but will go on doing the best we can in hopes of speedy supply ...[39]

As a result of his pleas, Potts became unintentionally involved in a bitter jurisdictional dispute between his superiors. Morgan's authority over the medical department in New York (and Virginia) was still not defined. Confident of Schuyler's support, Stringer assumed that he was independent of Morgan, and he tried to create a separate hospital department. Yet, far from populated centers, Stringer realized that he was heavily dependent upon Morgan for personnel and equipment. Sensitive to challenges of his authority, Morgan requested that Washington and Congress specify Stringer's subordination to him. Washington preferred to have Congress clarify the matter, but he tactfully recognized Morgan's direction over regional hospitals. When Washington received

Stringer's complaints, he merely forwarded them to Morgan. Congressional lethargy in this affair and the bureaucratic sparring of professional rivals caused such difficulties in hospital administration that sick soldiers were the victims.

To Potts's plea for the sick, Morgan responded that he was unable to help; "my hands are tied up." Frustrated by Congress and by quarrels with surgeons and generals at Manhattan, Morgan stated that he "could not presume to meddle in affairs out of my province, . . ."[40] Morgan insisted that he had not received "a single order, or instruction to supply you with Medicine, Surgeons, or Mates." Yet the volatile Morgan soon relented from his rigid stance and promised Potts that he would send some medicines. "However I cannot do it now," Morgan warned, "as two English Men of War are gone up the North River [the Hudson] and will intercept every vessel that attempts to pass to or from Albany."[41] Not until Congress ordered Morgan to assist Stringer did the Director General finally recruit staff for the north. In late July Morgan informed Potts that he was sending Dr. James McHenry and Andrew Craigie, the apothecary, to the lakes. In early August Congress resolved that Morgan was indeed head of all regional hospitals, and thus Morgan won his victory over Stringer.

Yet Morgan claimed that he was unable to supply Lake George; he was hard pressed with medical arrangements on Long Island, where the British were expected to attack. "It depends upon yourself to supply medicine not only to your hospital," Morgan curtly informed Potts, "but to [the] Regimental Surgeons with you."[42] Determined to humiliate Stringer further, the quarrelsome Morgan told Congress on August 12 that since he had not been consulted about the Stringer and Potts appointments, he doubted "whether these gentlemen have any right to depend upon me for assistance. . . ."[43] Congress responded by asserting again that Morgan was superior to regional directors, but to compound the confusion it added that regional chiefs were to appoint their own staff. Potts tried to avoid becoming enmeshed in this controversy. As a loyal and dependable bureaucrat, he good-naturedly acquiesced in his dilemma; as he informed

Morgan: "I am resolved to be governed by such regulations as our wise Congress shall think proper, wishing nothing more than to contribute my [might] toward the relief of our Distressed Country, and assure the Glorious Independent States of America."[44]

If Morgan could not assist him, Stringer reasoned, then he would have to find men and medicine himself. On July 24 Stringer described to Gates "the shocking condition of our hospital where men were dying for lack of attention," and he requested permission to journey to Manhattan for drugs and to "leave the care of the sick to Dr. Potts...."[45] Worried about his diminishing troop strength and about the British force mobilizing at St. Jean's, Gates quickly approved the request. As a consequence Stringer departed on a long hunt for medicine, and Potts was left to supervise the hospital.

Potts was desperate for drugs and supplies; as he notified Gates "We have no bandages and lint to dress our fighting men."[46] Assuming that Stringer would not return for weeks, Potts sent a mate to Albany for drugs, and he pleaded with the citizenry of Albany and Salisbury (in the Hampshire Grants) for help:

> As... the General Hospital at Fort George which is at present crowded and in great want of old linen for lint and bandages, etc. we therefore entreat all lovers of their country and humanity to send all the old shirts, sheets, aprons, etc. they can spare... as soon as possible, as well as the thanks of the public, they should receive a good price for every article.

Herbals were also needed, so Potts requested

> the good women to dry and cure as many herbs for the use of said Hospital as they can procure. Sage, Balms, Mallows, and Wormwood.[47]

The response from both towns was an indication of local public support in the war effort. Salisbury sent linen to Potts, which he forwarded to Ticonderoga.[48] The Committee of Safety in Albany informed Potts that Dr. Jacob Rosebloom was collecting rags and linen for shipment to Fort George, and it hoped that the troops would benefit "from what the good people of our Country can afford."[49]

Stringer meanwhile wrote Potts a pessimistic letter about his encounter with Morgan. Stringer was so incensed over his treatment by the director that he threatened to resign. His efforts to recruit personnel were also exasperating. Surgeons and mates were unavailable, he remarked, "I doubt if any [sic]." Some medicine, including thirty pounds of bark, had been shipped, Stringer promised, as he left for Philadelphia, "only when you'll receive them, God knows."[50] More bad news followed. Dr. McHenry, Morgan's appointee to Fort George, would not venture north. Caught in the Stringer-Morgan feud, McHenry informed Potts that "My commission for your Department made out by Dr. Morgan, is considered idle and nugatory by Dr. Stringer."[51] Although Craigie arrived on Lake George in late August to supervise the apothecary shop, the controversy between the medical chiefs impeded the recruitment of other medical men.

Medical conditions at Ticonderoga continued to be serious. Although smallpox cases were isolated and shipped to Fort George, the pestilence still struck some regiments. Micah Hildreth, a Massachusetts officer, indicated his preoccupation with disease as he cited men from his company unfit for duty:

> August ye 12 then left Isaac Clement with the smallpox at Castleton, August ye 17 then Corpl. Spaulding was carried to Lake George Sick with the smallpox, August——then Asa Coburn was carried to Fort George with the smallpox, August 25 then Elijah Hildreth was carried to Fort George with the smallpox, August ye 28 John Means was carried down to Lake George with the smallpox. August ye 28. Then Zachariah Fletcher was Carried to Fort George sick with the smallpox.[52]

The prevalence of sickness and inadequate medical care were major morale factors, reported Colonel Samuel Wigglesworth to the New Hampshire Committee of Safety. "It would make a heart of stone melt to hear the moans and the distresses of the sick and dying," he lamented. "I can scarcely pass a tent but I hear the men solemnly declaring that they will never engage another campaign without being assured of a better supply of medicine."[53]

Gates diligently enforced sanitary regulations for cooking, clothing changes, water supply, latrine use, and soap issues.[54] The general believed that Stringer would soon return from his trip with staff and drugs, and that as a result the health of his garrison would improve. When Gates discovered that Stringer traveled from New York to Philadelphia without his permission, he was indignant and assumed that the doctor was lobbying with Congress for a new appointment, "preferment hunting," Gates caustically termed it.[55] Medical conditions at the fort were so poor, Gates informed Morgan on August 22, that "the troops are almost ready to mutiny. . . ." Worried that his men were not receiving adequate medical care, Gates complained that the troops justifiably expected "the same attention paid to the health of the soldiers as elsewhere."[56] Continuing his complaints to Washington on August 29, Gates stated that "everything about the army is infected with the pestilence, the clothes, the blankets, the air, the ground they walk on. . . ." Even though smallpox cases were promptly shipped down the lake, Gates explained, "this care and attention has not yet effectively destroyed the disease, it is continually breaking out."[57] Gates was so concerned about the state of morale that in his Orders of the Day for August 21 he assured the garrison that he had "left no means in his power untried to provide medicines and comfort for the sick of the army . . ." Concluding his communique on a patriotic note, Gates stated that God would surely protect the Americans and that the British were confronted with similar environmental problems. "Tis the soldier's duty to maintain the post he is ordered to defend. The same climate and season that effects us, . . . effects our enemy. The Favor of the Almighty . . . will protect us from slavery and Death."[58]

In addition to smallpox, other serious diseases flourished at Ticonderoga. Exhausted by the task of treating three regiments unassisted, Samuel Kennedy, surgeon of the 4th

The Canadian Campaign and Fort Ticonderoga

Pennsylvania, informed his wife in late August that the men had numerous ailments. "They continue sickly with Putrid, nervous, Bilious, intermitting and Remitting fever with fluxes."[59] Surgeon Beebe noted that half his regiment was unfit for duty. "The dysentery, jaundice, putrid and intermitting fever were the principal diseases."[60] Colonel Jeduthan Baldwin, the post engineer, remarked that Colonel William Bond had recently died of malaria.[61] John Trumbull commented about a strange fever that struck the troops:

> The exhalations from the earth was now, for the first time, exposed to the rays of the mid summer sun, combined with the fog which rose from the lake, soon produced sickness in a new shape—a fever very nearly resembling yellow fever . . .—and it was not unusual to see the strongest men carried off by it in two or three days.[62]

The famous James Wilkinson, then a nineteen-year-old major with medical training, remembered that he was struck by typhus at Ticonderoga, which he claimed carried off one thousand troops. Removed to Fort George, Wilkinson stated that he was "under the personal attention of Dr. Potts, the surgeon-general."[63] On August 31 young Jonathan Trumbull, Jr., wrote Potts from Ticonderoga that "Our people fall sick by the dozens and not a penny worth of medicine have we for them, even in the virulent Disorders—." Cannily recognizing the psychosomatic value of drugs, Trumbull added:."'tis no matter whether the people die for real want of medicine or because they think they want it. 'Tis Death in each case."[64]

By late August the extent of pestilence was such that Gates ordered his surgeons to list the diseases, to suggest means to improve health conditions, and to make inventories of medical requirements. The fifteen surgeons at the camp, under Kennedy's leadership, agreed on basic measures. They stated that various diseases were present, that a stricter enforcement of sanitary standards was essential, that the sick lacked coffee, sugar, and oats, and that twenty-five basic drugs were needed. But their individual responses varied considerably, and as a result their comments provide a rare insight into the state of contemporary military medicine. A few surgeons diligently listed the diseases, the drugs, and their surgical instruments. Others merely cited names of sick men, medicine on hand, or the few instruments they possessed. The surgeons for the regiments of Colonels Joshua Wingate and Elisha Porter stated that they had few drugs and no instruments. Robert Johnston of the 6th Pennsylvania noted that he had forty drugs on hand. Beebe of Colonel Enoch Poor's regiment carefully filled two pages with names of sick soldiers. The mate for Colonel Ephraim Wheelock's regiment remarked that he had neither drugs nor instruments, as did the surgeon in Colonel John Stark's regiment. Dr. John Ross reported that he needed numerous medicines and that his men needed blankets. Benjamin Alison of the First Pennsylvania listed 123 sick and severe shortages: "I have no amputating instruments, no lancet, nor probe, or any kind of instruments. No lint, or bandages, but a few simple rollars." J. Proze, of some unidentified unit, needed Jesuit's bark. Colonel John Greaton's surgeon reported "I have no medicine, received a case of instruments from Dr. Potts." Thacher of the 6th Massachusetts had some bandages and an instrument kit. The best equipped was Kennedy, outfitted in Philadelphia, who had nearly a full supply of drugs and instruments. The five artillery companies had no surgeon, so an officer aptly summarized the gunners' plight by scribbling: "Medicine and surgeons none. Instruments none, Assistance none."[65] Compared to the drug and instrument inventories made at Boston and Manhattan, it is clear that the medical men at Ticonderoga were very poorly supplied with equipment.

Under the prevailing therapy of the era, doctors could do little to ward off pestilence, but Potts crossed the lake frequently to Ticonderoga to offer advice. On July 16 Reverend Ammi Robbins, the post chaplain, mentioned that he had asked Potts to prescribe for his "inflammatory camp disorder." "I took a solution of manna, cream of tartar, senna and anise seed, had a sick day."[66] When Gates ordered a medical inspection of a regiment on September 4, Potts was on hand to review the surgeons' reports and to discuss the construction of a hospital on Mount Independence.

The medical staff on the lakes became part of an effort undertaken by authorities to prevent troops at the Fort from becoming infected with smallpox carried by recruits coming to Skenesboro. Gates was so determined to eradicate the disease, that to prevent self-inoculation he issued the following certificate for men in his command to attest:

> I do solemnly swear by the Everlasting God that I have not received the infection of the smallpox by inoculation or by an application internal or external, but have taken the same in a manner entirely unknown to me, as firmly believed by the Oath I now take in the natural way, and no other so help me God.[67]

When Sullivan's army retreated from Canada in June, communities in New England feared Indian and redcoat attacks. As soldiers from the expedition returned to New York, to the Hampshire Grants, and to the rest of New England, a greater threat to the public was smallpox. "Fear of the infection," Governor Trumbull wrote Washington from Lebanon, Connecticut, "operates strongly to prevent soldiers from entering the service."[68] From Boston, Dr. Cotton Tufts, informed his relative John Adams that "the smallpox prevailing in our Armies and Country had much retarded the raising of Recruits."[69] Men in some areas enlisted so slowly for northern service that bounty money had to be raised. Massachusetts offered the high sum of £7 for service at Ticonderoga. Recruits for Washington's army on Manhattan received £3 from Connecticut, and an additional £3 was given for duty beyond lower New England and lower New York. As Trumbull explained on July 17, the horror of smallpox terrified some men more than the human enemy, and the disease was "represented in such a light [by travellers] as induced belief that it was inevitable by any who should join the army and greatly retards levies for that service, as scarcely one in twenty of our people have had this distemper."[70] Nevertheless by late July some brave New Englanders marched northward along the Connecticut River to upper New York. By early August these regiments assembled at Charlestown, a stopover on the march to Skenesboro. As Surgeon Thacher of Massachusetts remarked: "We took our route through Worcester, Springfield, Charlestown in New Hampshire, and over the Green Mountains to Skenesboro, which is the place of rendevous for the Continental troops destined for Ticonderoga."[71]

The authorities pondered a policy to prevent the spread of the contagion. They considered inoculating groups, segregating camp sites on the march, forbidding self-inoculation, and requiring soldiers to present certificates attesting to inoculation. Schuyler warned Washington on July 12 that uninoculated New Englanders on the way "will rather weaken than strengthen our army."[72] And on August 7 Gates echoed this sentiment by informing Washington that the large desertions from his army "were principally occasioned by the threat of smallpox." Urging that reinforcements be halted at Skenesboro for inspection and inoculation, Gates stated that otherwise, "it would be heaping a hospital upon another."[73]

Unfortunately it was difficult to coordinate a policy, and the measures were not implemented in time. Some troops were not inoculated during their march to the lakes, and to protect themselves they underwent unauthorized inoculation at Keene, Charlestown, Williamstown, Claremont, and Skenesboro. Such unofficial inoculation inevitably caused difficulties. Typical of the alarm voiced in western New England was that in Williamstown, where on August 4 the inhabitants protested to Gates that a company of Rhode Islanders had just inoculated themselves. To protect the community, the town fathers isolated the troops in a remote house. The Williamstown selectmen requested Gates to require that oncoming men present certificates, and that if they had not been inoculated, they be ordered to travel on roads far from their village.[74] Another incident occurred in Skenesboro, where the vessels for Arnold's fleet were being constructed. Schuyler

The Canadian Campaign and Fort Ticonderoga

notified General David Waterbury, the commander at the base, to enforce quarantine:

> You will please dispatch three or four trusty officers to the different roads which the military take in their ways to Skenesboro, with particular orders to remove all officers and soldiers infected with the smallpox to a distance from the road... The life of individuals is not to be put into competition with that of the state.[75]

How successful Waterbury was in enforcing these orders is partially documented. On August 12 Waterbury ordered a company of civilian carpenters heading for the shipyard and undergoing self-inoculation in Williamstown to avoid his post until cured. As Waterbury warned them: "We have got it out of this place and out of Ticonderoga, and we are determined to use every precaution to keep it clean, and for your men to go and inoculate and presume to come here among fresh Troops we think is monstrous."[76] As Gates remarked, "the excessive sickness of that place [Skenesboro] has greatly reduced the finishing of the row galleys. Very few of the Ship Carpenters are able to work."[77]

At Fort George, Potts was another link in the arrangements as he detained recruits who had slipped by the check at Skenesboro. As Potts remarked: "I am greatly surprised in having some patients sent here in the smallpox—from among the new levies. I have strictly examined them, I cannot as yet find they have been inoculated."[78] Although the inoculation system for the Northern Department was not as comprehensive as that performed for Washington's Army in the Middle Colonies, considering the shortage of personnel, the number of routes to be policed, and the vast area to be administered, this mass treatment, the largest attempted in the army until 1777, was generally effective in checking the pestilence.

As a result of such precautions, the health of the troops was reputedly improving by early September. On August 28 Gates informed Washington that "the smallpox is now perfectly removed from the army, ..." Indicating that since the pestilence was ebbing and that the fortress could be defended, Gates reported: "... I shall in consequence ... immediately assemble my principal strength to maintain this important pass and hope General Waterbury in a week at farthest will be able to come with three Row Galleys ..."[79] On September 2 Gates confidently declared: "Thank heavens the smallpox is totally eradicated from amongst us; ..."[80] Perhaps the healthier condition of his command in the early autumn may be attributed to the control of smallpox and to the strict imposition of sanitary regulations. Yet smallpox occasionally flared. As late as October 25 a New Jersey officer noted that forty men in his regiment were struck by the contagion.[81] According to the returns, on August 24 Gates had 13,013 troops in the north, of which 1,878 were sick present and 998 were sick absent. On September 29 out of 14,500 men, some 4,000 were sick present and 916 were sick absent.[82] Apparently, even though a large percentage of the men were sickly, smallpox was no longer the major problem.

It is obvious that morale gradually improved in the autumn. By early October the long-awaited drugs arrived, and the availability of medicine cheered the men. Even Morgan cooperated by sending a "large assortment, all capital items."[83] Stringer had traveled from Philadelphia back to New York, and then to Boston, where he purchased a large quantity of medicine from a cargo at Portsmouth. On October 5 the long-wandering Stringer was in Albany shipping boxes of drugs and casks of wine and vinegar to Potts. Colonel Persifor Frazer, who had complained to his wife in August about the "unwholesome" climate at Ticonderoga, remarked on October 2: "The weather is getting very cold. Almost the whole of our regiment have good chimneys built which makes them live much more comfortably."[84] Although shortages of clothing and blankets were common, provisions poured in—beans, potatoes, cheese, butter, beef, mutton, and even some soap. Traders and peddlers arrived at the post with rum, wine, and some fresh vegetables. Dr. Samuel Adams of Massachusetts noted in his diary that the men were becoming acclimatized to the privations of the wilderness. For him, service at desolate Ticonderoga was particularly beneficial: "I do not repent having come to this part of the world for especially it has given me a good opportunity in my profession, particularly in the branch of surgery."[85] By early October Thacher noted a marked improvement in the troops. "Our troops are quite healthy," he stated, "few cases of rheumatism and pleurisy comprise our sick-list, and it is seldom that any fatal cases occur."[86]

As supplies, weapons, and reinforcements were funneled into the garrison, the Americans strengthened their ramparts and awaited the enemy. They built entrenchments to the west and north of the fortress, and on Mt. Independence they erected redoubts, palisades, stockades, and placed cannon at strategic points. Thacher was impressed with the stout defense works at Ticonderoga, and he noted the floating bridge across the lake to Mt. Independence for the rapid shifting of troops. Colonel Anthony Wayne wrote Franklin that the fortress was strong and that it could withstand a siege. "Add to this our people are in high spirits," he commented, "tho' poorly clad—yet they will sell their Lives and Liberty dear—..."[87] Preparing for combat, Gates in early October ordered Potts to Ticonderoga to prepare a general hospital on Mt. Independence, and a field hospital at Wayne's headquarters near Ticonderoga. When an action occurred on the Ticonderoga side, Gates stated, the wounded were to be dressed, and then "to be carried to Doctor Potts at the General Hospital on the Mount."[88]

Fortunately for the patriots the British army had been immobilized since July at St. Jean's. Carleton was a cautious warrior. Uncertain of the American naval strength and concerned that his army had to be conveyed down Lake Champlain, Carleton willingly sacrificed weeks of campaign weather in order to possess maritime superiority with his fleet. His major logistical problem was that his larger vessels had to sail from the St. Lawrence to Chambly, be disassembled for the ten-mile portage south, and then be reassembled at St. Jean's. Not until early October was Carleton ready to sail with his twenty-nine heavily armed vessels, of which the frigate *Inflexible* carried so many heavy guns that unassisted it could demolish all the American vessels on the lake.

At Skenesboro, Arnold and Waterbury toiled through the summer to launch the American fleet. By early September, sixteen small vessels were ready. With this ramshackle collection of gondolas, bateaux, schooners, and row gallies, Arnold, the impromptu admiral, sailed to Crown Point. He then cruised the northern end of the lake, taunting the British to fight. But Carleton was still not ready. Unable to find a suitable anchorage to protect his ships, Arnold headed south in early October to pine-covered Valcour Island, above Crown Point, where he waited in a concealed bay.

Potts assisted Arnold in acquiring drugs and personnel for his ships. On August 12 Gates informed Potts that a surgeon was needed for the fleet.[89] Apparently Potts could not spare a man, so on August 16 Arnold wrote Gates remarking that "nothing but the surgeon and some few articles . . ." delayed his departure.[90] Potts sent him Dr. Stephen McCrea, who joined Arnold at Wind Mill Point on the schooner *Royal Savage*. McCrea, now a naval surgeon, notified Potts from Buttonmould Bay on October 2 that he needed an apothecary's scale. He also complained about his two so-called mates who cared for Arnold's 800 amateur sailors. One, McCrea stated, had "no practice and little theory, . . ." and the other "has neither theory or practice."[91]

On October 5 the British fleet sailed from St. Jean down Lake Champlain and searched for Arnold's ships. By October 10 Carleton's vessels cruised by Valcour Island. As the British ships passed, Arnold ordered his fleet to action. Tardily, he became aware of the enemy's superiority in ships and cannon and ordered his vessels back to the cove. But the American vessels were unable to beat upwind, and consequently, caught in the withering enemy bombardment, many sank, ran aground, or were burned by their crews. The battle of Valcour Island, the largest American naval engagement of the Revolutionary War, ended in darkness as the British penned Arnold up behind Valcour Island. In the eve-

The Canadian Campaign and Fort Ticonderoga

ning mists Arnold's few remaining ships slipped along the shore and eluded the British. Hours later Carleton overtook Arnold's leaky flagship; to escape, Arnold had to wreck his craft and flee to Crown Point. Only four small vessels and two hundred powder-singed American crewmen were left from the entire fleet. Soon after the action McCrea wrote Potts in what may be the only available medical commentary on the sea fight: "I am so hurried with getting off the wounded of our little navy that it is impossible to give you an account of our action which was bloody and unfortunately we have done them all the damage we could."[92] Although severely defeated, Arnold's fleet had won precious time for the Ticonderoga garrison.

With the lake cleared, Carleton seized Crown Point, and his ships reconnoitered the waterways near Ticonderoga. The Americans prepared for the assault. Thacher noted that "all our troops are ordered to repair to their alarm posts and man the lines and works; ... and our cannon and spears are in readiness for action."[93] Yet even with the preponderance of power, Carleton hesitated to attack the fortress. A sturdy gale thwarted his ships from maneuvering. The chilling winds, the falling autumn leaves, the honking of geese winging southward, and the frothing whitecaps on the cold water all signaled the coming of November storms and a frigid winter on the lake. The bastion was defended by 9.000 men, and its cannon bristled menacingly from the ramparts. Observing the scene, John Trumbull remarked:

> Ticonderoga must have had a very imposing aspect, ... when viewed from the lake. The whole summit of cleared land on both sides of the lake, was crowned with redoubts, and batteries, all manned with a splendid show of artillery and flags ... Our appearance was indeed so formidable, and the season so far advanced ... that the enemy withdrew without making any attack ... and we prepared for winter quarters.[94]

Fearful of supply problems in inclement weather and of the consequences to his troops exposed during a winter siege, on

November 1 Carleton returned with his force to St. Jean's to await the spring. Until the summer of 1777 at least, Ticonderoga was safe. Arnold's pathetic little fleet had given the Americans another year to consolidate their tenuous hold on northern New York.

As the campaign for the lakes subsided, a Congressional Committee, consisting of Delegates Richard Stockton and George Clymer, inspected medical facilities in the north. They reported to Congress on November 27, "that the sick have been greatly neglected and numbers to the prejudice of the service died from want of necessaries and attendance." They attributed the distress of the men to shortages of medicine, comforts, and "good female nurses." The accommodations at Fort George were so poor, they declared, that "those poor creatures [were] obliged to lay upon the bare boards." Without mentioning Stringer or Morgan, the Delegates concluded: "It is shocking to humanity, as well as ruinous to the public service, that such an evil has been so long without remedy."[95] Along with this report, Congress considered a reform of Continental army medical services resulting from the torrent of criticism leveled at Morgan. On November 3 Congress resolved that administrative controls for the hospitals in the north should be improved, that officers frequently inspect barracks and hospitals, that the Fort George and Mt. Independence hospitals be activated in the spring, and that a garden be planted at Ticonderoga to provide the troops with fresh vegetables.[96] Without castigating any medical officer at this point, Congress was determined to rectify the abuses and to find scapegoats for the inadequacies of medical care.

As the Canadian campaign came to an end, the medical department in upper New York consolidated its facilities. Fort George was crammed with sick, and it was difficult to maintain them in winter. Stringer had over 400 patients, and he was short of fuel, provisions, and accommodations. Fearful that "the poor wretches be exposed day and night" to the bitter cold, Stringer asked: "How in God's name am I to care for the poor creatures?"[97] With Schuyler's approval, Stringer removed the men to Albany, and by November 20 the Fort George hospital, whose significance had been long lost in history, was closed for the season. From July 11 to October 9, over 3,000 soldiers had been cared for in the Fort George hospital—probably the greatest number of patients treated in any one hospital during the Revolutionary War.[98]

As the threat of invasion subsided, only a garrison of 2,500 troops under Wayne was needed for bleak Ticonderoga. Enlistments for some troops expired; others were retained at outposts under Schuyler; and some regiments hurried south with Gates to assist Washington in New Jersey. Fortunately for Potts, McCrea volunteered to serve that bitter winter at Ticonderoga, so Potts could take a furlough. On November 12 Gates approved Potts's request for a leave, and ordered officers on the route to assist him on his journey home. "The doctor's bad health makes it necessary that he be moved with the utmost care, and be provided assistance to him on the road."[99] Traveling to Reading in a carriage, Potts was spared the misery of a winter on the lakes.

While a mantle of snow and ice covered the northern garrisons, the veterans of the Canadian campaign may have pondered the events of the past months. For the northern army, the year 1776 had been one of successive defeats—Quebec, Montreal, Three Rivers, St. Jean's, and Valcour Island. It was a year of heavy casualties, a year in which disease took an enormous toll of troops. For Potts it must have been a disillusioning introduction to war. Yet in December his country faced another crisis. The British under Charles, Earl Cornwallis, were marching to the Delaware, Washington's army was in full retreat, and the American rebellion was collapsing. Potts hastened to join Washington at Trenton and to participate in what would be a decisive moment in the Revolutionary War.

VI.
With Washington on the Delaware

While the Northern army prepared for winter quarters in late 1776, Washington's army in the Middle Provinces was driven out of Manhattan. Repeatedly defeated in battle, the Continentals retreated in November and December across New Jersey to the Delaware. The medical department was confronted with a crisis, and Potts, summoned from Reading to Philadelphia for the emergency, was ordered to organize hospitals.[1]

After the British evacuated Boston in March 1776, Washington believed that the enemy would attack New York in the summer. While he shifted his command to the lower Hudson during the spring, Morgan's medical department established facilities in Manhattan. Morgan displayed energy and imagination in anticipating the medical requirements of the army as he built a centralized administration for his department. He sent large stocks of drugs to the city from New England; he examined candidates and recruited an able staff; and he advertised for nurses and orderlies. He devised hospital diet tables, initiated procedures for weekly reports, purchased equipment, maintained accounts, wrote instructions about wound treatment, appealed to the public for herbals and dressings, drafted and enforced regulations, and explained his procedures to surgeons, generals, and politicians. He established general hospitals in Manhattan at

King's College, at the City Hospital, at the Workhouse, at the Exchange, and at vacant Loyalist homes in the Bowery. At the college was Dr. Solomon Drowne of Rhode Island, who stated in August that he worked in "a very elegant building, and its situation pleasant and salubrious . . . We have things in pretty good readiness at the Hospital," he explained, "for the horrid effects of a general action."[2]

Although the army had the experience of the Boston campaign in preventive medicine, the military were generally ignorant about the ramifications of disease. Furthermore Morgan's arrangements for combat had been untested in Massachusetts, and provisions to shift staff during the fighting to crucial battle zones and measures to transfer casualties to the rear were incomplete. Morgan experienced great difficulty with the regimental surgeons, with whom he quarreled incessantly. Most surgeons were poorly trained, and many were barely apprentices. Some fabricated medical excuses from duty for their townsmen; others falsified their returns or never sent any reports to Morgan. A few diverted hospital stores for their profit. Many of them retained the seriously ill in regimental hospitals, and yet they complained bitterly to Congress about Morgan's stingy dispersement of drugs and equipment. The tempermental Morgan castigated them as "unlettered, ignorant, crude to a degree scarcely to be imagined. Some of them . . ., were never educated to the profession of physick, nor had even seen an operation of surgery."[3] Annoyed with their bickering and their neglect of patients, even Washington called them "great rascals."[4] The regimental surgeons, usually supported by their colonels, who distrusted the general hospital system, deluged Congress with criticisms about the medical department, which helped to undermine Morgan's already faltering position.

Morgan's careful preparations in Manhattan, and those of James McHenry at Fort Washington and John Warren on Long Island, were affected by environmental problems caused by the transformation of an eighteenth-century metropolis into a major military base. The seasonal heat, the enervating toil of building defenses, the prevalence of venereal disease, the polluted water supply, and the primitive sanitary habits of the troops influenced the army's health. About seven thousand soldiers worked like busy ants that summer under the broiling sun at numerous fortifications—New York Island, Governor's Island, Brooklyn Heights, Paulus Hook, Fort Lee, and Fort Washington. Within the mile-long limits of Manhattan, men dug wells and ditches, erected thirteen forts and batteries, and barricaded streets and parks. On Long Island a large bastion was constructed at Red Hook, and from Wallabout Bay to Gowanus Marsh three more forts and two redoubts were built. From the Battery for a mile up the Hudson, and from Paulus Hook on the Jersey side, cannon bristled to threaten British ships. To prevent enemy use of the Hudson and East Rivers, huge obstructions were sunk to block the channels. Such continual labor, Washington noted, was wearing out his men. The sheer exhaustion from the work had weakened many troops even before the fighting began and may have left them prey for debilitating diseases.

Venereal disease was rampant. One section of the city, where some five hundred "ladies of pleasure" resided near St. Paul's Church, was termed "the Holy Ground." The area was frequently the scene of drunken riots and raucous street fighting, and officers and guards often had to restore order. Lieutenant Isaac Bangs of the Second Massachusetts was shocked at the prostitutes' coarse soliciting of the country bumpkins who thronged the streets. "Nothing could exceed them for impudence and immodesty . . .," he lamented. He was likewise appalled at the number of troops who visited the place "till the Fatal Disorder seized them and convinced them of their error."[5] About forty troops were contaminated weekly with syphilis or gonorrhea, and such men were usually unfit for combat.

Scabies, typhus, and particularly dysentery (or paratyphoid) incapacitated hundreds of troops. New York had a garbage-collection system, a framework of public-health regulations, and abundant wells, ponds, and springs for its water supply. But as troops poured into the city, the city's sanitary services collapsed, and the water supply became contaminated. Soldiers dumped filth over the streets, and the city government seemed unable to check the practice. By July, New York was a very unhealthy place. As Drowne remarked on August 9: "The whole of the city seemed infected, in almost every street there is a horrible smell."[6] Dysentery, probably caused by improper waste disposal, the breakdown of sanitary measures, and the long, hot spring and summer weather incapacitated 20 percent of the troops by August. Half of his regiment, stated Bangs, were sick with "the camp distemper."[7] What had been bright, clear ponds and bubbling brooks became malodorous pools due to unhygienic habits and to the practice of the soldiers who washed their bodies and clothes in the watersheds, and then used the same water for cooking and drinking. "The vile water sickens us all," remarked a clergyman at camp.[8] General William Heath of Massachusetts noted that many soldiers were ill, and that "in every lot, every farm and stable, and even under the fences and bushes, were the sick to be seen."[9]

Inasmuch as no one suspected the source of contamination, preventive measures were limited to instructions about cooking, bathing (only at sunrise and sunset), burying offal, finding sources of fresh water, and covering latrines. Washington ordered regimental commanders "to attend the cleaning the streets of their encampment, and especially to the digging and fixing of the Necessaries . . . for that purpose. . . ."[10] Nathanael Greene on Long Island, repeating rules given months before at Cambridge, ordered that fatigue parties clean the encampment, "cover vaults daily, and dig new ones, weekly, and attend the hospital." He was perturbed that "the troops were easing themselves in the Ditches of the Fortifications, a Practice that is Disgracefull to the last Degree." If the practice continued, Greene warned, "the stench Arising from such places will soon breed a Pestilence in the Camp."[11] Typical of eighteenth-century practice, Washington frequently issued commands about personal and camp hygiene, which were inscribed in orderly books and announced to the troops. Some American generals inserted information about sanitation into newspapers. For example, on

August 1, the *New York Packet* carried excerpts from Dr. Buchan's *Domestic Medicine* to demonstrate the advantages of cleanliness for the welfare of the men.[12]

One study made of dysentery during the campaign was by Ebenezer Beardsley, the surgeon for the 22nd New York. His regiment, quartered in the Bowery, was healthy until mid-August, when it was struck by a mysterious ailment. Noting that the men were housed in small, poorly ventilated rooms, he concluded that the disease originated in "the confined and putrid atmosphere which these uncomfortable men live in." When the troops were moved to more spacious quarters, their health improved. "This striking instance of the pernicious effects of putrid stagnant air," Beardsley concluded, "was of great service in the course of the campaign."[13]

By late August the rain fell and the torrid heat abated. But the men were still pestered by mosquitoes swarming from Jersey marshes. The draught, the lack of fresh water, and the array of debilitating diseases had weakened the army even before British ships appeared in the harbor. Washington warned Congress about the sickly condition of his troops, and that, because of illness, some regiments were severely short of officers.[14] Greene, in fact, was incapacitated by a serious fever just before the action. On May 29 Washington had 14,000 men around Manhattan, of which 1,000 were sick; by June 21 he had 18,000 troops, of which 2,600 were ill. For August, precise information is unavailable, but an estimate is that on August 7 out of 17,000 men, some 6,500 were sick. At Harlem Heights on September 8 Washington had 20,435 men, of which 7,725 were sick. Less information is available about the "Flying Camp" in New Jersey under General Hugh Mercer, where militia guarded routes to the Delaware. Mercer had about 3,300 men in August, of which 1,800 were ill. By early October at White Plains, Washington had 20,000 in his command, of which 7,900 were sick.[15] Clearly disease, as at Ticonderoga, diminished the army's effectiveness and contributed to the plummeting morale of the troops.

The Americans assumed that the British would reenact Bunker Hill for them by a frontal assault against their entrenchments, and that the Hudson could be blocked from the Royal Navy. Washington's staff was surprised indeed on July 12, when five British ships, part of an armada disembarking General Howe's 30,000 troops on Staten Island, sailed unscathed past rebel guns up the river to Tarrytown. The vulnerability of the Continental lines to British attacks above Manhattan was obvious, but the patriots were still obsessed with memories of Bunker Hill. On August 25, 15,000 redcoats landed on Long Island, occupied Flatbush and six miles of coastline. To prevent their march to Manhattan were 8,000 Continentals guarding Brooklyn Heights. Through a clever flanking maneuver, the British under Generals Henry Clinton and Cornwallis defeated the Americans in the battle of Long Island (August 27). A heavy rain, high tides, and Howe's dilatory tactics temporarily delayed the invaders, and Washington was able to extricate his troops to Manhattan. Yet Manhattan was another strategic trap; the enemy could utilize its amphibious power to storm ashore virtually anywhere above the American lines. Consequently Washington retired to Harlem Heights in September, fought a skirmish there, and then retreated further northward over Kingsbridge to White Plains. On October 26 the British again outflanked the Americans there, and Washington was driven across the Hudson. Dividing his army by entrusting Heath with 4,000 men to hold the Hudson Highlands, and General Charles Lee with 8,500 to guard Connecticut, Washington marched with the battered remainder to New Jersey, with the British close behind. The defense of New York was a disaster—600 combat casualties, 4,500 prisoners, thousands of desertions, and several thousand deaths from disease.[16]

During the retreat, Morgan's organization almost disintegrated; as the army scattered, he lost control of his staff. Some regiments lacked surgeons and some untreated wounded actually bled to death. Morgan operated on casualties; he organized the evacuation of the sick from Long Island to Manhattan, and then again to New Jersey. He seemed to be everywhere—dispensing drugs, visiting his patients, and establishing new hospitals. At the battle of White Plains, Morgan had only two surgeons and four mates to assist him. By mid-September he found sanctuaries for 1,000 patients at Hoboken and Weehawken. But when these centers were threatened by the fall of Fort Lee and Fort Washington in late November, Morgan had to move the sick to Newark and to Hackensack. The flow of sick and wounded continued to inundate his temporary facilities, and Morgan had to disperse his patients again to Amboy, Elizabeth, Brunswick, Trenton, and Morristown. The misery of these men, transported in open wagons in winter cold without blankets over miles of rutted roads, can be imagined. Threatened by invasion, Jersey could not provide sufficient shelters for the sick, so 500 patients ended up at Fishkill and Peekskill on the Hudson; another 2,000 from White Plains were sent to Norwich and Stamford, Connecticut. Perhaps another dozen villages served that winter as convalescent centers as Morgan tried to protect his patients from the inexorable British offensive.[17]

In such confusion the medical department was invariably blamed for defects in the handling of casualties. Washington remarked that his troops on Harlem Heights, "were exceedingly sickly and died fast." He noted the great difficulty in finding transportation across the Hudson for the ill. "The clamour was loud against the Department in general," Washington stated "and the miserable condition of the sick in all quarters, a fact too well known and remembered."[18] Greene complained to Hancock that surgeons were not provided with drugs and equipment, that much bitterness prevailed in the ranks about the hospital conditions, and that such feelings would prove "an unsurmountable obstacle to Recruiting the new Army." Greene was annoyed with Morgan's rigid insistence about bureaucratic procedures while men suffered. "It is wholly inmaterial, in my opinion, . . .," he declared, "whether a Man dies in a General or Regimental Hospital."[19] Dr. Josiah Barlett, a New Hampshire Delegate, demanded a Congressional inquiry into hospital matters.[20] But Morgan was not entirely at fault. His nurses and orderlies fled, and his surgeons deserted. Desperate to move his patients out of Hoboken as the British advanced, Morgan discovered that the panic-stricken militia had confiscated every cart and wagon in the area, regardless of the consequences for the sick. Morgan even encountered difficulties in finding accommodations for his patients, because some communities protested about the use of their homes for the soldiers. Some surgeons, dismayed with Morgan's obstinacy in supplying them, sought their own hospital accommodations in scattered locations. Colonel William Smallwood notified the Maryland Council of Safety that because the Director General was unable to assist him, he had withdrawn his sick from Morgan's hospitals, "and had them placed in a comfortable house in the country, ..."[21] From the Flying Camp came similar complaints. General James Potter of Pennsylvania complained that Morgan was unable to provision two hundred of his men, quartered in cold barns without blankets or provisions.[22]

Meanwhile Washington was in danger of being trapped by Cornwallis in New Jersey. As the British neared Hackensack, Colonel Benjamin Tallmadge of Connecticut noted that "all was confusion and dismay, it seemed as if we were on the eve of despair and ruin."[23] Washington crossed the Hackensack and Raritan Rivers late in November, passed through Trenton, and on December 6 led his 5,400 men over the Delaware. Young Wilkinson, back from Ticonderoga, remarked: "What a wretched spectacle did our troops present in retreating through the Jerseys! . . . without tents, or camp equipage . . . half clothed—badly armed—debilitated by disease, disheartened by misfortune, and worn out with fatigue."[24] Washington could not rely on Mercer's Flying Camp, disintegrating from disease and desertions. Surgeon James Tilton of Maryland commented: "The flying camp of 1776 melted like snow. They fell like rotten sheep as they straggled home, where they communicated the camp infection [typhus] to their neighbors and friends, of which many died."[25] New Jersey was abandoned to the enemy, and only isolated partisan leaders continued the resistance against the British.

During the retreat, Morgan faced another problem—the emergence of William Shippen, Jr., his arch-rival, to challenge his authority. In July Congress appointed Shippen as

Director of Hospitals for the Flying Camp. Shippen proceeded to organize facilities in Paramus, Fort Lee, Elizabeth, Perth Amboy, Trenton, and Brunswick. Confident that he could oust Morgan as director, Shippen began a crafty campaign to defeat his old enemy. Dissatistfied with Morgan's performance, Congress in August again reduced his power. It split Morgan's jurisdiction by restricting his authority to hospitals east of the Hudson and by authorizing Shippen to supervise hospitals on the west of the Hudson. As the army retired into Jersey, both doctors competed for staff, supplies, and locations, and they refused to assist each other in the crisis. By early December the Medical Committee of Congress, without notifying the exasperated Morgan, proposed that general hospitals be established in Philadelphia and in Bethlehem. By then Morgan was assailed from all sides as surgeons, generals, and politicians clamored for his removal. Arriving in Philadelphia on December 9, Morgan found himself without a staff, Congress evacuating to Baltimore, and Washington unwilling to intrude into the dispute. In fact Morgan issued only one directive, when Washington ordered him back to Connecticut. Washington indicated to Shippen, who was emerging as the logical candidate for the directorship, that he could not comprehend why Morgan hoarded stores during the campaign. Conscious of the bitter controversy, Washington later commented to Morgan, in a typical understatement, "I have understood this clashing between Doctor Shippen and yourself was no small cause of the Calamities that befell our sick in 1776."[26]

By early December wagonloads of sick reached Philadelphia, where the inhabitants expected that the redcoats would soon cross the Delaware to destroy Washington's force. Inasmuch as Morgan was unable to provide medical facilities, Washington requested Pennsylvania authorities to act in the emergency. Washington wrote that he hoped that the "House of Employment" could be utilized and that civilian doctors would assist his surgeons.[27] Before the first casualties arrived, the Pennsylvania Council of Safety considered the requests of Thomas Bond, Jr., and his father, Thomas Bond, Sr.

Young Bond, an army surgeon with forty patients in Elizabeth, did not have wagons and carriages to convey his sick to the Delaware. Fearful of the consequences to his wounded, jolted by bumpy roads, Bond hoped to evacuate them by boat to Darby, New Castle, and Wilmington.[28] The elder Bond promptly volunteered to assist his son. On December 4 he urged that the Council of Safety make preparations, and he suggested "that some able, judicious, and experienced persons may be empowered to fix proper places for supplying [the wounded] with all [the] conveniences which Art and Humanity can provide . . ."[29]

On December 5 the Council responded by requesting Potts to handle arrangements. The Council also designated Christopher Marshall, the apothecary, and three others, to establish army hospitals at the Pennsylvania Hospital, the Bettering House, the smallpox hospital on Pine Street, and at various stores and houses vacated by Loyalists. One indication of the tense state of affairs in the city, as Cornwallis approached the Delaware, was indicated on December 10, when the Council informed Potts: "You are to remove all the sick soldiers to Potts Grove or some other place of security for which purpose you are to procure wagons and every necessity."[30] Potts made preparations for evacuation of patients to the state of Delaware, but fortunately such a journey for the sick was not necessary. When Morgan arrived on December 9, Potts was already supervising facilities. As Morgan explained, "For the care of them, I gave the best advice I could to Dr. Potts, who was employed by the Council of Safety for that purpose."[31] Washington appointed General Israel Putnam to defend the city, and General Thomas Mifflin to bring reinforcements. Officers in charge of sick details were "directed to make returns to Dr. Jonathan Potts at Mr. John Biddle in Market Street of the number and place of residence of their sick that proper care may be taken of them."[32]

How many invalids were housed in Philadelphia during the winter of 1776–1777 is uncertain—perhaps five hundred in December and one thousand in January. Henry Hallowell of Massachusetts and six sick companions found a spartan haven there. The movement of casualties over the Delaware, he noted, "was so sudden to that city [that] small preparation was made for the sick . . . My lodging was a hard floor day and night, and no Nurse at first and not more than the Continental allowance [the standard food ration]." Three of his friends died that winter, Hallowell remarked, but with the help of some women, who provided him with tea, sugar, and a bed, he managed to survive. But without a clothing change, he remarked, "I got very lousy and flesh much gone."[33] Typhus killed many soldiers that winter. James Tilton remembered that hundreds perished in Philadelphia.[34] John Adams stated that 2,000 troops were buried in Potter's Field, the common ground for slaves and paupers.[35] Shocked by the daily sight of carts laden with dead, Nancy Shippen of Philadelphia exclaimed: ". . . it is too dreadful a scene to Attempt to describe. The poor Creatures die without number. Large pits are dug in the negroes ground—and fourty or fifty coffins are put in the same hole . . . The well soldiers are Quartered on private families."[36]

So many casualties were carried over the Delaware in December that other facilities had to be used. About 250 patients were scattered in Easton, Allentown, and Wilmington. Another 700 patients were sent to Bethlehem, the second largest convalescent center in Pennsylvania. Bethlehem was inhabited by the Moravians, a religious sect that had quietly indicated its neutrality in the war. Needing a place with large buildings, the military ignored the pacifism of the Moravians, and notified them on December 3 that wagonloads of sick were on the way. The patients arrived three days before staff and provisions, and the gentle Moravians, their peaceful village swamped with the victims of war, fed and clothed the soldiers in the Single Brethren's House until Shippen arrived with supplies.[37] Bethlehem is important as the first religious commune in the province occupied by the army for a hospital, and because of the 25 percent mortality rate there by March 1777, it acquired an understandable notoriety with Continental troops. Bethlehem was the headquarters of Shippen, who lobbied in Congress for the directorship. In contrast to Morgan's pessimism about developments, Shippen cheerfully informed the delegates and Washington that his patients were quickly recuperating: "I sent twenty or thirty weekly to join the army,"[38] he delcared, a statement quite inconsistent with the heavy sickness and mortality rates of the hospital. On December 17 Shippen wrote Richard Henry Lee in Congress that he hoped that drastic improvements would occur in the department, and that he was preparing a plan of reform.[39] It is evident that the medical department, wracked by controversy and blamed for every conceivable defect related to the welfare of the soldiery, was barely functioning as the organization devised by Morgan.

Cornwallis arrived at the Delaware on December 12, and he could have assembled boats and rafts for the crossing. But snow fell on December 13, and General Howe, assuming that the Continental army could be easily defeated in the spring, halted his troops on the river. At three large garrisons in eastern Jersey and at six outposts along the Delaware, the British prepared to winter. At Trenton were 1,400 Hessians, contemptuous of their beaten foe.

Washington had only 2,500 men by Christmas, although reinforcements under Gates and Mifflin were coming, and guerrilla units were active around Morristown and Hackensack. Hoping to regenerate American morale and to hit and isolate enemy detachments, Washington planned a surprise attack on Trenton. Neither the supporting force under General John Cadwalader nor that under General James Ewing could row over the ice-choked Delaware that night. But at McKonkey's Ferry, in one of the most daring exploits of the war, Washington and his men made a dramatic night crossing in the swirling snow and sleet. Washington quietly maneuvered his troops near the town, and in the dawn light of December 26 he surrounded and defeated the Hessians. Washington finally had a victory and with only four casualties, but three men froze to death on the return march to Pennsylvania. Neither Morgan nor Shippen was involved in the fighting, but John Warren was at Trenton, and so too was Dr. John Cochran, whose home in New Brunswick had been destroyed by the British. "I had the pleasure to see the Garrison of Trenton lay down their arms and submit prisoners of war," Cochran wrote in glee. "Never was a set of beings so panic struck since the Creation as the whole Garrison on the Delaware when they heard of the fate of Trenton."[40]

Expecting that the British would quickly retaliate, Washington was delighted to learn that the Hessians had evacuated the other river posts and had retired to Princeton. Capitalizing on his luck and faced with the expiration of enlistments, Washington returned to Trenton on December 30. With the militia brought by Mifflin, Washington had 4,600 troops concealed behind Assunpink Creek to await the attack. With 5,000 redcoats, Cornwallis reached Trenton at dusk on January 2, 1777. After probing the American lines, he terminated the fighting for the night, confident that at dawn he would bag Washington the fox.

Medical services for this second battle of Trenton were perfunctory. On December 25 Washington had summoned Shippen to join him, but the message arrived days later at Bethlehem. Washington barely kept Morgan informed of developments. Disappointed with the director general, Washington merely told Morgan that he had no medical staff for the pending fight. "In case of need, I have nobody here to take direction, I think it very strange."[41] Yet Warren and Cochran were on hand, joined by Potts and Rush with the militia. Potts arrived in Trenton on January 2 as "surgeon-general" in Mifflin's brigade of Pennsylvania militia.[42] Rush served with Cadwalader's brigade of Philadelphia Associators. Twenty men had been badly wounded in the Assunpink Creek skirmishing, and Rush and Cochran treated them that evening. "It was now for the first time war appeared to me in its awful plentitude of horror," Rush commented. "I lack words to describe the anguish of my soul excited by the cries and groans and convulsions of the men who lay by my side."[43]

On January 2 Washington considered whether to fight at Trenton, to retreat over the Delaware, or to make a surprise attack on Princeton. After sending the baggage to Burlington and ordering camp fires maintained all night to dupe the enemy, Washington took the enormous risk of a march in darkness around the British flank. The night was clear and frigid. Captain Stephen Olney remarked that the road, wet and muddied the previous day, had congealed, "hard as a pavement."[44] Shivering in his tattered uniform, Private John Howland remembered that he marched in frozen mocassins which "chapped my toes till they bled."[45] As the sleepless and frightened men stumbled along the rutted road, Sergeant R, as he is known, commented: "The ground was literally marked with the blood of soldiers' feet."[46] Although evidence is lacking, Potts probably trudged along in the darkness with Washington on this desperate venture. Apparently Washington was so preoccupied with preparations for this march that he neglected to make hospital arrangements; only a few regimental surgeons accompanied the column. Warren, Rush, and Cochran were still in Trenton, not even aware that Washington and the troops had moved out. At 4:00 A.M., Cochran awoke to inquire about the army's movements, Rush remembered. "He returned in haste, and said they were not to be found. We now produced wagons and after putting patients in them directed they should follow us to Burlington . . .," to where the doctors assumed Washington had retreated.[47]

At sunrise on January 3 Washington's troops paused near Stoney Brook Bridge, two miles from Princeton, where the half-frozen men gulped from buckets of rum. "The morning was bright, serene, and extremely cold," Wilkinson recollected, "with a hoar frost which bespangled every object."[48] Moving on to Princeton, Washington ordered one column under Sullivan to hit the village from the rear, and a second column under Greene to destroy the bridge, and then join in on the attack on Princeton. Greene sent an advance party of 350 men under Mercer to wreck the crossing. Just as Mercer neared the stream, two British regiments from Princeton under Colonel Charles Mawhood suddenly appeared against the icy-blue sky. Both sides raced for higher ground. Taking cover in the orchard of William Clark's farm, the Americans began firing their slower-loading rifles. The better-armed

British volleyed with muskets and then charged with their deadly bayonets. For militia, untested in combat, the menacing sight of that naked, glistening steel intended for their chests and stomachs may have been unbearable. They bolted and scattered to the woods. Trying to rally them near Clark's house, Mercer fell from his horse. Trapped by British soldiers in a murderous mood, Mercer was clubbed and stabbed repeatedly by a dozen vengeful redcoats.

Hurrying to assist Mercer's shattered brigade came the Philadelphia militia. Mawhood's troops fired deadly volleys at the untrained levies. For men unaccustomed to the butchery of battle, it was a horrible experience to witness their comrades screaming in pain and writhing in agony. Sergeant R recalled that "my old associates were scattered about groaning, dying and dead ... The ground was frozen, and all the blood which was shed remained on the surface, which added to the horror of this scene of carnage."[49] Potts candidly described his own fears. Terrorized as his comrades toppled to the ground or scattered to the woods before the advancing British, Potts admitted that he "was obliged to flee before the rascals or fall into their hands, and leave behind my wounded brethren."[50] Just as the patriots were losing the fight, Washington rode up on his horse with Continentals to rally the frightened men. The Americans re-formed, advanced, and now outnumbering their opponents five to one, they fired withering blasts that broke Mawhood's line. Meanwhile Sullivan had driven the last redcoat regiment out of Princeton, and the Americans triumphantly marched into the village. In one of the most decisive events of the war, Washington had won another victory.

Washington remained in Princeton two hours to assemble his men, to collect the wounded, and to acquire wagons. At the bark of musket fire from Cornwallis's troops in the distance, Washington hurriedly evacuated Princeton and headed for Brunswick, a large enemy depot eighteen miles away. Washington soon realized that his men were too few and were too weary for another engagement. As Henry Knox, Washington's artillery man, explained to his wife, "If we could have secured one thousand fresh men at Princeton and to have pushed up for Brunswick, we should have struck one of the most brilliant strokes in all history."[51] Washington reluctantly ordered his men to bear left on the road at Kingston to Somerset Court House (Millstone), where that night the troops fell exhausted on the frozen ground. The next day Washington resumed the march to Pluckemin, and on January 7 he reached the sanctuary of Morristown, well protected by the rugged slopes of the Watchung Mountains. Outwitted, outmarched, and outmaneuvered, the British withdrew from most of Jersey, retaining only sectors around Elizabeth and Perth Amboy. Even with his skeleton army, Washington had kept alive the flame of rebellion.

Potts did not accompany Washington to Morristown; he remained at Princeton to treat the wounded. Writing to Owen Biddle on January 5 from the village, Potts mentioned that Major Anthony Morris, a mutual friend, had died in battle and that Mercer was still alive. "But I have little hope for him," Potts explained, "the villains stabbed him in five different places . . . Would you believe that the inhuman monsters robbed the General as he lay unable to resist on his bed [in the Clark house], and insulted him all the time? . . . The dead on our side amount to fifteen," he continued, "that of the enemy twenty three . . . The number of prisoners we have taken I cannot of yet find out, but they are numerous . . . They have never been so shamefully drubbed and outgeneraled in every respect."[52] With Potts was Rush, who performed amputations on four British casualties in the Clark home; surprisingly they all survived. On January 7 thought Rush, Mercer would live, but the soldier bled profusely and he died on January 10. His corpse was taken to Philadelphia, his wounds were displayed, and the city held a public funeral for this war hero. Inasmuch as Princeton was a no-man's-land, the casualties were evacuated to Trenton and Bristol, where Potts assisted in their treatment. William Bryant, a Loyalist surgeon at Trenton, pleaded with Potts on January 19 for surgical instruments. "There are 4 or 5 [Hessians]," he wrote, "who must be submitted to operations soon or lose their lives."[53]

1. Pottsgrove Manor, the home of Jonathan Potts built by John Potts in 1752. (Courtesy of Marjorie Potts Wendell.)

2. Dr. Jonathan Potts (1745–1781).

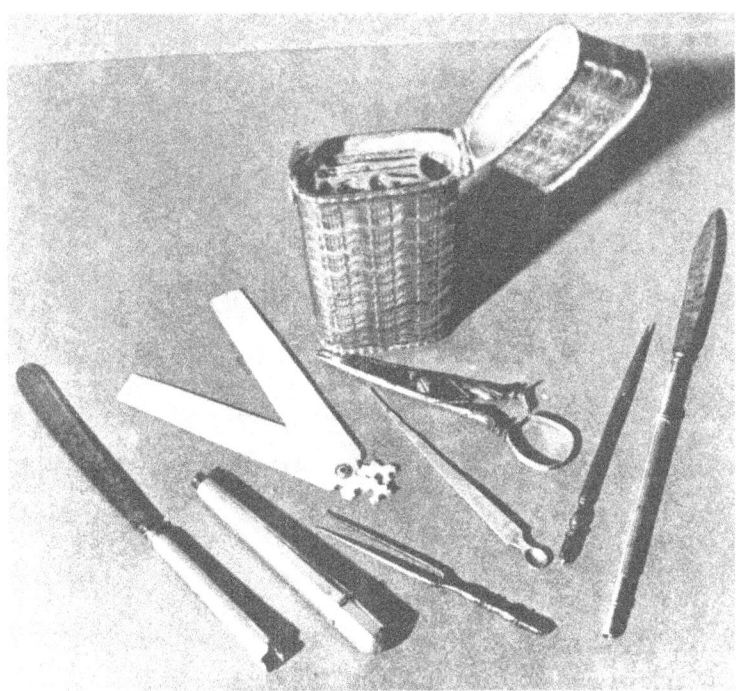

3. Surgical instruments in four inch silver case used by Dr. Jonathan Potts. (Courtesy of Marjorie Potts Wendell.)

IN CONGRESS.

The DELEGATES of the UNITED STATES of *New-Hampshire, Massachusetts-Bay, Rhode-Island, Connecticut, New-York, New-Jersey, Pennsylvania, Delaware, Maryland, Virginia, North-Carolina, South-Carolina,* and *Georgia,* TO *Jonathan Potts Esquire*

WE, reposing especial Trust and Confidence in your Patriotism, Valour, Conduct and Fidelity, DO, by these Presents, constitute and appoint you to be *Deputy Director General of the Hospital in the Northern Department* in the Army of the United States, raised for the Defence of American Liberty, and for repelling every hostile Invasion thereof. You are therefore carefully and diligently to discharge the Duty of *Deputy Director General* by doing and performing all manner of Things thereunto belonging. And we do strictly charge and require all Officers and Soldiers under your Command, to be obedient to your Orders as *Deputy Director General*. And you are to observe and follow such Orders and Directions from Time to Time, as you shall receive from this or a future Congress of the United States, or Committee of Congress, for that Purpose appointed, or Commander in Chief for the Time being of the Army of the United States, or any other your superior Officer, according to the Rules and Discipline of War, in Pursuance of the Trust reposed in you. This Commission to continue in Force until revoked by this or a future Congress.

DATED at *Philadelphia the 11th April 1777*

By Order of the CONGRESS,

John Hancock PRESIDENT.

ATTEST. *Cha Thomson secy*

4. Appointment of Dr. Jonathan Potts by the Continental Congress to the rank of Deputy General of the Hospital in the Northern Department, April 11, 1777—signed by John Hancock. (Courtesy of the Fort Ticonderoga Museum.)

5. Fort Ticonderoga. (Courtesy of the Fort Ticonderoga Museum.)

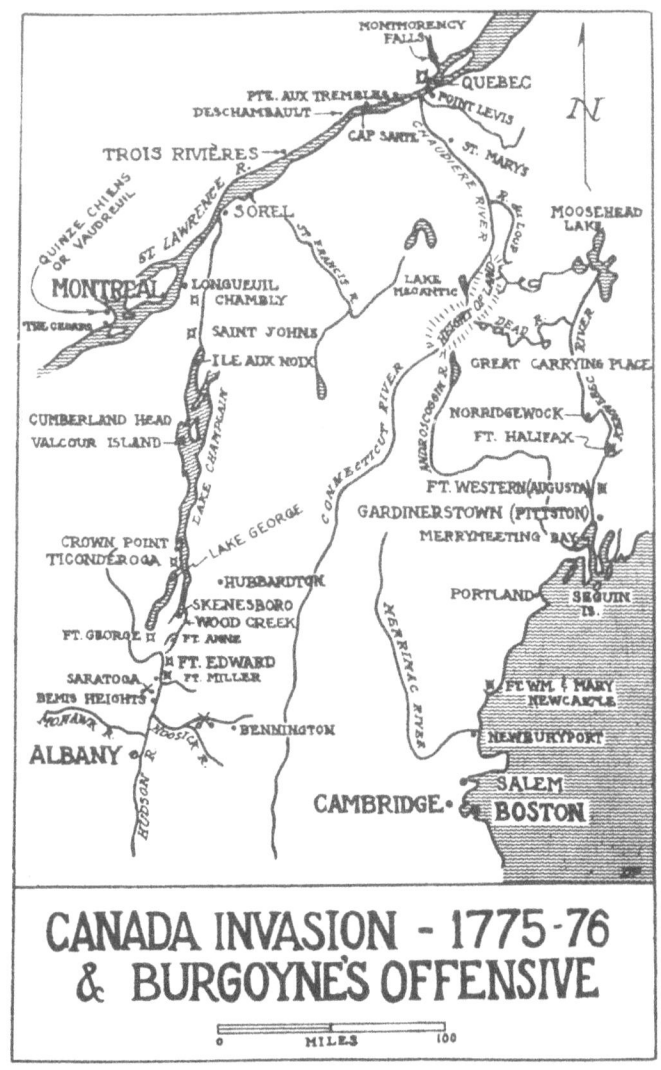

6. Canada invasion, 1775–1776, and Burgoyne's offensive. (Reprinted with permission from *Encyclopedia of the American Revolution* by Mark Mayo Boatner, III, New York: David McKay Company, Inc.)

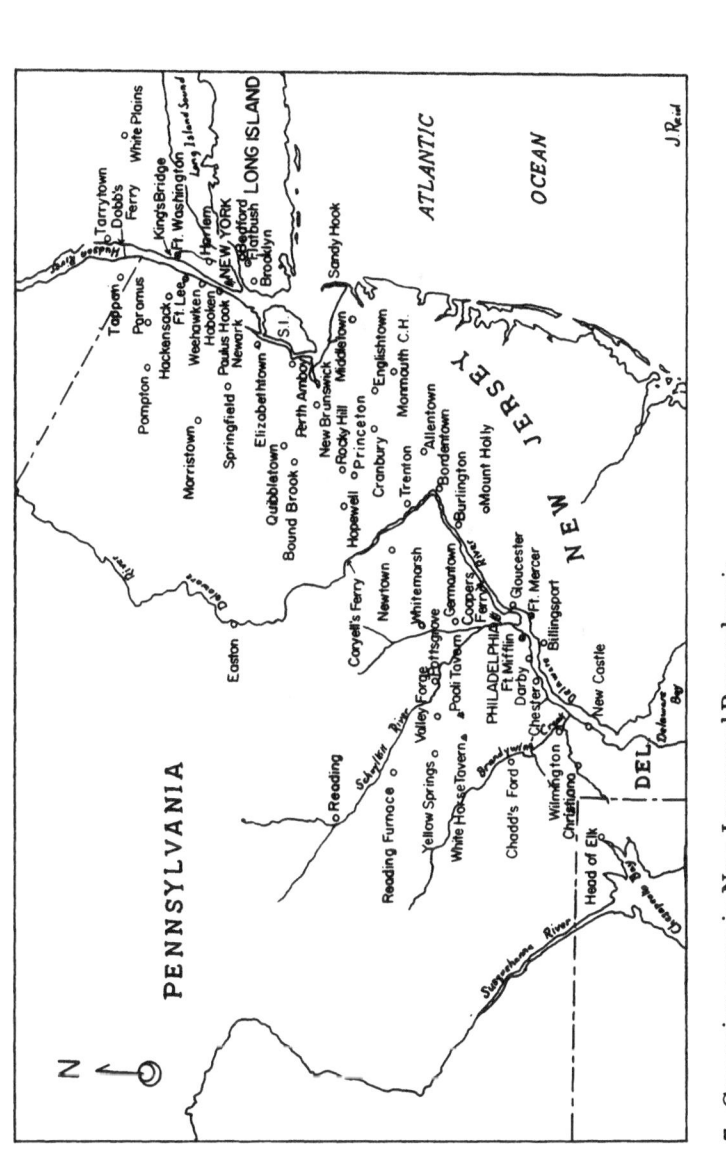

7. Campaign areas in New Jersey and Pennsylvania.

8. The medical chest of Dr. William Shippen, Jr. (1738–1808). (By permission of the Mütter Museum, College of Physicians of Philadelphia.)

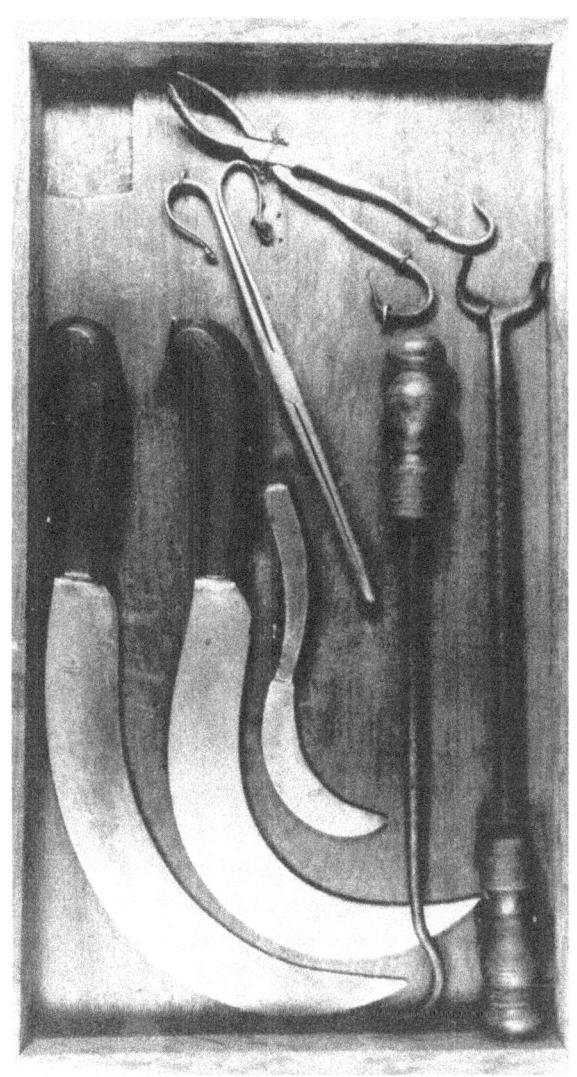

9. Field case of surgical instruments owned by Dr. Charles McKnight (1750–1791). By permission of Morristown National Historical Park.)

10. The surgical instruments of Dr. Charles McKnight (1750–1791). (By permission of Morristown National Park.)

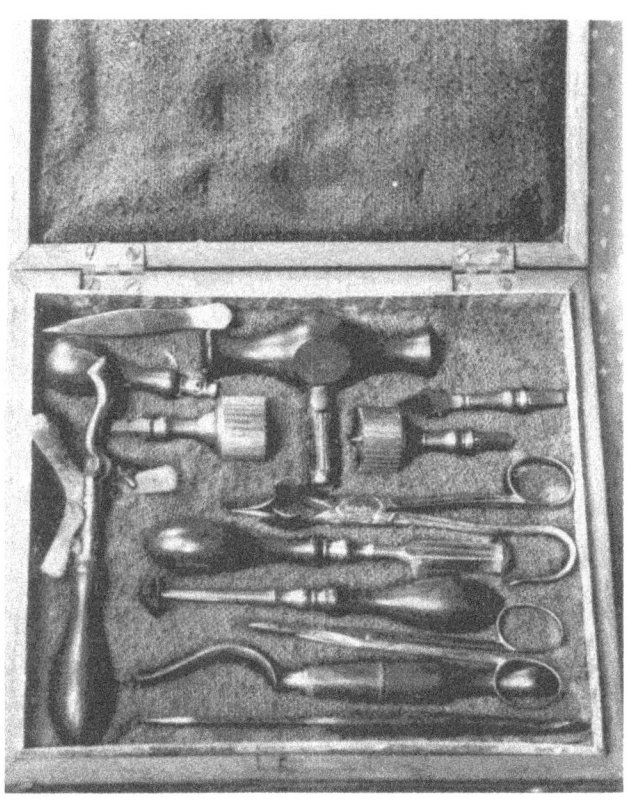

11. The trepanning instruments of Dr. Charles McKnight (1750–1791). (By permission of Morristown National Historical Park.)

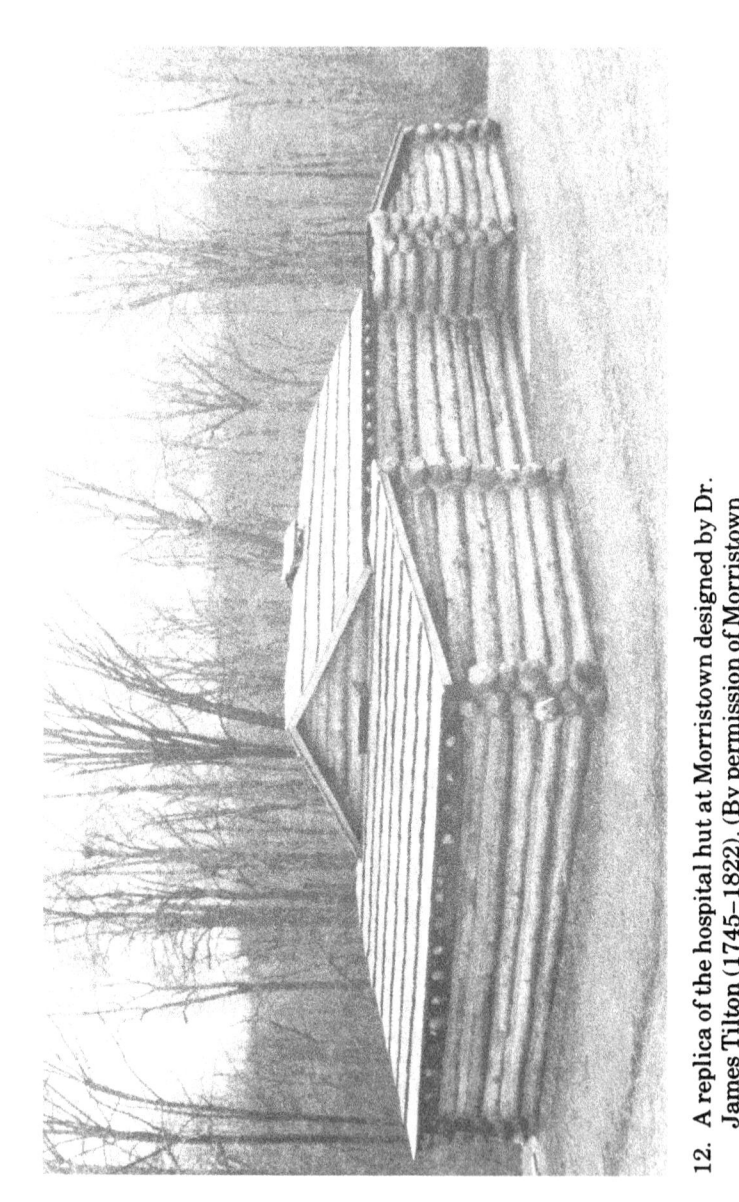

12. A replica of the hospital hut at Morristown designed by Dr. James Tilton (1745–1822). (By permission of Morristown National Historical Park.)

As Washington prepared for the spring campaign, he pondered improvements for the army. The medical department obviously required new leadership as Morgan and Stringer were completely discredited with the officer corps and with the medical staff. Typical of this sentiment was the commentary of Dr. William Brown of Virginia, who wrote Rush a long letter lamenting the state of army hospitals.[54] Isaac Foster, a Connecticut surgeon, informed his father from Fishkill that "complaints against Dr. Morgan are so many and so loud that I believe if he does not resign he will be superceded [sic], ..."[55] Morgan was castigated by innumerable critics for excessive casualties, mistreatment of patients, corruption in his department, and the demoralized conditions of regiments. Shippen called him "a damned rogue" who speculated in medical stores.[56] Richard Henry Lee confided to Shippen: "As for Morgan, the very air [in Congress] teems with complaints about him."[57] And Sam Adams wrote John Adams that "great and heavy complaints have been made of abuses in the Director-General Department of both our armies. I have no doubt that Morgan and Stringer will be removed as I think they ought ... the reason (as I take it) was the general disgust and danger of the loss of an Army arising there from."[58] Stringer was also severely criticized, and as a New York associate of the haughty Schuyler, he invariably shared in the anti-Schuyler bias directed at his patron by New Englanders. Both Morgan and Stringer had been assigned incredible tasks, and under the circumstances they had performed remarkably. Because of his arrogance and the chaotic conditions of the department, Morgan was an inevitable scapegoat. Although Stringer erred in leaving his post to hunt for drugs, he too was the victim of Congressional ineptitude and of inadequate war preparations. Without holding an inquiry into their performances and without providing the doctors an opportunity to defend themselves, Congress on January 9, 1777 curtly dismissed them.

Assuming that he was the prime candidate for Morgan's position, Shippen had forwarded a plan of administrative changes to Lee in Congress in late December 1776. In mid-

January Shippen sent his suggestions to Washington. With the general at Morristown were his favorite army doctors—James Craik, his old Virginia friend, and John Cochran. Impressed with Cochran's skill and experience, Washington had him consult with Shippen in Philadelphia. The Shippen-Cochran plan was sent to Washington on January 31, and Washington soon submitted it to Congress. He wrote to Hancock that his army could not continue to function effectively under previous medical arrangements, that he had been swamped with complaints about hospitals "from every Quarter," and that he could not understand why the army "is permitted to moulder away by Sickness . . ."[59] After some procrastination, Congress on April 11 approved the Hospital Bill. Shippen was appointed Director General with control over four regional departments—Northern, Eastern (New England), Middle, and Southern—which were to be supervised by Deputy Director Generals. Some able physicians such as Rush, Brown, Craik, and Cochran were rewarded with high posts in the Middle Department, and Potts, because of his work at Lake George and Princeton, was appointed Deputy Director General for the Northern Department. Praising the appointments of Potts and Cochran in particular, Shippen wrote Washington: "These gentlemen are known to be possessed with great humanity, industry, and knowledge of what is necessary for the health of soldiers."[60]

In the Hospital Bill, Congress offered higher pay for medical men. Colonels in the army then received $2.50 daily, Captains $1.33, and Lieutenants $1.00. An indication of Congressional willingness to pay increased wages to doctors is demonstrated by the fact that the pay for Deputy Director Generals was $5.00, that of Senior Surgeons $4.00, and Junior Surgeons $2.00. As John Adams remarked about the improved pay scale: "A most ample and generous liberal allowance. The expense will be great, but humanity overcame avarice." Under the new leadership, Adams hoped, the medical department would attract "the best abilities in Physic and Chirurgery that the country can afford."[61]

To recruit such talent, Shippen had the following notice

inserted in several newspapers on June 4 in the Middle Department:

> The liberal provisions made by Congress in the new medical arrangements, joined with a humane desire to prevent a repetition of the distress which afflicted the brave American soldiers the last campaign, have drawn men of the first abilities into the field, to watch over the health and preserve the life of the soldiers—many of them from very extensive and profitable practice and every species of domestic happiness ... Under these [circumstances] none but gentlemen of the best education, and well qualified, are employed as senior Physicians and Surgeons, etc. The Eastern and Other Departments are filled with gentlemen of the first character in these counties; and the public may depend upon it that the greatest exertions of skill and industry shall be constantly made and no cost spared to make the sick and wounded soldiery, comfortable and happy. As a consequence of the above liberal arrangement of the Honorable Congress, we do so with great pleasure and equal truth, assure the public, (notwithstanding the many false and wicked reports propagated by the enemies of American liberty, and only calculated to retard the recruiting service) that all the military hospitals of the United States are in excellent order, and the army enjoy a degree of health, seldom to be seen or read of.[62]

This advertisement is unique. One of the few of its kind published during the war, the item indicates that medical care was closely related to the morale of, and the recruitment for, the army.

Another aspect of the attempt to improve conditions was Rush's essay printed on April 22, 1777, in the *Pennsylvania Packet*. His *Directions for Preserving the Health of Soldiers* occupied the entire front page of the issue. Addressing combat officers, who seemed indifferent to sanitary matters, Rush noted that regardless of the medical profession's efforts to protect health, "Your authority is absolutely necessary to enforce the most salutary plans and precepts for preserving the health of soldiers." He then listed preventive measures in four categories—dress, diet, personal hygiene, and camp sanitation. Rush remarked that officers were often praised for their tactical ability, which prevented casualties of their men. "But if it be meritorious to save the life of a soldier by skill and ability in the field," Rush inquired, "why should it be thought less to preserve them by skill and ability of another kind in a march or encampment?"[63] Though the essay contained little that had not been expounded by British military doctors, the fact that the article was reprinted several times during the war may have helped to popularize concepts of sanitation in the army—orders that generals promulgated year after year for their careless officers and troops.

Combat casualties in 1776 were 1,156 men; about 5,200 were prisoners. How many died from disease is conjectural, but one estimate is that several thousands died from sickness. In May 1776, about 32 percent of the army was reported sick. After an autumn decline in the sickness rate, it increased to 35 percent in the winter.[64] Hence for the last six months of the year, about one-third of Washington's army was unfit for duty. Obviously the army could not again sustain such losses, or it would disintegrate as a fighting force.

VII.
With Gates at Saratoga

As Potts prepared for his assignment in early 1777, a major step in preventive medicine was under way for the army. At Morristown, Washington decided that his troops should be inoculated for the spring campaigning. As he explained on January 6, "I have determined that the troops be inoculated . . . Necessity not only authorizes it, but seems to require this measure, for should the disorder infect the army . . . and rage with its usual Virulence, we should have more to dread from it than from the Sword of the Enemy."[1] If levies of the south and middle states, expected on the Delaware in February, could be inoculated efficiently, Washington believed the disease could be checked, regiments would have time to recuperate from the treatment, and recruitment would be encouraged.

From February until May Shippen's staff inoculated regiments at Germantown and at Province Island and Fort Island in the Delaware. While the variolation occurred, the clothing of the men was washed, smoked, and cleaned. Similar procedures were devised for mobilization centers at Boston, Providence, Hanover (Hampshire Grants), Trenton, Peekskill, Fishkill, Baltimore, and in Virginia at Dumfries, Colchester, and Alexandria. Washington instructed generals Gates at Germantown, Schuyler at Albany, and Samuel Holden Parsons at Boston about the timetable of inoculation; he also informed state officials about the undertaking. Governor Trumbull of Connecticut wrote Washington on February 24 that he hoped the measure would prevent a repetition of the year's past disasters: "Our returning soldiers [from Canada] have spread the infection into every other town in the State; . . ."[2]

The inoculators eliminated antimony from the treatment and salt and spices from the predominantly vegetable diet. They prescribed niter and calomel for alternate days, and two carthartics—one taken a week after the inoculation and the second when the pox appeared on the skin. During the eruptive stage of the pustule, the doctors kept the soldiers in cool quarters and warned them about excessive exercise. The inoculation at Morristown was successful, remembered Colonel Ashbel Green of Pennsylvania, and the treatment only briefly incapacitiated the troops:

> The most troublesome aspect of the system experienced was the sore which was formed on the arm at the place where the virus had been introduced by the puncture of a lancet. Many of these sores continued to discharge pus for two or three months, and in some instances were large and a degree painful. Yet none of them proved dangerous ... I believe that there was not a day while they were under inoculation, in which they might not have been, with a few exceptions, marched against the enemy.[3]

Mass inoculation for the army was quite effective. Although death caused by the natural infection averaged 16 percent, the mortality rate for Washington's troops who underwent supervised inoculation averaged well under 1 percent.[4] In early March Cochran wrote to Schuyler, his brother-in-law, that "our army is in fine spirits and pretty healthy where the smallpox is and has been troublesome. We have now under inoculation about 300 and as one set gets out we take in another 'till we inoculate the whole of our regular troops."[5] Though thousands of Continentals and militia still had to be inoculated during the succeeding years, the program of 1777 was a success. The adoption of mass inoculation eliminated a major obstacle to recruiting, and in the spring thousands of men converged upon the Delaware to join Washington's pox-free army. Pleased with the program, on April 22 John Adams wrote from Philadelphia: "We are crowding along soldiers to the General, as fast as they get well of inoculation."[6] No medical doctor in the nation had the prestige or the authority to convince his countrymen of the necessity for inoculating the troops. More than any other contemporary figure, Washington deserves the credit for popularizing the treatment and for making the greatest contribution to preventive medicine during the war.

Smallpox appeared near Lake Champlain in February 1777. Wayne had only 1,200 men at Ticonderoga, and he feared an enemy attack in the spring when the ice broke upon the waters. Wayne learned that the pestilence, supposedly caused by unauthorized self-inoculation, had broken out at Skenesboro. Determined to check the contagion before it spread to his post, Wayne dispatched Captain Henry O'Hara to investigate, and to arrest the culprits.[7] Fortunately, the alarm was exaggerated, and only a few smallpox cases appeared at Skenesboro, which O'Hara reported, "must have come in the natural way."[8] Schuyler stated to Hancock that he intended to inoculate all his troops. "It appears highly necessary," he remarked, "but I will not venture upon it until Dr. Potts arrives, . . ."[9] Intent on avoiding the calamities of the preceding campaign, Schuyler had agents scouring New England for drugs, and he ordered a hospital built on Mt. Independence, "sufficiently large to contain six hundred sick, besides the necessary apartments."[10]

Potts was not officially designated Deputy Director General for the Northern Department until April 11, but he acted in this capacity since January. His letter to Congress in February may have convinced delegates that a pay increase was necessary to attract talented men to the department. . ."The dearness of Every Necessity of life and the Difficulty of procuring Gentlemen of Ability," he stated, ". . . induce me to beg your attention to this matter. I have the highest sense of honor conferred upon me by the Honorable Congress," Potts declared, "and I shall exert every nerve to merit their notice."[11] His staff for the general hospital—six senior surgeons, six assistant surgeons, seven mates, two clerks, one steward—was a decided improvement over Stringer's small cadre the previous year. Traveling north in early March, Potts received a letter from Wayne, who urged him to hasten. "For God's sake," Wayne scribbled, "push on to this place . . . [and] fly to your friend."[12] Potts's little wagon train of supplies and equipment was seen passing through Bethlehem on March 14 by the Moravians.[13]

On April 2 Potts arrived at Albany, where he found that his supplies were adequate and his staff complete. He was needed not only to supervise inoculation procedures but also to administer a scattered medical establishment. From Philadelphia Schuyler ordered him to prevent smallpox patients at Fort George "from straggling among the troops."[14] And there were other problems. Surgeon Joseph Young at the Albany hospital, for example, was clearly perplexed about the scope of his responsibilities; he asked Potts the following:

> Should not the blankets of such Soldiers as die in the Hospital, be kept in the Hospital Store, and account of them taken?
> Should not their Arms etc. be returned . . . [to the quartermaster]?
> Should not their cloaths [sic] and other effects be bound together and a label affixed thereto, to be delivered to their friends?
> What quantities of Soap and Candles, may be allowed to each Ward per Week, or is this affair regulated?
> May the Regimental Surgeons be supplied with Medicine for the sick?
> Or would it be better to take them into the Hospital and take care of them there?
> If a Hospital patient has not a Shirt, or not a change, must I draw one from the store for him?
> If a Soldier is dismissed to join his company, and his Officers all absent, and he is destitute of money, what is to be done?
> Are the Nurses etc. to be allowed any liquor?
> If a Nurse be emply'd, and takes sick are they [sic] entitled to nurses wages during their illness?

What number of bandages will it be proper yet to make, if linen can be procured?
What number of each kind?
Shall I purchase vinegar, if it can be procured, and what quantity?
I want Bottles for Tinctures, etc. Shall I take them out of a Chest in the Cellar, or shall I purchase some?[15]

George Smyth at Fort Edward required lancets and utensils for his twenty-three sick: "They have not a Pot, Kettle, nor Pan to cook with, nor a Cup to Drink out of, which renders it very disagreeable."[16] Treating patients who had been maimed by hostile Indians terrorizing the Mohawk Valley, James Thacher needed assistance, particularly for three men "cruelly wounded by the savages."[17] Patients awaited Potts at Ticonderoga, Wayne indicated. "It will not be amiss for you to come with your sleeves rolled up and your amputating instruments, etc. placed in proper order."[18]

Potts established three hospitals in the north—one at Albany for troops in transit, the second at Fort George for smallpox care, and the third at Mt. Independence, where combat was expected. Pointing out to Shippen that "one prevention is worth two cures" in the treatment of disease, Potts explained that he would advise the military about food preparation and about camp sanitation. Smallpox, Potts was pleased to advise, "is not on the line of march at all."[19] Potts also explained to the Medical Committee of Congress that he planned a vegetable garden at Mt. Independence. "I can with confidence assure you," he wrote, "that no step will be left untaken by me to support the health of the troops and do my duty to the sick . . ."[20] The committee responded by praising Potts for his endeavors, adding that, with respect to recruiting medical men, "as handsome salaries are now allowed, . . . we expect none but persons of the best abilities will be employed."[21]

Owing to various administrative matters, Potts was detained in Albany. Because of local Loyalist sentiment, for example, Potts had difficulties in acquiring wagons.[22] His jurisdiction encompassed not only Albany, Fort George,

Ticonderoga, and Skenesboro, but also Fort Anne, Fort Miller, and Fort Edward along the Hudson, and Fort Stanwix, German Flats, and Schenectady along the Mohawk. For each post Potts provided medical arrangements. In Schenectady he appointed Dirk Van Ingen, a local physician, to treat militia wounded in Indian fights. As he told the Schenectady Committee of Safety: "It is my determination that every care and precaution should be taken respecting our sick . . ."[23] Inasmuch as Potts had been ordered to improve discipline among regimental surgeons, he warned surgeons and mates who were on leave to rejoin their units. "No excuses will be taken," he informed them, "such as neglect this notice may expect to be succeeded [replaced] without distinction."[24] He also sought to improve the quality of surgeons. Colonel Samuel Brewer notified Potts that he had appointed Dr. Thomas Binney as his regimental surgeon. "How far he will be able to answer your Scholastic questions, I can't say." the officer admitted, "but can only say that I know he has had long and successful country practice at home, and has been on two or three Campaigns in the army, and has given very good satisfaction."[25]

Potts finally arrived at Ticonderoga in early May. Here he was undoubtedly flattered by a testimonial from five surgeons in the regiments of Colonels John Nixon and John Glover who, in contrast to the typical acrimony between surgeons and Morgan, thanked Potts profusely for supporting their efforts and congratulated him on his appointment. "It has been owing to your assistance you have at all times so generously lent us that we have been able to discharge with benefit and advantage to our patients, with care and convenience to ourselves that great and important duty toward the sick of the army."[26] Potts found that the 2,500 troops at the garrison under Colonel St. Clair (replacing Wayne, who had joined Washington) were well quartered and adequately provisioned. Two cases of smallpox were detected at the post, but they were quickly isolated; at Fort George eight men were reported with smallpox, but they too were quarantined. The construction of the hospital on Mt. Independence was under way. Colonel Baldwin, the post engineer, had the timber cut in March, the ground cleared in April, and on May 5 he noted in his diary, "laid out the area for the hospital."[27] By early June one side of the building was erected. Visiting the site that month, Chaplain Enos Hitchcock commented, "250 feet long and 24 feet wide—warm and pleasant."[28] Another measure for helping casualties, instigated by Schuyler, was the construction of six large bateaux, "covered with old tents as awnings to be kept as Hospital boats conveying the sick from Ticonderoga to Fort George."[29] Schuyler repeatedly ordered his commanders to inspect the dress, rations, and quarters of their men, and St. Clair frequently issued instruction about cooking facilities, proper rations, and the use of latrines. Assuming more the function of a purveyor, Potts not only acquired many casks of wine for his patients, but he also purchased 200 sheep, 20 cows, tubs of butter, and a steady stream of provisions. The sickness rate of 16 percent in Ticonderoga in June was probably the lowest at the post since the war began.[30] Morale was high, Potts informed his brother Samuel, and "never were the troops more healthy." Summarizing his projects for the summer, Potts confided that "in short, I hope to have a happy campaign."[31]

Potts communicated the same enthusiasm to Shippen. "I shall excite every nerve to preserve cleanliness," he informed his former professor, "paying particular attention to the method of dressing the provisions delivered to the troops, and above all that the Garden will be taken care of."[32] In late May Potts told his friend Owen Biddle, President of the Board of War, that the garrison was preparing to repulse Burgoyne's attack expected that summer. "As to my department," he added, "it gives me great pleasure to assure you that I have but 200 in the General hospital [Albany] and 11 in the other place [Fort George]. In short, the troops are extremely healthy." Indicating his humanitarian concern for his charges, Potts added in a revealing comment: "My only concern is to preserve the health of soldiers and to tenderly nurse the sick."[33] In that phrase, Potts neatly summarized the creed of dedicated army doctors in the war.

Yet Schuyler viewed Potts with suspicion. Schuyler frequently confided in Stringer, but was quite cautious with Potts. The proud Albany patroon had been reprimanded in January 1777 for his intemperate language during a quarrel with delegates in Congress, and he realized that inasmuch as he symbolized the defeats in the north for 1776, a movement was under way to replace him with Gates. Under the circumstances Schuyler regarded supporters of his rival with concern, and Potts was a known admirer of Gates. When Potts arrived at Albany in April 1777, Schuyler was in Philadelphia, seeking support in Congress for confirmation of his command. Rumors had abounded for months about Schuyler's dismissal, and he was anxious to learn what Potts knew about the matter. Richard Varick, Schuyler's aide in Albany, informed him about the political viewpoints of newcomers to the area. During long dinner conversations with Potts, Varick probed him for information about possible changes in the military leadership for upper New York, but typically Potts avoided comment. Varick notified Schuyler that Potts seemed to know more about the situation than he would reveal, and that the doctor was "most violently attached to [Gates]." Varick again tried to obtain some clues from Potts, but Potts refused to discuss the affair, and as Varick remarked, the doctor "seemed determined to keep secret what he knew about the matter."[34] Schuyler clearly distrusted Potts, and this attitude may account for the fact that Schuyler provided Potts with very few instructions, and Potts, doubtless aware of the hostility, corresponded very seldom with Schuyler. One historical consequence of this tense relationship is that relatively little information about medical matters is available for the northern campaign in 1777, although Schuyler did provide Potts with full authority to administer the department.[35]

Meanwhile a British invasion from Canada was under way. Burgoyne planned to conquer upper New York by capturing Ticonderoga and Albany with two widely separated armies. While a force of 1,100, based at Oswego, seized Fort Stanwix and pushed eastward through the Mohawk Valley, Burgoyne's main command of 6,600 troops would descend the lakes and the upper Hudson. As rebel resistance disintegrated, General Howe in Manhattan was expected to send an expedition up the Hudson in order to link with Burgoyne at Albany. Yet Howe tinkered with the strategy that could have ended the war with British victories; he assumed that he could easily conquer the Delaware Valley and that Burgoyne's army, unassisted, was powerful enough to crush American opposition. The fine British force assembled at St. Jean's in May appeared so formidable that the collapse of the rebellion in New York that summer seemed inevitable.

At Ticonderoga, St. Clair had only 2,500 effectives to man lines so complex and extensive that 10,000 troops were needed. No American squadron guarded Lake Champlain, reinforcements of militia were slow to arrive, and Washington, uncertain of the destination of Howe's army mobilizing in Manhattan, hesitated to commit veteran battalions to the lakes. Until mid-June Schuyler was uncertain of the enemy's strength and of the pace of Burgoyne's mobilization on the Richelieu. Soon after, he realized that Burgoyne's expedition was majestically gliding down Lake Champlain and that Ticonderoga could not sustain a long seige. Consequently he made efforts for evacuation of the post. Schuyler curtailed shipments of military equipment to the garrison and made preparations to move the sick. "Not a single room of the hospital is yet finished," he informed Congress, "nor will it be in a condition to receive a considerable number of sick."[36] On June 21 Schuyler ordered Potts to evacuate his hospital. "You are to remove the principal part of your medicine and stores to Lake George. All sick patients as labour under chronic complaints and are not likely to be fit for duty in a short time should also be sent over the lake. You will, therefore," Schuyler instructed, "have every wounded, maimed, and other patients labouring under infection or lingering disease, removed to the Hospital at Fort George."[37] Potts supervised the transfer of the sick across the lake, and he remained at Fort George while the attack of Ticonderoga occurred, moving his patients to Albany as the enemy neared, and setting up field hospitals along the Hudson for the retreating American army.

By June 30 the British fleet was only fifteen miles from Ticonderoga. On July 2, after disembarking his troops, baggage, and heavy artillery, Burgoyne ordered an advance to the citadel. Probing the American lines, the British were repulsed at Mt. Independence, but they found an opening to Mt. Defiance, an undefended steep hill south of Ticonderoga. The British had artillery positioned on its summit by July 5 and began to pound Ticonderoga with devastating effect. Nearly surrounded and under heavy bombardment, St. Clair sought to save the Northern army for another battle.

Two escape routes were available. Crossing the bridge in darkness to Mt. Independence, St. Clair hurried his troops to the eastern shore, down the south arm of Lake Champlain, and along a trail to Hubbardton in the Hampshire Grants. Guarded by a regiment, the women, children, and casualties evacuated the post by bateaux to Skenesboro, sixty miles to the south. As the vessels approached Skenesboro the following morning, enemy gunboats were not detected. But while disembarking, the escape party was astounded to hear the boom of enemy cannon and to see redcoats landing above the settlement. After burning the facilities at Skenesboro, the fugitives fled along Wood Creek to the southwest, finding sanctuary sixteen miles away at Fort Anne. Unable to defend this tumbledown stockade, the escape party continued to Fort Edward on the Hudson, where Schuyler and 700 men provided protection. St. Clair meanwhile led the main army to Hubbardton, where he left a rear guard that fought a bloody battle with pursuing redcoats. On July 7 St. Clair marched to Castleton, and then, taking a circuitous route to Rutland, his force finally reached the Hudson by July 13. Here, said Thacher, who supervised the evacuation of casualties from Ticonderoga, the survivors of the retreat huddled, "greatly distressed and worn down with fatigue."[38] Now, as Schuyler retreated toward Moses Creek on the Hudson, he had the awesome task of rebuilding the army and of delaying Burgoyne.

The American cause on the Hudson seemed doomed. Ticonderoga, Fort George, Skenesboro, and Fort Anne had toppled to the British; the enemy moved its artillery from Lake George without interference; Indian war parties terrorized American settlements; and only a shattered and dispirited patriot army stood in Burgoyne's path to Albany. Yet the British and Americans exaggerated Ticonderoga's importance, and at first both sides overlooked Burgoyne's logistical problems. Fortunately for the Americans, Burgoyne inadvertently provided them with time to prepare new defenses. While regrouping his forces at Skenesboro, Burgoyne decided to hack his way through the twenty-three miles of forest to the Hudson. The British march of conquest through this wilderness was greatly impeded by environmental difficulties, and by Schuyler's determination to impede his opponent. Schuyler ordered hundreds of woodsmen to push boulders and trees into Wood Creek, so that the nearby trail was flooded. They destroyed every bridge and causeway on the route. His men dug ditches to divert streams and turned stretches of trail into muddy quagmires. They cut huge stands of pine and hemlock to block other portions of the path, and flooded ponds and streams that interlaced the area to make it into a logistical nightmare. As a result of Burgoyne's own lethargy, his ponderous baggage and equipment, and the shortage of transportation, the British army took twenty-four days to cover the distance. The force took seven days to move the sixteen miles to Fort Anne, and not until July 24 was the road cleared to Fort Edward. By August 9 Burgoyne finally had his ponderous force assembled on the east bank of the Hudson. Again he paused to re-form, and not until September 13 was his army poised on the west bank of the river for the final thrust to Albany.

While Burgoyne and Schuyler prepared for battle, Potts continually shifted the field hospitals farther and farther southward as the army retreated to a defensible position. Potts had saved most of his stores from Ticonderoga, and as he noted, Schuyler's decision to encamp near Moses Creek (with 4,500 men) in early August, "was a prudent step, at this spot we are daily getting supplies."[39] Yet the shortage of tents, the constant rain, and the strain of continual defeat demoralized the army. As Jonathan Trumbull, Jr., remarked to his father on August 4: "Disease and sickness is pressing upon our army. Dr. Potts had just showed me a letter in which he informs me that from disease and other causes our army is reduced to not more than 4,000."[40] Schuyler informed Washington that "desertion prevails and disease gains ground; nor is it to be wondered, for we have neither tents, houses, or barns . . . we are in want of every kind of necessities, provisions excepted."[41] The constant evacuation of casualties caused a temporary dislocation of medical facilities. Surgeon John Browne reported to Potts that he had to continually move his sick.[42] From Moses Creek, Robert Johnston commented on July 30 that he required wagons to transfer his patients to safety.[43] Jonathan Bartlett pleaded for aid, stating that his patients were now "wretched sick creatures . . . bones grinding on hard oaken planks . . ."[44] Perhaps overburdened with a multitude of tasks during the emergency, Schuyler provided Potts with very little help. Potts, in fact, had to return to Albany to request the local Committee of Safety on August 7 for wagons to move his patients from the Hudson to safety.[45]

As the British advanced down the Hudson, their Indian allies roamed the frontier. The entire Allen family was massacred in its cabin, and the Barnes family was slaughtered on the trail to an American outpost. The most publicized atrocity in the region occurred to a young girl on July 26 near Fort Edward. Jane McCrea was waiting for her Tory lover, a member of Burgoyne's staff, when she was seized and scalped by Iroquois raiding the area. Surgeon Bartlett hurried to the site and reported to Potts the grisly details. The woman was "taken by the savages, led up a hill to where there was a body of British troops," Bartlett wrote, "and the poor girl was shot to death in cold blood and left on the ground." Fearing another Indian attack, Bartlett begged for some equipment. "There is neither an amputating instrument, or a crooked needle in all the camp. I have a handful of lint and two or three bandages, and that is all. What in the name of wonder am I to do in case of attack, God only knows, without assistance, without instruments, without everything!"[46] The massacre of Jenny McCrea assumed legendary proportions, because the event provided propaganda about the fiendish enemy for the patriotic cause. Overlooking the girl's Loyalist affiliations, the Continental military dramatized the incident as an example of the martyrdom of American women in order to rally support for Schuyler's army. As a result some farmers from New York and New England, fearful of the consequences of Indian raids on their communities, joined the army. Although Burgoyne actually had tried to restrain his scalp-hunting allies, Potts regarded the incident as deliberately contrived by the British command to terrorize the area. No quarter should be given to such an enemy, Potts declared to his brother Samuel. "Now for Lex Talionis, by heavens." Potts was so enraged at the deed that he vowed: "No [British] officer or soldier shall have mercy from my hands."[47]

Although still confident of victory in early August, Burgoyne realized that his invasion plan was impeded by supply and transportation problems. He needed oxen, horses, and cattle for his army, which were available on farms in Vermont. Burgoyne realized that some American militia under John Stark was massing near Manchester and Bennington, but he did not consider this force a threat to an expedition into the area. On August 11 Burgoyne sent Colonel Fredrich Baum and 800 Hessians through the Green Mountains to comandeer mounts and livestock. As the British force neared Bennington on August 18, Stark's 1,700 men stung the invaders like angry hornets. Assailed from all sides, Baum retreated back to the Hudson, his force saved only by the timely arrival of 600 troops sent by Burgoyne. Nine hundred British and German troops were casualties or were captured in the fighting, and the army still lacked enough draft animals. Naturally the Americans were jubilant over their victory; at last it seemed that Burgoyne could be repulsed.

Potts had sent Stark a medical chest before the battle and dispatched Surgeon Francis Hagan after the fighting. On August 17 Hagan received permission from the Bennington selectmen to use a church and the town meetinghouse as hospitals. "I want for nothing but stores to render their situation comfortable," Hagan wrote about his patients.[48] Two captive Hessian surgeons treated their own casualties in the meetinghouse and notified their superiors that they were well treated. Yet Hagan had problems in caring for the American wounded; because they were "scattered about the country," he reported to Potts on August 22, making it difficult to locate them. To add to his difficulties, the local citizenry seemed reluctant to help him. "The inhabitants can nor will not furnish me with any furniture, and it is impossible to find houses in town for them."[49] Hagan's difficulties were soon resolved. Potts sent Surgeon Samuel McKenzie to assist him with additional stores, and more shelter was made available. On August 25 General Benjamin Lincoln, commanding in the Grants, stated that the wounded were being treated in "a very good hospital."[50] On August 30 McKenzie needed only bark, scalpels, and bandages. "Our patients seem to do well," he added, "we hope to have our hospital well regulated in a few days and have everything that will contribute to the recovery of the wounded prisoners."[51]

Soon after Bennington, Burgoyne met another defeat. The western wing of his army—a force of Indians, Loyalists, and regulars—invaded the Mohawk Valley, and by August 3 it surrounded Fort Stanwix (Rome). On August 6 Colonel Nicholas Herkimer marched to the relief of the stockade from Fort Dayton with 800 New York militia, accompanied by Surgeon Moses Younglove. Even with Oneida scouts, Herkimer's men were ambushed at Oriskany, where Younglove was captured and Herkimer badly wounded. Potts sent Robert Johnston to treat the casualties. On August 16 Johnston wrote that he had thirty patients at Oriskany and that Herkimer, ten days after the battle, was in agony from injuries to his leg and thigh. Herkimer's wounds, Johnston stated, had been dressed only once since the battle. The old Dutchman was in such pain on August 17 that the surgeon had to amputate, "there not being any hope of recovery without it." The operation was unsuccessful, Johnston reported:

With Gates at Saratoga

". . . Alas, the patriotick hero died in the evening, the cause of his death God only knows."[52]

A force of 500 men under Arnold hurried to retrieve the defeat at Oriskany and to relieve Fort Stanwix. The wily Arnold duped Colonel Barry St. Leger's Indians into believing that he headed a huge force bent on severe retribution. At the news the Indians fled to Lake Ontario, and without their aid St. Leger had to withdraw from the siege on August 22. Nicholas Scull, a surgeon's mate, was with Arnold when the fortress was saved, and he reported to Potts on August 28 that "the Cowardly Rascals" had fled in such haste that they had left their supplies behind.[53] Arnold's men then rejoined the army on the Hudson, which was daily increasing as hundreds of militia joined to fight the redcoats. Another portion of Burgoyne's army was defeated, his Indian and Canadian allies were deserting, Loyalists were not flocking to his standard, and the American forces were rapidly expanding.

By August 19 Gates commanded the American forces on the Hudson. Schuyler's accomplishments in delaying Burgoyne were remarkable, but Congress replaced him in order to regenerate its Northern army. Gates was a popular leader, and he appreciated the role of militia in supplementing the Continental line. Washington sent him some veteran regiments, and after the news in late August that Howe's expedition was sighted off the Delaware Capes headed for Philadelphia, Washington spared Gates additional troops. With these reinforcements Gates had 8,300 men on September 17.

Gates knew that Burgoyne had depleted his manpower and his resources, but rather than risk an assault against the disciplined British-Hessian brigades, Gates planned to defend a sector along the Hudson against which Burgoyne would have to hurl his legions. Gates selected a densely wooded slope overlooking the river, twenty-five miles north of Albany, called Bemis Heights. By September 15, when the American entrenchments had been dug, the breastworks erected, and the artillery positioned, Burgoyne had 5,500 troops at Saratoga prepared to attack. With only the haziest notion of the extent and depth of the enemy lines, on September 19 Burgoyne ordered a wide flanking maneuver through the thickets and ravines on the American left. The armies clashed in a bloody struggle north of Bemis Heights at Freeman's Farm. Although outnumbered in the seven-hour battle, the British held the field, but they suffered heavy casualties. Assuming that they had been beaten, the Americans waited for a renewal of the attack. But the British forces had been badly mauled, the American defenses were difficult to penetrate, and Burgoyne hesitated to attempt another frontal assault. As he contemplated another probing of enemy positions on September 21, Burgoyne learned that Clinton had sailed up the Hudson from Manhattan with 4,000 men to attack rebel defenses in the Highlands. Now the British prepared defenses of their own at Freeman's Farm and hoped that Clinton would relieve some of the American pressure.

For the next three weeks Burgoyne waited in vain. After advancing to Kingston, Clinton returned to Manhattan by October 9. His force encountered large masses of militia hovering all along the Hudson banks, and he had been ordered by Howe (to compensate for losses in the invasion of Pennsylvania) to dispatch an army to the Delaware. Burgoyne's troops went hungry on half rations, they spent sleepless nights listening to the militia hooting and howling like Indians, and they shivered in the crisp autumn weather. All the lake posts had fallen to the Americans, the last escape routes to the north were closed, and Gates's force was rapidly increasing to 11,000 men. In a desperate effort to extricate his army from the trap, Burgoyne led another attack on October 7 below Freeman's Farm. Again he encountered fierce resistance and had to retreat. But this time the Americans stormed the British redcoats and captured a chunk of the British defenses. Burgoyne had to move his army back to Saratoga, leaving his wounded behind. After the battle Captain Henry Dearborn of New Hampshire noted in his journal: "We found the enemy had evacuated the whole of their lines and had left about 500 sick and wounded on the ground."[54]

Potts was at Bemis Heights supervising medical arrangements in a hospital tent. On September 12 he had been issued a dozen musket balls,[55] presumably not to fire at the enemy as he may have preferred, but probably to provide the wounded with lead to bite on during periods of excruciating pain. With 200 Americans wounded on September 19, another 100 on October 7, in addition to several hundred British casualties, Potts and his surgeons were inundated with casualties. They treated men with skin scorched by powder burns and by artillery explosions. They saw men with limbs partially shot away by cannon fire, bones splintered by bullets, hands and feet left hanging by a few threads of flesh, joints torn and shattered, horrible bruises, and massive hemorraging from gaping wounds. As Colonel Varick remarked to Schuyler on September 19: "The groans of the many wounded which are at Potts's in the neighborhood affront me so much that I can't recollect any thing more..."[56]

Amid scores of mutilated bodies brought from the battlefield, surgeons had to determine quickly what men could be saved by prompt treatment, what cases could be temporarily delayed, and what injuries were so destructive to the human frame that little could be done.[57] The surgeon could postpone treatment of men with sprains, dislocations, and simple fractures. His mate could treat the numerous powder-burn cases—caused by a flashback in the musket pan from the accumulation of residual powder in an uncleaned barrel or from a premature explosion in the touch hole of a cannon—with linseed oil, olive oil, and compresses of tea or vinegar. Men with severe head injuries had to wait for trepanning, because this operation was too complicated to attempt near the scene of the action.

Likewise, wounds of bodily cavities were considered so dangerous that they were invariably accepted as fatal. Thoracic and abdominal penetrations were practically impossible to treat—a surgeon could only bleed the soldier in order to reduce hemorrhaging at the site of injury, plaster over the wound, and hope for the patient's recovery. As the surgeon appraised those patients who required immediate attention, his task was complicated by the variety of war wounds. About half the wounds caused by musket balls were embedded in fleshy parts of the body; they often produced little immediate pain, and during the excitement of battle soldiers were sometimes unaware of their bodily damage. Other casualties exhibited more immediate and violent reaction to injuries by vomiting and convulsions. Some superficial wounds appeared massive; others seemed slight, but the undetected internal damage was enormous. Most surgeons delayed treating soldiers who bled little, preferring to treat first those who bled profusely. Why some wounds bled intensely and some wounds relatively little was a question that baffled the surgeons. Some men with lesser wounds sobbed and screamed in agony; others lay mute or groaned quietly in a state of shock.

Punctures made by swords, sabers, and bayonets were usually clean wounds with sharp, deep gashes. Penetrations caused by smooth-bore musket balls produced torn, jagged wounds. Unlike the hardened bullets of the late nineteenth century, the low-velocity lead balls flattened on impact in the body, tore flesh savagely, traumatized tissue, splintered bones, and implanted bits of clothing in the injury. Blade and bullet wounds of the face, neck, and bodily extremities required most of a surgeon's attention. He tried to arrest hemorrhage, to clean the wound, and to remove foreign bodies. He could restrain bleeding by pressure of bandages and by ligature. As Morgan advised:

> In applying a common tourniquet to stop the flow of blood from any principal artery in a limb, till it can be otherwise properly secured, care must be taken not to twist it too tightly above the limb; and to prevent the tourniquets from slipping so as to endanger a fresh loss of blood, it must be fortified with a ligature of thread or tape; . . .
>
> What the surgeon has chiefly to attend to, in case of person being much wounded in the field of battle, is to stop the flow of blood, either by tourniquet, ligature, lint and compress, or a suitable bandage, as the case may require; to remove any extraneous body from the wound, to reduce fractured bones; to apply proper dressings to wounds; take care on one hand not to bind up the parts too tightly, so as to injure

blood circulation, increase inflammation, and excite a fever; or, so loosely as to endanger the wound bleeding afresh, or to allow broken bones, after they are properly set, to be again displaced.[58]

Before a surgeon probed, he gave his patient a slug of rum or a grain of opium. He then opened the wound with his knife, making additional incisions in the belief that healing was promoted by changing the shape of the wound and that prolonged bleeding was part of the recuperative process. When he located the ball, he removed it with a spoon, a forceps, or his own dirty fingers. "But when [the object] is sunk too deep, and lies absolutely beyond the reach of the fingers," Ranby admitted, "I could never bring myself to thrust those long forceps the Lord knows where, with scarce any probability of success."[59] After the surgeon extracted the metal, he displayed it to the wounded soldier—if he was still conscious—in an effort to improve the man's morale. If the bullet was lodged too deeply, it was left to extricate itself. The wound was cleansed with dry lint or lint soaked with oil; it then was stuffed with lint soaked in wine, brandy, or vinegar and bandaged. Frequently the only medication available was water, and if a surgeon did not have lint, he placed some other material into the wound—moss, grass, leaves, a piece of rag, or even a piece of a tattered flag. In the second stage of the treatment, infection of the wound invariably followed with suppuration and a free discharge of pus encouraged on the assumption that the evacuation would dislodge any retained foreign bodies. "Laudable pus" was believed to be part of the healing process, and many surgeons left a piece of lint or sponge in the wound, theorizing that inflammation of the injury would hasten healing. Later, in the third stage, the wound was washed with a "digestive," a substance used to draw pus, and then covered with a bread-and-milk poultice, with oil for moisture. In the belief that a patient should be kept cool to avoid the chance of infection during the prolonged process of granulation, the doctors prescribed a special "cooling regimen" of special foods and drugs.

Richard L. Blanco

An amputation was the most serious operation that surgeons performed in the field. Amputation of the bodily extremities was considered necessary for anything more serious than a simple fracture of flesh wounds that missed a main artery. The general rule was that amputation was essential if limbs were partially or completely shattered; if bones were smashed and much flesh and arteries were missing; if the bones were intact, but the muscles, nerves, and small bones were too disordered; or if the joints were smashed and the hope of limb movement was abandoned. Another rule was that of primary operation, or operation within twenty-four hours of the injury. As Jones explained: "If a wound be of such a nature as to require amputation, which is frequently the case where it happens in a large joint, it is of the utmost importance to perform the operation immediately; as the consequent pain and inflammation, renders it improper during these symptoms; . . ."[60]

Although uncertainty about the proper time to amputate continued through the Napoleonic era, primary operations were considered essential, because the body healed most rapidly from a wound by the removal of the injured limb. Though the wound usually became infected, the incision was made through healthy tissue, and consequently a patient could survive. The blood vessels were tied, the cautery iron (or boiling oil, or pitch, or chemical caustics) was used to seal off the severed arteries and veins, the skin flap was sewn tightly, and the wound was covered with ointment and bandaged. The advantages of amputating a damaged limb were ending unbearable pain, avoiding the danger of long convalescence, and leaving the patient—if he managed to survive—with a relatively simple wound. Of course, some soldiers, for example, the intrepid Benedict Arnold, wounded while storming a British redoubt on October 7, disdained an amputation, regardless of the consequences. When the fractured thigh bone of his right leg, the same one injured at Quebec, was examined by a surgeon who urged immediate amputation, Arnold reputedly exclaimed as he stormed out:

"Goddam it, sir, if that is all that you can do with me, I shall see the battle out . . ."[61]

Wound surgery occurred under frightful conditions. Operations were performed on tables on doors or on planks placed across barrels. The table, instruments, and the doctors' coats were covered with blood and with secretions from previous operations. Frequently there was little heat or light, and tying the end of arteries in flickering candlelight was a complicated task. A single wash basin served to cleanse the sponges, hands, and instruments. With complete disregard for elementary hygienic procedures, the surgeon used one surgical knife to probe dozens of men, the same filthy sponge to clean wounds, and if a rag was not available, he wiped his hands on his surgical coat. Gangrene was epidemic under such conditions, and few wounded men escaped its ravages. In this preanesthetic age, even if patients survived the operation, they were confronted by the triple threat of pain, infection, and hemorrhage. It is amazing that wounded men actually survived this ordeal.

The treatment of the wounded was the subject of messages exchanged between Gates and Burgoyne. Their notes, carried by flags of truce, began on September 6 and continued through the fighting. Burgoyne requested Gates for permission to send a British surgeon to treat some of his officers held behind American lines. "I trust sir," he wrote, "that it is understood between us that the Surgeon shall have safe conduct . . ."[62] Gates responded on September 16 by authorizing British Surgeon Vincent Wood to enter the American camp. As Burgoyne withdrew from the carnage at Freemans Farm on October 9, he informed Gates that he was leaving 300 wounded behind. "The state of my hospital makes it advisable to leave the wounded and sick officers which you will find in my last camp than to carry them with the army. I recommend them to the protection," Burgoyne continued, "in which I feel I should show to an enemy in the same case."[63] Burgoyne sent Dr. John McNamara Hayes, his medical chief, to an American outpost to meet Gates's emissary. Awaiting Hayes in the evening fog was Major Wilkinson, who watched Hayes gallop toward him with a white flag. Wilkinson rode back to the British hospital tents with Hayes, and he assured the wounded British officers that they would be protected from the American militia.[64] Writing to Burgoyne that night, Hayes mentioned that Gates would respect the conventions of war regarding enemy casualties.[65] Gates informed his British opponent on October 11 that two wounded British officers, Sir Francis Clarke and Major John Acland, were being well treated. "Every sort of tenderness and attention is paid to [them]," Gates promised.[66] Hayes meanwhile told Potts he had 254 casualties, who needed to be removed to a general hospital. Potts sent him six wagons, presumably all that he could spare. Hayes responded on October 12 by requesting stretchers and bearers for fifty men so badly maimed that "their wounds will not admit the motion of carts."[67]

The seriously wounded American, British, and Hessian troops were transported to the general hospital in Albany, where Thacher described his experiences. He worked with thirty other surgeons of different nationalities in a large building (built in 1756) situated on a hill overlooking the town. By late September the hospital had 550 patients, of which 173 were wounded. As another 500 sick and maimed poured in, Potts requested local officials for additional space; he was granted the use of a church, the home of Abraham Cuyler, and several "untenanted houses," a euphemism for vacant Loyalist homes.[68] As additional casualties continued to arrive in October, Potts had to send ninety-six Americans, English, and Hessians another sixteen miles to Schenectady.[69] The enemy wounded, remarked Thacher, had their own surgeons, and "were accommodated in the same hospitals with our men and received equal care and attention." Impressed with the skill of the British surgeons, Thacher was appalled at their German colleagues. "Some of them were the most uncouth and clumsy operators I have witnessed and appeared to be destitute of all sympathy and tenderness toward their suffering patients."

With twenty surgical cases assigned him by Potts,

Thacher had ample opportunities to perform a variety of operations. "Amputations, trepanning fractured skulls, and dressing the most formidable wounds have familiarized my mind to scenes of woe." One of Thacher's patients had been scalped by Indians; another had been struck with a missile that split his face and tongue; another's head had been smashed by a cannon ball. One man who at first seemed doomed had a musket ball lodged in his forehead. Thacher was able to extricate it, remarking that it was "fortunate for the brave fellow that his skull proved too thick for the ball to penetrate." On October 13 the wounded Arnold was finally brought in, writhing in pain. "He is very peevish ...," Thacher noted in his journal, "and required all my attention during the night."[70] The long excruciating journey for the wounded to distant hospitals in open jolting wagons along rutted roads, and days of inevitable delay that typified the transfer of casualties in the eighteenth century undoubtedly increased the incredible agony that these men endured.

Behind British lines some soldiers' wives witnessed the horrors of war. Near the battlefield at the Taylor homestead used as a hospital were Baroness Frederick Von Riedesel, the wife of a German general, and other ladies, including Lady Christian Henrietta Acland, whose husband lay wounded in Gates's camp. Jane Crumer, the spouse of a British sergeant awaiting a dangerous operation, was also in the Taylor farmhouse. As the ladies and children huddled in the cellar, American cannon pounded the farm, and frequently a heavy missile penetrated the roof of the building. Upstairs, surgeons were performing amputations on four men, whose shrieks of terror rang through the house. In one amazing tragedy, the Baroness recalled, just as a surgeon severed the leg of a screaming man, a heavy cannon ball ripped through the walls and smashed the soldier's other leg.[71]

Jane Crumer performed a remarkable act of heroism for her mate and his companions, who were begging for water. An orderly had run to a nearby creek with a pail, but he was struck down by American bullets. Exclaiming that "the Americans were not beasts to fire on a woman," the young girl darted out of the farmhouse, "paused by the dead orderly to unclasp his fingers from the pail that they still clutched," stated Sergeant Roger Lamb, a surgeon's mate in the Royal Norfolk regiment, in admiration. "She continued to the water-side, drew water, curtsied her gratitude, and returned. Not a shot was fired at her. She went to and fro with her pail until she had fetched sufficient for all," remarked Lamb, who eventually married the brave widow after the war.[72]

Lady Acland had gamely accompanied her often drunk husband across the Atlantic, up the St. Lawrence, and down the Hudson. After Major Acland was captured, she appealed to Burgoyne for permission to visit American lines in order to comfort her injured spouse. On October 9 Burgoyne wrote to Gates: "Whatever general impropriety that may be in persons acting in your situation and mine to solicit favors, I respect the perseverance and exhaltation of the Lady."[73] Although Gates was indignant at the British destruction of farmsteads during their retreat ("without precedent among civilized nations"), he willingly offered to assist the distressed woman. "Considering my preceding conduct with respect to those of your army who the circumstances of war placed in my hands," he remarked, "I am surprised that your Excellency should think that I consider the great attention to Lady Acland in the light of an obligation."[74] Accompanied by a chaplain, in one of the few romantic episodes at bloody Saratoga, Lady Acland was rowed to the American side, escorted to Gates's headquarters, and then taken to Albany to comfort her dying husband.

Burgoyne meanwhile contemplated surrender. By October 13 he was completely surrounded by 18,000 troops. Neither Clinton in Manhattan nor Carleton in Canada could relieve him. His demoralized men were famished, and musket balls and cannon shot rained on his camp day and night. Accepting the gravity of his situation, Burgoyne on October 14 offered to negotiate a convention with Gates, and on October 17 his 4,700 soldiers surrendered their weapons. By positioning his men behind strong defenses and forcing the British to attack, Gates had blunted the enemy offensive. Saratoga was the greatest American victory in the north, and it was a decisive event of the war, bringing France by April 1778 into the struggle on the American side.

From a medical aspect the conduct of the campaign was impressive. Few complaints about shortages of drugs or staff were voiced. In July Shippen sent Potts a large drug supply, and in August Craigie dispatched bark and instruments to supplement Potts's stores.[75] As a result Potts may have had the largest stockpile of drugs and equipment of any other northern campaign, with the exception of the siege of Boston. Even though Schuyler's command after the evacuation of Ticonderoga suffered from fatigue, exposure, and lack of shelter, the health of the new army assembled on the Hudson, two-thirds of which were experienced Continentals, was high. William Weeks, Paymaster of Scammel's Third New Hampshire, noted on August 7 that after widespread "Fever, Ague, and Dysentery ...," the army "begins to be more healthy as they get hardened to this Method of living—...."[76] The low incidence of sickness that prevailed may be explained by the eradication of smallpox, the infrequency of typhus cases, the constant change of camp sites, the generally favorable late summer and fall weather (As Wilkinson remarked: "The weather in the autumn of 1777, on the Hudson's river, was charming, ..."),[77] an ample supply of drugs, and the work of a conscientious hospital staff. Whether the healthy state of Gates's army was due, as Rush suggested, to the fact that the most of the army was composed of New Englanders is problematical. In contrast to the widespread complaints about medical arrangements that invariably typified American campaigns, very little criticism of the department emerges from the documentation. From March 1 to December 16, 1777, Potts lost only 205 men in his hospitals,[78] a figure lower than in any major northern campaign, with the exception of the siege of Boston.

Potts and his staff received praise for their work from many quarters. Wilkinson applauded the doctors "for care and attention to those unfortunate brave men [which] deserves the greatest attention."[79] In Albany, Surgeon John

Browne wrote Potts on December 29 that Dr. (John) Jones had visited the hospital and had commented upon its efficiency. "Everything has been carried out with so much satisfaction," Browne mentioned, "as to have no room for complaint."[80] Another compliment came from the French General, Matthias Roche de Fermoy. After visiting the Albany hospital wards, de Fermoy informed Potts that he was extremely pleased "with the care and attention and humanity with which the patients are treated. . . . I shall report the same to the General and the Gentlemen in Congress." Symbolizing the pending French alliance, de Fermoy remarked that he left some money for the wounded "to convince them that the King of France is in alliance with the United States and will afford them all he can in his power."[81] Rush had kind words for his former classmate, praising him for his commissary work in supplying the hospitals. Comparing the enormous sickness and mortality rates of the 1777 campaign in Pennsylvania under Shippen's direction, Rush stressed that Potts lost comparatively few patients. "The putrid fever," Rush claimed, "never made its appearance in any one of his hospitals."[82]

The finest accolades to Potts came from Gates and from Congress. On October 20 Gates described to the Delegates "the great care and attention with which Doctor Potts and ye gentlemen of the general hospital conducted the business of their department." He requested that "some Honorary mark of favour" be conferred upon the medical men.[83] Delighted with the astounding victory at Saratoga, in contrast to the dismal military situation under Washington's direction along the Delaware, Congress could hardly refuse its triumphant general. On November 6 Congress resolved:

> That the unremitting attention showed by Dr. Potts and the Officers of the General Hospital in the northern Department . . ., to the sick and wounded soldiers under their care, is a Proof not only of their humanity, but of their Zeal, so deeply interested in the Preservation of the Health and Lives of the gallant assertors of their Country's Cause;

With Gates at Saratoga

and therefore that Congress cannot but entertain a high Sense of the Services which they have rendered during this Campaign by a diligent discharge of their respective Functions.[84]

For Potts, now thirty-two years old, who returned home on November 16, it had been "a happy campaign." He emerged from his trying experience in the north with compliments from doctors, generals, and politicians. The Congressional praise of Potts and his staff was the only such testimonial to the skill and bravery of army doctors during the entire Revolutionary War. For the medical department, frequently charged with corruption and mismanagement, it was a prized tribute.

VIII.
The Valley Forge Hospitals

During the summer of 1777 the Americans and British fought for Pennsylvania. Determined to capture Philadelphia and thereby end the war, Howe sailed with 13,000 troops on July 23 from the Hudson to the Delaware. Off the Jersey coast he received information about the sturdy American defenses below Philadelphia, and consequently he shifted the destination of the expedition to Chesapeake Bay. Not until August 24 were his weary and seasick troops disembarked at the Head of the Elk (River) in Maryland for the conquest of Pennsylvania.

The fifty-seven-mile march from the Chesapeake to Philadelphia was an arduous task for the British, who had hoped to be hailed as welcome liberators. Instead the redcoats were scorned as hated invaders, and they were harassed by militia who denuded the countryside of cattle, mounts, and provisions. Unwilling to match his inexperienced troops in pitched battle with Howe's disciplined brigades, Washington withdrew from the enemy, until certain of a defensive advantage, he positioned his 11,000 soldiers along the north banks of the Brandywine, twenty-six miles from Philadelphia. The Americans had faulty information about their opponents' movements, and Washington failed to detect a wide-flanking maneuver by Cornwallis through an unguarded ford. The battle of Brandywine on September 11 was a decisive defeat for the Continental army, which had losses of 1,000 men killed and wounded, double the British casualties. Fortunately for the Americans, Howe neglected to exploit his victory and permitted Washington's troops to retire northward.

Unable to defend Philadelphia without risking another defeat and worried about his supply depots in the interior, Washington marched and countermarched in vain efforts to block the British advance to the Quaker City, and to protect his major magazines at Warwick and Reading. But Howe outmaneuvered him. He defeated Wayne's brigade at Paoli (September 21), destroyed the mills and iron works at Valley Forge, threatened the American stores at Reading, and then, encountering little opposition, he led his troops to Germantown. On September 26 the British marched triumphantly into Philadelphia. Howe had accomplished his objective of capturing the rebel city, but he still encountered difficulties—his supply line from the Chesapeake was long and tenuous, his ships were unable to reach Philadelphia, and Washington's command, although severely battered, was still capable of combat.

Washington now took the initiative. Aware that Howe had committed troops to guard supply lines from the Elk and to beseige the Delaware forts, Washington ordered an attack on the enemy encampment at Germantown. The night assault on October 4 was difficult for uncoordinated regiments to execute, information about enemy dispositions was inaccurate, and the Americans had incredibly bad luck. Washington lost another 1,000 men, yet he forced Howe to evacuate Germantown, and he demonstrated that the American army could still fight. Beaten in two major engagements, the Continentals displayed a determination to wage war that impressed the French court at Versailles. Yet the British continued the bombardment of the rebel defenses on the Delaware, and by November 23, when the last American bastion on the river toppled, Howe had a secure base to provision his army from the sea. By late December the British were comfortably ensconced in Philadelphia for the winter, while the pathetic American army destitute of food and supplies, tried to survive in the bleak environment of Valley Forge.

The Valley Forge Hospitals

Because of Washington's uncertainty about strategy in September, medical arrangements for Brandywine were incomplete. Shippen knew that Howe's fleet was sailing up the Chesapeake, but the British did not leave the Elk until September 8. Typical of preparations for field hospitals in eighteenth-century warfare, Shippen did not have sufficient wagons or stretcher bearers. Nor had he established adequate emergency centers. At a meetinghouse on the Brandywine during the battle was Captain Samuel Dewees of Maryland, who penned a rare description of casualty evacuation:

> Those engaged in bringing them [the wounded] in drove as fast as they could possibly drive under existing circumstances, and upon their arrival they would hastily lift the wounded out of the wagons, place them in front of the hospital and return as soon as possible to the field of carnage for another load. To hear the wild and frantic cries of the wounded, the groans and cries, and to see the damaged and bloody state of the soldiers upon their arrival in the wagon, to see them all covered with blood and blood running in numbers of places from the wagons and bodies was enough to chill the blood in the warmest heart.[1]

After the battle the 500 wounded were moved to nearby cities and towns—Reading, Bethlehem, Philadelphia, Northampton, Trenton, Burlington, Wilmington—and to settlements at Trappe, Hanover, Skippack, Evansburgh, Lancaster, Falkner's Swamp, and Pennypacker's Mill. Major Moses Bloomfield of the Third New Jersey, wounded at Brandywine, left a commentary about the disorganized handling of casualties. Unable to find medical aid after the fighting, he rode unescorted for two miles with a musket ball in his arm, when luckily he encountered "a stranger who dressed my wound . . . and wrapped my arm in a handkerchief . . ." With his limb swelling in pain, Bloomfield continued another seven miles to Chester, looking for aid. Not until he reached Trenton on September 13 ("53 hours after I was wounded. 20 hours of which it bled . . .") did an army surgeon treat his injured arm.[2] Reverend Henry Muhlenberg, noting the confusion in handling casualties, remarked that the wounded were pouring into Philadelphia after Brandywine, "that the church at Reading has been turned into a hospital and is filled with wounded," and that many casualties were quartered "in houses here and there."[3]

Little information is available about the hospitals in Trenton and Burlington, but Rush and Tilton commented about their experiences at Princeton. "The sick and wounded flowing promiscuously without restraint into the hospitals," wrote Tilton, "it soon became infectious and was attended with great mortality."[4] Preparations for the patients was so inadequate, Rush complained, that 100 men under his care would have perished from the cold and dampness had not local inhabitants assisted with blankets and clothing. "Our hospital affairs, grow worse and worse," he wrote, "... the fault is both in the establishment and in the Director General. He is both *ignorant* and *negligent* of his duty."[5] And General Greene, in charge of troops in New Jersey, wrote Washington on November 24 that he encountered much criticism of the medical department: "The hospitals in the Jerseys are greatly complained of."[6]

At Philadelphia, in a repetition of the 1776 campaign, the Pennsylvania Hospital, the Bettering House, the Smallpox Hospital, various stores, and vacant Loyalist homes were used as army hospitals. When Howe threatened Philadelphia in late September, Shippen transferred army patients from the capital into the interior of Pennsylvania. Shippen's problem in New Jersey was complicated by Washington's uncertainty about strategy, by the continual movements of Continental army, and by the constant flow of casualties from Red Bank, Fort Mercer, and Fort Mifflin on the Delaware. Even after the battle of Germantown on October 4, in which the Americans suffered 650 casualties, Washington contemplated another attack in early November on British lines. Not until November 25 did Washington direct Shippen to evacuate the Jersey hospitals, informing him that "we must always keep the sick in the Rear of the Army, or they will be subject to captivity."[7] Because of the fluid nature of the campaign, the large number of casualties, and the lack of available sanctuaries for the sick and wounded, the preparations for the hospitalized were disastrous. Never before had Pennsylvania been confronted by such masses of helpless troops, and the state did not have facilities to house them. The British held Philadelphia and its large buildings, the Continental army was severed from many routes to the Delaware, and the province had few areas where casualties could be safely quartered.

Under such circumstances Shippen again had to occupy the large buildings at Bethlehem. On September 18 he informed Reverend John Ettwein, the leader of the Moravian community, that the army had to commandeer Bethlehem's Single Brethrens' House. "It give me great pain to be obliged by order of Congress to send my sick and wounded soldiers to your peaceful village—but so it is. We will want room for 2,000 at Bethlehem, Easton, and Northhampton ... These are dreadful times," Shippen continued, "the consequences of unnatural wars. I am truly concerned for your Society, and wish sincerely this stroke could be averted, but 'tis impossible."[8] By September 24 the first wagonloads of wounded were hauled into Bethlehem. Within a week the three-storied Brethrens' House, which had a capacity for 360 patients at four feet of space per man, was crammed. The Sisters' House was seized for the overflow, and additional wounded were sheltered in tents and barns. By October 22 about 500 soldiers were quartered in Bethlehem, a hamlet with a civilian population of 300; and by Christmas the number of patients soared to 700. The medical staff was so inundated with patients that Dr. Moses Scott was unable to keep records of admittances. Watching the convoys of casualties pour into the small commune, Ettwein noted that the houses were so crowded by late November that the excess had to be transported to Easton. Many of the soldiers, he noted, "came here in rags, swarming with vermin, while others during their stay had been deprived of their clothing by their comrades."[9] In such overcrowded and unsanitary conditions under which filthy, emaciated men shivered in tattered uniforms, typhus struck.

Tilton had assumed that the situation in the Princeton hospital was terrible, but he was stunned at conditions at Bethlehem. One company of forty Virginians sent to recuperate there ended their convalescence with three survivors; some two hundred North Carolinians perished in Bethlehem that winter, about half the total casualties of that state for the entire war. Even the medical staff were victims of typhus—ten of the eleven attending surgeons caught the pestilence and three of them died. By the spring of 1778 about five hundred patients had perished in the little village. Bethlehem inevitably acquired an unwholesome reputation for inhumane treatment to suffering soldiers.

Many other small villages were used for casualties moved from Jersey and from Philadelphia, Reading, and Bethlehem. By late October the army established additional convalescent centers in Easton, Warwick, Mendham, Allentown, Rheimstown, Sheaferstown, and Buckingham. Lititz was occupied on December 19, and Ephrata on December 24. Although hundreds of men were sheltered in private homes, such places were usually too small and often too isolated to be more than temporary quarters. Barns were spacious but they were damp and dirty. Churches at least had pews for beds, but they were cold and were usually poorly ventilated. Taverns and schoolhouses were frequently used, even though their rooms were usually cramped. But in the frenzy to house the sick, such inconveniences were disregarded, and even a shoe factory was used. In Reading, for example, where Potts was on furlough, accommodations for sixty-nine soldiers were found in the Court House, the Trinity Church, the Reformed Church, the Friends Meeting House, the Potter's Shop, and in various residences.[10] Potts had been working with the local Committee of Safety on the production of muskets when he was requested to assist in the emergency. On December 14 Shippen wrote him from Bethlehem, asking for help:

> You were so kind to offer your assistance on your arrival from ye north. Now I have great need of your best exertions because the late movement of ye army make it necessary to

move all our sick to the west side of the Schuylkill. All must pass through Reading, and you can do much toward making their stay comfortable, and their transportation to the place assigned to them easy and safe. I am sure if your inclination is equal to your abilities, the business will be done, and there is no doubt with me that you are an honest fellow, and I, in return will be as ever have been, your affectionate friend.[11]

Unfortunately, conditions at many of these new locations were little better than before. Casualties were moved greater distances and were given similar wretched attention. Private Elijah Fisher, placed on the sick list at Gulph Mills on December 16, remarked that he was sent to Reading, "but when we came there the Sick belonging to the other regiment had taken it up so we was sent to Dunkertown [Ephrata] to the hospital there."[12] At Ephrata on Christmas, remembered Joseph Kimmel, an inhabitant, "the troops arrived in open wagons at night time, almost naked; many of them were without shoes, stockings, or blankets to cover them. Neither were they accompanied by nurses or other attendants, and left there by the waggoners . . ." The sick crept to the houses, he stated "in a piteous condition . . . and entreated to be saved from perishing." Hans Baer, Ephrata's miller, testified that his parents died from "camp fever" transmitted by the troops, and "that the disorder raged through the neighborhood and proved fatal to a great number of all ages."[13] Tilton remarked that the large house selected for a hospital in Ephrata was "ill choosen, being cut into small monks cells, that would admit of but little ventilation."[14] Another horror was Lancaster, where Captain Charles Lloyd remembered that with 500 others, he spent six weeks on a cold floor without straw or blankets.[15] Lititz, which received much of the Reading overflow, became another Bethlehem. By mid-December, eighty patients were here. On January 1, 260 men crammed its wards, of which 120 patients, five nurses, and the local pastor died from typhus. About 2,800 soldiers were quartered in these hospitals by late 1777, and perhaps another 2,000 were scattered elsewhere over eastern Pennsylvania. The prevalence of disease undoubtedly contributed to the demoralization of the army. Over 17 percent of the army was listed sick in October, 26 percent in November; and when the Continentals trudged off to Valley Forge in late December, 32 percent of Washington's army—sick present, sick absent—was listed unfit for duty.[16]

In late December and early January the stream of sick was such that additional hospitals had to be established at Red Lion (Lionville), French Creek, Uwchlan, and Yellow Springs. Ignoring local protests, army officers seized any available shelter. Muhlenberg noted that the Lutheran and Reformed Churches in Lionville were filled with casualties. "Yea, they even filled the parsonage, and afflicted [the pastor] with all kinds of persecution, because he publicly refused to pray for Congress, and because he was thought to be a Tory." The minutes of the Quaker Meeting House at Uwchlan included this dramatic notation: "The key of the meeting house was demanded by some of the physicians of the Continental army in order to convert the same to a hospital for their soldiers. The Friend who had care of the house refusing to deliver it, forcible entry was made into the house and stable."[17]

Dysentery, and perhaps typhoid, may have caused havoc in the ranks that winter, but typhus was the greatest scourge of the army. Many men hospitalized for lesser ailments caught typhus from their bedfellows. "Many a fine fellow have I seen brought into the hospital, for a slight syphilitic affliction," Tilton remarked, "and carried out dead of a hospital fever."[18] Inasmuch as nothing was known about the contagion, newcomers to a ward were usually provided the same straw and bedding of patients who had just died of typhus. Rush noted how frequently men with respiratory ailments were struck by the disease. "Whenever a hospital was removed in winter, one half of the patients generally sickened on the way, or soon after their arrival to the place where they were sent. There were many instances of patients with slight sickness," he continued, "who suddenly fell dead after being removed from a hospital."[19]

Infected by typhus at Princeton, Tilton described his languor, severe headaches, feverish state, and stiff, dry tongue. "Besides enduring obstinate deliriums," he remarked, "I had a crust on my tongue as thick as the blade of a knife and black as soot." Tilton was treated by Rush and aided by a lady who provided him with several gallons of wine. "I drank freely of the liquid and took at the same time Huxham's tincture. My tongue soon after began to moisten on the edges, and in the course of some days, the whole crust fell off . . ." Therapy for typhus, stated Tilton, was bark, bleeding, vomiting, blistering, and pills made of opium, calomel, and tartar emetic. When the fever began, he advised bleeding; if the fever continued, he urged caution in bloodletting. "We are disposed to avoid it altogether when not demanded by a full pulse, and other pressing circumstances." More important for the patient's survival, Tilton claimed, was vomiting, which benefited the patient "by opening and squeezing all the glands of the body, and thus shaking from the nervous system the contaminating poisons, before the impressions are fixed."[20]

With such therapy the doctors were virtually helpless to combat the infection. If the hospitals had been heated, cleansed, and provisioned, some of the destruction caused by the disease may have been averted. Complaints about shortages of food, straw, bedding, medicine, blankets, and clothing filled the contemporary literature as the medical department was castigated again for contributing to the heavy incidence of sickness and death. Governor William Livingston of New Jersey stressed the chronic inadequacy of supplies at hospitals that he visited. Calling for an inquiry "into the astonishing mortality which now rages in our hospitals," Livingston stated that Shippen was so involved with his commissary duties, that he "never saw the interior of any of our hospitals. . . ."[21] Washington bitterly lamented the situation, and on December 31 he wrote: "I sincerely feel for the unhappy Condition of our poor Fellows in the Hospital, and wish my powers to relieve them were equal to my inclination. It is but too melancholy a truth," he continued, "but our Hospital stores are exceedingly scanty and deficient in every instance. . . ."[22] Rush had the most sarcastic comments. Advising Greene about how to defeat the enemy with disease, Rush asserted: "A sure and certain method of destroying Howe's whole army without powder or without any of the common implements of death [would be to] lead them through any of the villages in Lancaster country where we have a hospital, and I will ensure you that in 6 weeks there will not be a man of them alive or fit for duty."[23] To these criticisms, Shippen, who had received little assistance from the disintegrating Quartermaster and Commissary Departments, acknowledged that the sick suffered needlessly, but he insisted that it was not his fault. The trouble arose, he claimed, because many of the troops were unaccustomed to campaign hardships, that they had retreated continually, that they lacked clothing and blankets, and that "the sick were removed great distances in open wagons."[24] Under a torrent of invective for his supposedly inept, inhumane, and dishonest supervision of hospital affairs, Shippen would be subject to a Congressional investigation.

Meeting in York, Pennsylvania, Congress in January considered reforms of the department, and it gathered evidence about Shippen for submission to a special committee. One significant letter came from Dr. William Brown of Virginia, in the service since 1775, and now Surgeon General of the Middle Department. Brown noted that the basic reason for the chaotic state of the hospitals was that the Director General had excessive duties which he could not possibly perform, and as a result the commissary aspects of administration were neglected. "It is very distressing to see men die," Brown noted, "apparently for want of things which a little industry might obtain." Without castigating his superior, Brown called for a reform of the procurement functions under the control of a purveyor.[25]

Rush was the most vitriolic critic of the medical department. In letters to generals and politicians, Rush wrote polemical commentaries on hospital conditions, and he denounced Shippen for inefficiency, corruption, and indifference to suffering. Yet, as he admitted to Delegate William Duer of New York, Shippen was not entirely to blame for the mismanagement of hospital affairs. "If he possessed the abilities of a Bacon, the industry of a Boyle, and integrity of a Aristides, he could not be expected to complete one half of the extensive power you have given him." Rush also urged the appointment of a purveyor, as in the British system ("the most perfect in the world"), who would be divested of medical duties. Such an official, Rush stated, would "represent a share of industry, and a capacity which falls to the lot of few men in the world." It was due to the excessive centralization of controls, the absence of discipline in the wards, and the shortages of every kind, Rush asserted, that accounted for the heavy toll of sickness and death. "Nothing like this has happened in the northern department," Rush claimed. "Dr. Potts has confined himself solely to the Purveying, and Dr. [Malachi] Treat [Potts's surgical chief] introduced the British system in the most minute parts into the hospitals under his direction."[26]

By December Rush became increasingly embittered. To Washington he wrote that the worst thing that could happen to a sick soldier was to be committed to an army hospital. To Patrick Henry, the Governor of Virginia, Rush claimed on January 17 that more men died in army hospitals, "than perished in the field during the whole of the last campaign."[27] Rush was so frustrated that he contemplated resigning. He confided to his wife, Julia, in late January that he was tempted to quit the service, but inasmuch as Congress was planning some drastic changes of the department, he would testify. "If this system is altered and Dr. Shippen can be restrained by proper checks from plundering the sick," he promised, "I shall not resign my commission and shall serve another campaign."[28]

In late January 1778 a Congressional committee heard testimony from Rush, Shippen, Tilton, Brown, and Bloomfield. Brown asserted that one-half the casualties for the year perished in army hospitals. John Thaxter of the committee remarked that Rush "presented a shocking picture indeed . . . by all accounts it is a just one . . . a bad system and a bad administration, peculation and embezzlement of stores prevail in the [medical] department as in the others."[29] Against such tirades, Shippen ably defended himself. He insisted that the high incidence of sickness and mortality was not due to departmental laxness, he denied charges of corruption, and he blamed supply problems on other departments. He even had the temerity to write Henry Laurens, Chairman of the committee, "that our sick are not crowded in any hospitals, . . ., no fatal disease prevails . . . very few die, and the hospitals are in very good order."[30] Though there were strong indictments against the director general, and even though Rush was on cordial terms with the committeemen, he did not have specific proof of Shippen's activities. Shippen had influential friends in Congress, he still retained Washington's confidence, and the Delegates hesitated to recommend measures that would embroil the castigated medical department in further controversy. Given the choice between retaining Shippen or Rush in office, the committee decided to seek Rush's resignation.

Rush went into semiretirement in early February 1778. Yet he still penned caustic letters about Shippen, and he continued to gather evidence about his former professor in the hope that he could have Shippen court-martialed. As data about the numbers of hospital deaths were difficult to obtain, Rush concentrated on Shippen's supposed profiteering in hospital stores. "Dr. Potts informed me," Rush claimed, "that he knew of Dr. Shippen having sold several hogsheads of brown sugar to a person in Reading." Thoroughly embittered over his defeat, Rush insisted that Shippen had repeatedly lied to the committee, that he had falsified reports, and "that he spent his days and nights in revelry and debauchery. . . . While the poor soldiers were dying," Rush asserted, Shippen "was feasting with the general officers, or bargaining with tavern-keepers in Jersey or Pennsylvania over the sale of Madeira wine from our hospital stores. . . ."[31] In his efforts to discredit Shippen, Rush was assisted by Morgan, who had been gathering evidence about his old enemy Shippen. Rush and Morgan now became staunch allies in their crusade to destroy Shippen's credibility, and in the process they would rock an already demoralized medical department.

The Valley Forge Hospitals

Some minor reforms of the medical administration took place. The power of the Director General was trimmed, the department was decentralized, and district hospital directors became almost autonomous. The main result of the legislation was that Shippen was relieved of his commissary functions, and that on February 4, 1778, Potts was named Purveyor General and Deputy Director General of the Middle Department. Rush wrote Washington to congratulate him on the changes for the department and to praise the appointment of his old friend Potts, "a gentleman of established character for integrity, humanity, and capacity in the managing of . . . the duty of a director of a hospital."[32] For Potts a purveyorship was not a major impetus to his medical career, but the post was a significant one in the departmental hierarchy. The Rush-Shippen feud left vestiges of suspicions and partisanship as surgeons, mates, stewards, and storekeepers took sides in the controversy, contributed evidence to Rush and to Morgan, or, perhaps intimidated by Shippen, they remained silent. The medical organization would be regarded with suspicion on financial matters by Congress, and requests by Shippen and Potts for money to operate the department were intensely scrutinized. When Shippen submitted his budget for 1779, Congress cut it in half.

How effective could Potts be in his new role? One of his many responsibilities was to dispense wages and salaries to the staff in the Middle Department, yet Joseph Shippen, the Director General's brother, was the Paymaster for the hospitals. William Shippen, Jr., had influential contacts in Congress, he had had close links with army contractors, and he may have profited financially from such arrangements. As James Tilton remarked: "It was found to be very difficult to remove any part of . . . the purveying function from that of the direction; even when Congress had ordained that the direction and Purveyorship should be separate, such was the influence of interested men," he explained, "that the utmost efforts of the [purveying] level have never been able to carry into the full and complete policy intended by Congress."[33] Under such circumstances Potts, who avoided becoming embroiled in the

Rush-Shippen controversy, could only try to improve the supplying of the army hospitals, a process which was part of the general reform of the army at Valley Forge.

After maneuvering against Howe in early December, Washington searched for winter quarters. After considering several locations, he selected Valley Forge, a 3,000 acre wooded plateau that had belonged to John Potts, Sr. In 1760 Isaac Potts built his house there, and with co-owner William Dewees manufactured pig iron and household implements. The tract was protected on the north by the Schuylkill, on the west by Valley Creek, and on the south and east by steep hills. Only twenty-two miles from Philadelphia, the encampment was close enough to British lines to intimidate the enemy, and yet it was a sanctuary safe from redcoat raids. From Valley Forge, the Continentals could cow Loyalists, inhibit British foraging, and develop links to provision the army. Besides its strategic advantages Valley Forge had the remnants of a iron foundry, a sawmill, and a grist mill; it also had transportation links to surrounding communities. Roads from Valley Forge connected to magazines, hospitals, armories, ordnance factories, artillery parks, cavalry quarters, infantry garrisons, and prisoner-of-war camps.[34]

With this communications network, the general support of the populace, the fertility of local farmlands, and the availability of light industry, the army at Valley Forge could have been adequately supplied during the winter of 1777–1778. Although severed from connections to manufacturing centers in the Delaware Valley, the army could be equipped by many small villages in the interior. Scattered in scores of hamlets were the facilities to weave blankets, to fabricate uniforms, to cobble shoes, and to package foodstuffs. But it was extremely difficult to feed, clothe, and shelter 12,000 men encamped in a relatively small area during a winter—virtually a new city had emerged in the wilderness. Furthermore the near collapse of the Commissary and the Quartermaster Departments complicated the difficulties. Because of inflation, poor roads, shortage of basic commodities, and problems in procurement, the troops at Valley Forge were destitute by

The Valley Forge Hospitals

December 20. At Christmas, 3,000 men lacked even the clothing to protect them from the biting wind. Fearing that famine and cold would destroy his army, Washington warned Congress on December 26 that unless the troops were fed and clad quickly, "this army must inevitably ... starve, dissolve, or disperse."[35]

The first task was to shelter the men from the snow and sleet. Until the wrecked sawmill was repaired, planks were unavailable for construction. Undaunted, the troops cut trees and hauled the timber to camp. Ebenezer Davis, a Rhode Island chaplain, wrote on December 22: "The whole army comes here to build huts to winter in. The Huts are to be 14 by 16—in height 6 1/2—twelve soldiers to a hut ... They are now laying out the ground. toMorrow I expect to take the axe."[36] Using logs and other building materials, the troops constructed huts large enough for twelve men, each hut with a door, chimney, fireplace, and sometimes a window. The roofs were covered with sod, saplings, evergreens, or canvas. The doors were constructed of slabs, the space between the log sides were chinked with dirt or clay, and the windows were usually covered with oil paper, if that rare item was on hand. Floors were merely hard earth; few men were lucky enough to have straw. Exercising their provincial individualism, the men built a variety of shelters, regardless of the official specifications. Some of the shanties were built partly below ground. Many had no windows; in some huts the fireplace did not function; and in others the fire continually blew smoke on the occupants. In most huts the calking leaked during rain and thaws, and blasts of cold air constantly chilled the men.

By early January, 900 huts were under construction, and Washington had moved into the Potts house, using its barn as a hospital and nearby ovens for baking bread. By the end of the month, in a remarkable demonstration of toil and energy, most of the shelters were completed. In a somewhat exaggerated account, Surgeon Albigence Waldo noted in February that "the soldiers are nearly covered with good huts, and our camp begin to look like a spacious city."[37] Characterized by the ravages of disease and chronic suffering of troops, Valley

Forge symbolized the determination of Washington's troops to maintain the semblence of an army, whatever the obstacle. Amazed at the selection of the cantonment in such bleak terrain, Baron Johann de Kalb, a French mercenary serving with the Continentals, remarked that "it is unparalleled in the history of mankind to establish winter quarters in a country wasted without a single magazine."[38] In such an environment it was inevitable that the sickness rate from scabies, typhus, pneumonia, and other respiratory ailments would be high.

If the housing problem was resolved, that of acquiring provisions and clothing seemed insurmountable. Not only were supply routes dislocated, but foodstuffs were difficult to obtain because of Congressional unpreparedness, inefficient procurement, and the temptation of British gold for Pennsylvania farmers compared to the depreciated Continental currency. Likewise Joseph Trumbull, the Commissary General, was ill and wished to resign, and his deputies were unable to cope with the crisis. Thomas Mifflin, the Quartermaster, also wished to quit, and he plotted with some discontented officers against Washington. When the troops moved onto Valley Forge, only twenty-five barrels of flour were available. By Christmas the standard ration was "fire-cake," a mixture of flour and water cooked without salt or seasoning over the campfire. Surgeon Waldo of the First Connecticut was so disgusted with the sickening fare that he prayed "that our Commissary of Issues may live on fire cake and water, till their glutted guts turned to pasteboard." No bread or meat, the shortage of clothing, and the frigid climate all contributed to withering morale. Commenting on the scene before him, Waldo wrote a classic commentary on the soldiers' plight:

> There came a soldier. His bare feet are seen through worn out hose, legs nearly naked from the tattered remains of his stockings, his breeches not fit to cover his nakedness. His shirt hanging in rags... I am sick, feet lame, legs are worn, my body covered with the tormenting itch, my clothes worn out, my constitution is broken.

The Valley Forge Hospitals

In a lament familiar to generations of servicemen, Waldo wondered how long he could withstand the cold, the wretched food, and the debilitating fatigue. "Why are we sent here to starve and freeze?" he asked himself. "What sweet felicity have I left at home; a charming wife, pretty wife, good bed, good food, good cooking, all agreeable, all harmonious. Here all confusion, smoke and cold, hunger and filthiness. A pox on my bad luck."[39]

Some men were so poorly clad that they were unable to stand guard. "The Army was not only starved, but was naked," remembered Private Joseph Plum Martin, "the greatest part was not only shirtless ... but destitute of all other clothing, especially blankets."[40] Some sentinels performed duty in moccasins; their feet were so cold from the blustering wind that they had to stand on their hats to keep their toes from freezing. The bitter cold caused frostbite. Lafayette remarked on February 13 that "the unfortunate soldiers are in want of everything.... Their feet and legs have frozen until they became black and it is often necessary to amputate them."[41] Garments were so scarce that some helpless sick were robbed of their shirts and breeches, and the dead were stripped naked by shivering messmates. By February 5 some four thousand men were listed as unfit because of clothing shortages. Congress could only appeal to the states for assistance in the crisis, and call on the clergy to urge their parishioners to donate garments. In late January Wayne's men found some blankets in Lancaster and Wilmington, and Smallwood's regiment captured an enemy sloop in the Delaware with enough British uniforms to clothe four American regiments. Under Greene, the new quartermaster, search parties hunted the countryside for lost shipments and located some garments. Owing to these efforts, some troops were better clad, and in April some shoes were distributed. But throughout the spring Washington complained about the chronic shortage of garments; even by June 1 about one thousand men were unable to march to the Delaware because of clothing deficiencies.

Fresh water was difficult to obtain. Even with the ample

supply of potable water available in wells, springs, streams, and the river, a shortage occurred. Some men even drank from muddy puddles near their huts, until an order forbade the practice. The supply of water should have been sufficient, but the troops polluted it by washing, laundering, and dumping waste in the same watersheds. Private Elijah Fisher remarked that "the warter we had to Drink was out of a brook that ran along by the Camps and so many a dippin and washin it [sic] which maid it very Dirty and muddy."[42] A related ecological factor was the weather, usually cited as contributing to the misery of the troops. Compared to the difficult winters at Ticonderoga in 1775-1776 and at Morristown in 1779-1780, the weather at Valley Forge was not particularly severe. Except for twenty-nine days in the five-and-a-half month period of encampment, the temperature was above freezing. Snow, sleet, or rain fell only on thirty-six days from December 19 to March 31, and judging by contemporary records it was not a bitter season.[43] Yet the rough weather, in addition to the difficulties of housing, clothing, and provisions, contributed to the high incidence of sickness.

Because of the hasty construction of the camp and the general ignorance about hygiene, sanitary practices in the camp were primitive. Little attention was paid to the proper disposal of waste, latrines were inadequate or were often not used by the troops, and few facilities existed for washing, bathing, or laundering. The weather permitted few hygienic practices. Horses died by the hundreds, and their carcasses lay unburied for weeks. On January 7 Washington ordered that dead animals be buried, that offal from slaughter pens be covered, and that garbage pits be dug. But it was difficult to dig in the cold ground without shovels, and the order may have been ignored. In cold weather the men were particularly careless about using vaults, and Washington had to issue repeated injunctions about covering the waste and orders about the use of latrines. He warned, "that much filth and nastiness, is spread among ye Hutts, which will soon be reduced to a state of putrefaction and cause a sickly camp." When his commands were disregarded, Washington issued sterner de-

The Valley Forge Hospitals

crees: "As the above orders were absolutely necessary to preserve the health in camp, no plea of ignorance will be admitted, and the least breech thereof, will be severely notic'd." One brigadier was so incensed at the carelessness of his men that he had sentries posted "to Fire on any man who should be found easing himself other than in ye vaults." In early April Washington discovered some clean camp areas during his inspection, but "the smell of some places is intollerable, ... oweing to the want of necessaries or the neglect of them." Finally the very patient Washington posted guards to arrest men who did not use latrines, and authorized a penalty of five lashes to the offenders. The problem continued through the spring to such a degree that by June 10, "due to the unwholesome exhalations of the ground," the entire encampment was moved one mile away to a new location.[44]

A poorly provisioned army, or fleet, in the eighteenth century was usually stricken by scurvy, and because of the inadequate diet of troops at Valley Forge one would expect to find evidence of this disease. Yet no record of scurvy is mentioned at the encampment, although Hessian troops in Philadelphia were so afflicted in January 1778. The only clue about the matter is an invoice to Potts mentioning that barrels of lime juice were being shipped to camp.[45] A more common problem was scabies, or "the itch." As men huddled together in frigid and filthy habitats for weeks without washing, scabies became rampant. De Kalb noted in early January that "our men are infected with the itch ... I have seen the poor fellows covered over and over with scabies."[46] The treatment for the skin disease was that the men be isolated in separate barracks where they cleansed themselves and received a mixture of sulphur and hog's lard. The prevalence of scabies was so serious that on January 8 Washington ordered the surgeons "to look attentively into this matter ...," and the brigade quartermasters to increase the soap rations.[47] One colorful account of combating the itch survives. Private Martin and his companions managed to acquire some sulphur, mixed it with tallow, and merrily prepared to rid themselves of the affliction:

Richard L. Blanco

> The first night one half of the party commenced the action by mixing a sufficient quantity of brimstone and tallow, which was the only grease we could get . . ., at the same time not forgetting to mix plenty of hot whiskey toddy, mixing up a hot toddy and laying an oxhide upon the hearth. Thus prepared with arms and ammunition, we began to cover the other's outsides with brimstone and tallow and to drink the hot whiskey sling.

Some men got so drunk in the process that they lay naked all night before the fire, remarked Martin. "The rest of us got to our berths, as well as we could, but we killed the itch, and we were satisified, for it nearly killed us. It was a decisive victory, and the only one we had achieved lately."[48] Martin and his friends were fortunate to find the necessary ingredients; most troops had to wait for soft soap, for medical aid, and for warmer weather. With the distribution of new clothing and milder temperatures, scabies became less a problem. By May 14 the troops were marched to Schuylkill for weekly baths, and henceforth Friday was designated as the day for cleaning, laundering, and preparing for inspection.

Another common affliction was venereal disease, but how widespread it was is difficult to determine. Congress resolved that officers with the disease would be fined $10 from their pay, and enlisted men $4. As a consequence most men suffered in silence, or they tried to secure applications of mercurial ointment. One clue about the problem came from a medical officer at Yellow Springs, who repeated the ancient joke to Potts about treating many "officers, wounded in the conflict of Venus as well as of Mars."[49] Smallpox was still a threat. To replace troops who died or deserted, recruits entered the encampment through the winter and spring, and most of them had not been inoculated. On January 6 Washington ordered the medical staff to determine which men needed to be inoculated, but owing to the shortage of drugs and hospital foods the mass treatment was delayed. By April the program under Cochran's supervision was finally under way. As William Weeks of New Hampshire noted: "The small pox was nothing

The Valley Forge Hospitals

to me than dieting—I took the Air every day whilst I had it, and had only one sick Turn worth mentioning, and that was when the Pox was coming out—." All the New England troops had to be inoculated, he wrote, "but very few died."[50] Rejoining his regiment after surviving Ephrata, Private Fisher remarked: "I was annockulated for the small pox and had it pritty favorable to what others had it . . ."[51] Although hundreds of men in general hospitals, in isolated garrisons, and on foraging parties had not been inoculated by June, the program was successful, and out of four thousand men inoculated at Valley Forge only ten died.

Hospital conditions during the early weeks of the encampment were shocking. Waldo lamented on Christmas that "the poor Sick suffer much in tents this cold winter."[52] Wayne stated that he would prefer to fight the enemy under great odds than be required to visit the wards in camp.[53] The administrative system was typical of earlier phases of the war—regimental hospitals, flying hospitals, and general hospitals. Although barely recognized in Congressional legislation, the regimental hospitals actually handled the greatest number of sick. Yet as far as Shippen was concerned, the regimental hospitals had little importance. "Each regiment has a number called sick," he stated, "that are not proper subject for the [general] hospitals [because of minor ailments], and are under the care of regimental surgeons, though there are no regimental hospitals."[54] Whether regimental hospitals existed or not according to Shippen, they were fundamental to medical supervision in camp and were scattered throughout regiments in any available huts. Regulations for flying hospitals were more precise. In early January Washington ordered the construction of two flying hospitals per brigade, with dimensions of 14-by-25-by-9 feet, with windows and two fireplaces. These shanties were erected about three-hundred yards behind a brigade encampment; their roofs were built of boards or shingles, because sod or dirt was not permitted. These shelters soon became crowded, and some regimental surgeons, without authorization, moved their sick to general hospitals or to areas outside the camp limits. Washington forbade this practice and on January 21 admonished that, "a contrary practice have been attended with great inconveniency and probably occassions the Death of several men; many have been sent to Hospitals already crowded with patients, or to places where no provision had been made for the Sick."[55] Henceforth, under Cochran, the chief surgeon of the Flying Hospital, the medical staff determined the disposition of patients who had serious ailments.

Special efforts were made to ease the plight of the sick in camp. Washington had officers visit the regimental sick weekly to determine if they were properly treated. On January 15 surgeons were instructed to provide patients with straw for bedding, but straw was a scarce commodity for months. Potts supplied the hospitals with rice, sugar, barley, Indian meal, port and Madeira wine, and on rare occasions with beef. In May brigade quartermasters contracted with farmers for deliveries of milk to the wards. The regimental and flying hospitals held 1,500 men in January, 3,200 in February, and some 3,800 in April and May. On June 17, when Washington broke camp, 2,800 soldiers were sick at Valley Forge, and another 1,200 were at the general hospitals.[56] About 2,100 men supposedly perished at Valley Forge that winter,[57] but few graves have been found; apparently no central burial ground existed.

If the camp hospitals held most of the sick, what then was the purpose of the general hospitals? Dr. James McHenry stated that the general hospitals were not designed to accommodate all the sick, "but [they were] for the reception of that overproportion of sick that can be provided for in camp or at regimental hospitals, and on extraordinary occasions when the sick and wounded become so numerous that the regimental doctors cannot attend or provide convenient places for the reception of their proportion. This is the first and we say the only intention of a general hospital."[58] Administrative controls of the general hospitals were inefficient at first. Doctors were uncertain of how many patients they treated, some men deserted the wards for home, medicine and stores were unavailable, guards stole clothing from patients, and orderlies often neglected the helpless sick. Unless properly supervised, general hospitals frequently became the scene of riots. Donald Monro, of the British army, described how frequently the uproar in the wards was caused by drunken patients provided with wine or spirits by unscrupulous orderlies.[59] Washington was clearly distressed by such reports. On January 30 he noted that "irregularities and disorders are reported at our hospitals in the interiour parts of the State. Some sick are not tended with due care."[60] Two brigade officers were sent to visit these hospitals to ensure that discipline was maintained, that desertion be minimized, and that inventories of clothing and equipment be taken.

The only surviving report of general hospital conditions made by a field officer was completed in late April by General Lachlan McIntosh, brigade commander of the North Carolina regiments. Washington designated McIntosh to inspect the hospitals, to provide him with information about their conditions, to return laggards to duty, and to discharge the infirm. Because of the confusion about the transfer of casualties in late 1777, few doctors could provide McIntosh with records of admittances. The Carolinian admitted that he was uncertain about when some locations opened, about how many patients had been housed in a particular hospital, or even about how many had died or deserted. Only Reading hospital had records from September 18, Ephrata from December 25, and the rest—though most of them had functioned since October—had reports beginning only in January or February. At Allentown, occupied since the early autumn, McIntosh found "no account of the general hospitals can be found before March 10." Tallying his figures, the general reported that since October these hospitals had treated 3,612 patients. Of this number, 2,000 had been returned to duty, 690 had died or deserted, and 910 remained. Half the remaining sick, McIntosh noted, "were disabled by old wounds and chronic disorders . . .," and should be discharged.[61]

The number of locations listed as general hospitals in December and January remained unchanged, and during the spring no additional major hospitals were established at Valley Forge. All these general hospitals occupied temporary and requisitioned quarters. Yellow Springs, however, was unique. Located ten miles from Valley Forge, Yellow Springs was a famous health spa where Rush and Morgan had sent their patients. By the early 1770s the area was a noted summer resort where some five hundred convalescents yearly enjoyed the bubbling spring waters. In 1774 the tract was purchased by Samuel Kennedy, the surgeon in Wayne's regiment who had served at Ticonderoga with Potts. After the abortive "Battle of the Clouds" on September 18, American troops briefly encamped there and Washington wrote hurried dispatches from the tavern. In late December the inn and the barns were used as hospitals. Requiring a permanent hospital building to house the seriously ill, Washington on January 3, 1778 ordered the erection of a three-storied structure at Yellow Springs with broad porches and with kitchen and bathing facilities. Construction began in March, and the building was completed in August. In contrast to the unwholesome reputation acquired by some other military hospitals, Yellow Springs had a better record, due mainly to Kennedy, the supervising doctor, who died in May of typhus.[62]

Potts was continually in communication with the personnel at Yellow Springs. He provided Kennedy with provisions, candles, and bedding; and Kennedy repeatedly thanked him. Andrew Craigie, the pharmacist, informed Potts on April 7 that the hospital was "in excellent order."[63] Reverend James Sproat, a chaplain making his rounds of army installations in late April, noted that the "Hospital seems to be very neat, and the sick comfortably provided for."[64] On May 13, Washington, in the company of James Craik, visited Yellow Springs to console the sick. Craik commented to Potts that the Commander in Chief found the wards "in excellent order. He spoke to every person in their bunks, which pleased the sick exceedingly."[65] In contrast with Bethlehem or with Lititz, Yellow Springs had a record as a fairly healthy place. By August some 1,300 patients had been treated there, of which 445 were discharged, 124 had died, and 725 remained.[66] Not only was Yellow Springs the largest hospital in Pennsylvania outside of Philadelphia, but it was probably the first military hospital built by Congressional order.

As the Purveyor, Potts was the individual responsible for supplying these hospitals. His primary task was to acquire provisions and equipment—the numerous food items for the special diets, the beds, bedding, clothing, straw, candles, eating implements, and kitchen utensils. His responsibility to the medical staff was to provide drugs, instruments, and surgical dressings. He supervised teams of clerks, storekeepers, and teamsters; he maintained detailed records of his transactions for a Congress suspicious of the department's financial activities. Although Potts acquired some supplies from James Mease, the Clothier General, from Nathanael Greene, the Quartermaster General, and from Jeremiah Wadsworth, the Comissary General, he usually had to devise his own procurement arrangements to feed hospital patients.

Potts assumed the task with his typical energy. From Albany he ordered drugs and equipment from the captured British stores to be shipped by sleigh and wagon to Valley Forge. By March Potts was supplying the flying hospitals with bark, sulphur, camphor, molasses, coffee, and Indian meal. In April Potts sent Craik sacks of rice and barley and barrels of wine and lime juice. At Wilmington Potts procured wooden bowls and utensils for his patients; from Lititz he acquired lint needed by surgeons, and at Dover he found them some amputating instruments. From Baltimore he procured bark and cantharides, and from Boston he had brown sugar and molasses shipped.[67] Potts was assisted by Captain Anthony Morris, appointed on March 23 as Commissary General for Hospitals. Morris found horses and wagons in Jersey, Indian meal in Baltimore, rice in Maryland, wine in Delaware, and vinegar and molasses in Virginia.[68] To what degree Potts was assisted by the other supply departments is unclear. He did apply to Mease for shirts and blankets for the sick. Potts also corresponded with Greene about acquiring wagons and sugar, and apparently the doctor located some missing provisions, because Greene wrote: "I am much obliged to you in behalf of the publick for searching out their stores where they are concealed or neglected."⁶⁹ Ephraim Blaine, the Deputy Commissary General, answered Potts's request for beef in early May, stating that he could hardly even provision army troops with meat, but that he would cooperate with Potts's commissary in acquiring some cattle for hospital use.⁷⁰ Potts's job was not a glamorous one, but the supplying of army hospitals that bleak year of Valley Forge was a vital function.

Few army doctors received compliments from the military those stormy months of departmental controversy, yet Potts earned some praise from his colleagues. At Boston John Warren, who would become one of New England's most renowned physicians, praised him on April 20 for his efficiency.⁷¹ At Yellow Springs on May 2 Craik lauded him, stating, "the hospitals here are in fine order and are much approved of. I think that if they are sufficiently supplied, I hope they will keep up their character."⁷² Likewise Kennedy at Yellow Springs wrote Potts a gushing letter of praise: "To you, dear sir, we look up for the support of all our wants not doubting but that the almost patriotic benevolence which have ever distinguished your character . . . will still continue to render the brave sons of liberty as happy as possible."⁷³ And Craigie wrote Potts from Baltimore; "It is the peculiar felicity of your generous soul to make all your acquaintances happy . . ."⁷⁴ Potts acquired such a stock of supplies by the late summer that he could provision New England hospitals. As he informed the Medical Committee, "I am fortunate in having large stores on hand so that it will be easily in my power to furnish everything wanted . . ."⁷⁵

One of Potts's major responsibilities was to acquire drugs, which were still scarce in early 1778. Congress had not devised a consistent policy for drug procurement, and Potts had the task of locating supply sources. In 1775 Congress had Craigie collect drugs with John B. Cutting, his assistant. Later that year Morgan prepared regimental chests at Cambridge and in 1776 at Manhattan. Congress also paid physicians for their stocks, it appointed a Continental Druggist (whose accomplishments remain a mystery), and it dispatched agents to Europe and to the Caribbean in search of the precious bark, opium, ipecec, camphor, calomel, and other scarce items. In January 1778 Washington ordered that the regiments be provided with complete medical chests, but little could be done until the spring. Dr. William Brown, supervising the Lititz hospital, had the responsibility of determining the necessary items, and on March 27 he sent Potts a list of the requirements.[76] By April, Potts, Craigie, and Cutting were purchasing drugs from numerous sources, storing them at warehouses in Reading and Mannheim, and setting up laboratories at Carlisle and at Yellow Springs.[77] The druggists prepared two types of chests, a large one for general hospitals and a smaller one for regiments. Precisely what drugs were manufactured at Carlisle and at Yellow Springs is uncertain. The apothecaries probably compounded powders, elixirs, tinctures, spirits, and plasters. Perhaps they manufactured niter, cream of tartar, Glauber's Salts, castor oil, oil of turpentine, and red precipitate of mercury, but many of the essential drugs were beyond their rudimentary level of manufacturing. Until large quantities of drugs arrived from Marseilles in late 1778, the most important sources were British ships captured by American privateers, and hence Boston and Baltimore were important markets. Potts acquired two tons of bark at one time from Boston, and at Baltimore Craigie found a large shipment of bark and cantharides that came from Martinique. Continental agents found drugs on the French and Dutch islands in the Caribbean, and they searched in Spain and Holland for additional items. Because of the improved policy of drug procurement, by June most regiments at Valley Forge were equipped with a standardized list of eighty drugs, surgical dressings, and amputating equipment.

Related to this pharmaceutical procurement was a major achievement of the medical department that difficult year, the compilation of a pharmacopoeia for military medicine. Until the Revolution no American had written a formulary or dispensatory, but Brown wrote the "Lititz Pharmacopoeia," published at Philadelphia in July 1778, a landmark in the history of American pharmacy. Printed entirely in Latin, with information extracted from four or five European pharmacopoeias, the thirty-two-page book was designed to assist surgeons and mates who had little training in pharmacy, and to standardize the drugs and equipment in regimental chests. The chronic hardship of the era is indicated in the subtitle, which read in part that the work was "especially adapted to our poverty and straitened circumstances caused by the ferocious warfare of the enemy...."[78] It advised about the simplest, cheapest, and most available drugs, particularly the botanicals that were indigenous to the region. The hardship of the period is also shown by recommendations that linseed oil be substituted for olive oil, cider and vinegar for wine, molasses for sugar, and crude ammonia for volatile salts. Brown also suggested that the root, bark, or wood of a plant could sometimes be used instead of a liquid solution. Many of the drugs, such as rhubarb and sassafras, were of local origin; some, such as volatile salts and cream of tartar, were probably manufactured at Yellow Springs. But many of the eighty drugs had to be imported, and most of them had to be compounded by an apothecary. The importance of the "Lititz Pharmacopoeia" was to demonstrate the need for the professional services of pharmacists, to stimulate the production of chemical manufactures in America, and to provide a standard for an official, national pharmacopoeia.

The amelioration of hospital services was part of the general reorganization of the army that occurred at Valley Forge. After a dismal beginning in the winter the department began to function effectively—medical chests were filled, inventories of stores were kept, registers of sick became standardized, the transfer of convalescents proceeded efficiently, and thousands of men were inoculated. Complaints about scarcities of hospital provisions tapered off by late spring, and the severities of the earlier months were overcome. Linked to this improvement of health care was the regeneration of the troops through superior training, better leadership, and the imposition of regulations—a process in which Baron von Steuben stands as an inspiring force. Best remembered as the Prussian mercenary who trained recruits in musketry, the

The Valley Forge Hospitals

bayonet, the manual of arms, and in field maneuvers, Steuben was also instrumental in stressing sanitary matters. Steuben urged the men to pride themselves on their personal cleanliness; he advised that straw and bedding be changed frequently, and that officers consider the welfare of their men. "The captain cannot be too careful for the company of men that the state had entrusted to his care," advised the German, "and he should gain the love of his men by threating them with every possible kindness and humanity."[79] Tilton was so impressed with Steuben's performance that he commented: "He introduced a number of sanitary reforms which contributed more to the health of the troops than all the utmost efforts of the medical staff."[80]

The experience at Valley Forge was decisive in the Revolution. The determination to keep an army in being—however tattered, hungry, and diseased—inspired the nation and impressed America's allies. The appalling suffering of the troops that characterized the winter months was gradually eased by the spring. Sullivan's bridge over the Schuylkill expedited the shipment of provisions; and with the flow of higher water in the spring, boats with foodstuffs came from Reading. Greene had many bridges repaired and roads improved; he formed teams of wagoners; and his search parties located lost cargoes of clothing. The army that survived the ordeal at Valley Forge was a disciplined, confident force ready for combat. With this assurance that his troops were prepared, Washington was eager to pursue the British as they evacuated Philadelphia.

In late May Clinton, who had replaced Howe, prepared to leave Pennsylvania for New York. By June 18 his 15,000 troops left Philadelphia and crossed the Delaware into New Jersey. Washington's army of 14,500 was close behind and eager to hit the enemy, strung out over twenty miles of road. On June 23 the British troops were resting from the march and from the torrid heat near Monmouth Court House (Freehold). Sensing a victory Washington ordered an attack. But he erred in appointing the erratic General Lee to the field command. Lee bungled the maneuvers, and the battle became a rout for the Americans. Washington barely managed to regroup the retreating troops, who then threw back repeated enemy assaults, and who held their ground. After the battle Clinton's regiments slipped away at night and reached the safety of Sandy Hook, where the Royal Navy convoyed them to Manhattan. Washington marched through Jersey, crossed the Hudson, and camped at White Plains. The strategic situation was now similar to that of the summer of 1777, but the sheer endurance of the Continental army was gradually wearing down the British war machine.

Hospital preparations for the battle of Monmouth were again confusing and uncoordinated. Shippen certainly knew that a fight was pending, but, typically, the medical staff under Cochran, the senior officer, was uncertain about hospital locations. The battle was not only bloody (106 killed, 100 wounded), but it was a hot one as well. In the struggle was Lieutenant Samuel Smith, who remarked about the broiling temperature: "In fact, the heat was so excessive that I could not tell by which most died, whether by the heat, or the [musket] balls."[81] After the fighting Private Martin noticed a wounded American captain whose thigh bone had been shattered by a cannonball:

> I found [him] . . ., lying on the ground, and begging his sergeant, who pretended to take care of him to help him off the field or he should bleed to death . . . I asked the sergeant why he did not carry his officer to his surgeon. He said he would directly. "Directly!" said I, "why he will die directly." I then offered to assist . . . in carrying him to a meetinghouse [the Old Tennent Church] a short distance off where the rest of the wounded and surgeons were. I helped him to the place, and tarried a few minutes to see the wounded to my party again, . . ."[82]

Dr. Samuel Adams recorded that he had treated the wounded at Monmouth Court House, and stated that "it was very fierce and very hot indeed." After the combat he strode over the battlefield, and remarked that it was "a shocking

The Valley Forge Hospitals

sight."[83] Bandages were so scarce, Dr. William Read of Georgia recalled, that he had to tear off shirts from the dead. Without any assistance from medical personnel Read had to beseech "some country people and negroes . . . to assist in lifting and turning these [twenty one] wounded men, and, at length, procuring wagons and straw to remove them to the court-house." Four days after the battle he remembered, two army surgeons finally came to help.[84] Eventually the wounded were removed to Trenton and to Princeton.

After Monmouth, the last major engagement fought in the north, the war in the northern states became a stalemate. The Americans could not expel the British from New York without sufficient French naval and military aid; the British, clinging only to Manhattan and to Providence, dared not mount major expeditions into the interior. In November 1778 Washington shifted his army to Middlebrook, New Jersey, for the winter. With the exception of Yellow Springs, all the hospitals in Pennsylvania were closed, and the chemical laboratories were transferred to the Pennsylvania Hospital. The frenzy of the past months was over, and Potts's task was facilitated. On August 27 he informed the Board of War with pride: "I am certain our hospitals at this time are in the neatest order, and as comfortable as hospitals can be . . ." Proud of his accomplishments for the year, he added: "I cannot forgo mentioning His Excellency General Washington having visited some of our large hospitals before he left [Pennsylvania] was highly satisfied with them. I further hear," Potts went on, that "the Baron Steuben and other gentlemen of humanity and distinction have visited our hospitals in New Jersey and speak very favourably of them."[85]

After Monmouth the welfare of the army improved. The percentage of sickness in Washington's army declined from 21 percent in July to 16 percent in November and December, figures that were far lower than those for the same months in preceding years.[86] With the termination of combat and maneuvers for the year, the heavy incidence of disease tapered off. Tilton indicated that in late 1778 the army was fairly healthy. "Our troops have not been harassed and have not been on hard marches; and the troops being provisioned with a variety of other circumstances contributes to good health..."[87] As Purveyor, Potts had contributed to the survival of the army at Valley Forge.

IX.
Potts's Last Years

During the winter of 1778-1779 Washington quartered some regiments at Danbury, Paramus, and the Highlands, but the majority of the troops encamped at Middlebrook in the Watchung Mountains of New Jersey. The dispersal of brigades in several states enabled Washington to observe enemy movements in Manhattan and to acquire provisions for his command from various areas. As Washington explained to Gouverneur Morris: "I have made a disposition of our Army for the Winter more adopted to our circumstances in point of supplies, than if the Troops remained in a collected State."[1] On December 11 the men began to build huts, and by February 11 shanties for 10,000 men, based on the Valley Forge model, were finished. "Our soldiers have been employed six or eight weeks in constructing log huts," Thacher remarked, "which at length are completed, and both officers and men are under comfortable covering . . ."[2] After the cabins were built, the army was adequately housed, and because of the fairly mild winter and the efficient functioning of supply services, the intense suffering of the preceding year was not repeated.[3] In March Washington commented to Lafayette that the soldiers were again in huts, "but in a more agreeable and fertile country, than they were last Winter at Valley Forge, and are better clad and more healthy than they have ever been since the formation of the Army."[4]

The general hospitals for Middlebrook were located in

Morristown and Brunswick, but the majority of the sick were housed in regimental hospitals and in flying hospitals at Millstone and Bound Brook. Because of the moderate weather, a strict supervision of hut construction, and a rigid enforcement of sanitary standards, the incidence of sickness at Middlebrook was low. Dr. William Brown even had sufficient time to offer a course in medicine and surgery for his staff. The sickness rate for the five months of the encampment—15 percent in January 1779 which decreased to 9 percent in May—was the lowest since the war began, and compared to the 2,094 men who perished at Valley Forge, only 100 died at Middlebrook.[5]

The encampment broke up in late May, when two regiments under Sullivan departed for the invasion of the Iroquois country in western New York, and in June Washington led the rest of the army back to familiar positions around Manhattan. The only significant combat for the summer in the north (except for Indian fighting) was Wayne's capture of Stony Point on the Hudson. Acquiescing in the checkmated nature of the war in the north, the British concentrated on the southern colonies, and in October they repulsed a French-American attack upon Savannah.

In late October, after the French fleet sailed from Georgia for the Caribbean, Washington searched for winter quarters. He selected an area near Morristown that had ample water and timber. By mid-December 11,700 troops were at Jockey Hollow and at nearby camp sites constructing log cabins. On Christmas some of the shivering men were fortunate enough to move out of tents into warmer quarters. Owing to the severity of winter storms, the building of most huts was delayed, and not until late February 1780 were all troops sheltered under timber. In early January fierce blizzards dumped high drifts of snow on the encampment and made roads impassable for weeks. "Our soldiers are in wretched condition for want of clothing, blankets and shoes,..." complained Thacher, "and these calamitous circumstances are accompanied by want of provisions."[6] The veterans of the army had never witnessed such weather. De Kalb, who had served at

Valley Forge and Middlebrook, stated that no winter he had witnessed could compare with "the cruelties of this one."[7] Food was so scarce that Private Martin recalled that during four days and nights he had nothing to eat but a "little black birch which I gnawed off a stick, if that could be called victuals."[8] As the storms abated in late January, Washington managed to impress supplies from nearby counties and to enlist the support of local magistrates to feed and clothe his men.

As at Middlebrook, sanitary regulations and direction of hut construction were strictly enforced, and Washington issued frequent orders about cleansing the bunks and airing the bedding. Flying hospitals were maintained at Basking Ridge, Pluckemin, Mendham, and Jockey Hollow. For the first time since early 1778 medical supplies ran short—because of depleted Continental finances, uncoordinated procurement policies, and Congressional indifference. Bandages were so scarce that old tent cloth was used to cover festering wounds. On March 18 Cochran lamented to Potts that he had 600 men to treat, but that he had few supplies. "I flatter myself that you have no blame in this matter ...," remarked Cochran. "It grieves my soul to see the poor worthy fellows pining away for want of a few comforts..." Washington could do little in the matter, Cochran observed. The Commander in Chief would refer the matter to Congress, Congress would refer it to the Medical Committee, "who would probably pow-wow over it for a while, and no more will be heard of it."[9] By April 11 Cochran was so desperate for supplies that he appealed directly to the Medical Committee. Stating that he had recently requested help from Potts, Cochran declared that "I have for answer that he has neither stores nor any money to purchase any."[10] Though the Morristown winter was severe, it is remarkable that the illness rate was relatively low. The incidence of sickness, that was 11 percent in January 1780, tapered off to below 10 percent by May, and from December 8 to June 3 only 86 men died.[11] Perhaps the troops were inured to hardships, and they were better able to fend for themselves; perhaps the medical staff may have learned something about preventive medicine. Even the use of a novel type of hospital building, the "Tilton hut" may have contributed to the reduction in deaths.

Tilton was convinced that a basic cause of the high death rates in buildings used as army hospitals was their crowded, unsanitary, and poorly ventilated condition. Trying out new log huts in 1776 for convalescents, he discovered that the entry of air through crevices in the timbers seemed to check the spread of typhus. Testing his ideas at Jockey Hollow, Tilton had a one-story log cabin erected to house twenty-eight patients in three separate sections—a central ward of 78 square feet for twelve patients, and two side wards, measuring 50 square feet apiece, for eight patients each. The structure had only one entrance, no windows, and the floor was merely hard earth. Each ward had a fireplace and a 4-inch hole in the roof. From Tilton's sketches, it is apparent that the building provided a small, amply ventilated, fairly spacious hospital in which groups of patients could be secluded from other convalescents. Noting the importance of isolation, Tilton remarked that "the importance of separating those ill of fever, fluxes, etc. from the wounded and such as have only slight topical effects, will be imagined." The smoke from the fires circulated in the hut above the patients' heads; it exited through apertures in the roof, and it thus provided a partial disinfectant of the interior. Tilton recalled that "the smoke contributed to combating infection ... [and] that there was little spread of contagious disease in these huts." Although little evidence exists to indicate if these shelters were duplicated in other army encampments, the Tilton hut represented the most practical achievement of the medical department that year. "This was the experiment I employed in the hard winter of 79–80," Tilton concluded, "and I was satisfied with the result."[12]

Potts's task was less burdensome during the years of the Middlebrook and Morristown encampments, but in 1779 he encountered stubborn resistance to his budget requests. Because of suspicion that the entire medical department was corrupt, Congress was increasingly stingy with appropriations. Concerned that inflation would inhibit his purchasing power and worried that the long delay in paying back salaries to the staff was eroding departmental morale, Potts on April 10 made a cautious request to the Medical Committee for funds. By August the committee had still not responded to Potts's inquiry, so he wrote again, stating that thus far "the sick were never better provided for or taken care of in any age or country," but that such a level of care would deteriorate without adequate funding.[13] On December 24 he again made another request, but Congress continued to grant him only small sums of money intermittently, as if the delegates distrusted all the financial transactions of the department.

Potts's dilemma was typical of hospital problems in 1780. Staff morale was low, and Shippen was unable to provide adequate leadership. Army doctors were offended not only by their two-year wait for salaries, but by the fact that Congress refused to grant them the same pension and bounty land privileges that it extended to line officers. Overshadowing such personnel problems was a Congressional investigation under way concerning Shippen's notorious administration of hospitals; but there were other major criticisms of ranking medical officers. Congress questioned the need for the large staff that Shippen maintained at Philadelphia for few patients. Regardless of Congressional resolves about his next post, John Warren refused to close his hospital in Boston, nor would he accept reassignment. Philip Turner of Connecticut lobbied openly for a hospital to be built in New London, from which, it was suspected, he would materially profit. Isaac Foster, the District Director in New England, was known to have stockpiled army hospital stores for his own use. Consequently, Congress was so disenchanted with the medical men that inevitably it viewed their budget request with grave doubts. As Dr. Barnabas Binney expressed it: "The dirtiest and basest actions are everyday deprecating the profession ... 'till the very appellation [of doctor] has become the butt of satire, ridicule, and contempt."[14]

The overriding factor in this deplorable situation was the renewal of the Morgan-Shippen controversy in 1779. Since his dismissal in January 1777, Morgan had attempted to have Congress vindicate his conduct as Director General. Congress became weary of Morgan's endless tirades against Shippen, and it had numerous problems to consider far more important than the woes of a heartbroken physician. In April 1777 Morgan published a long polemic in which he defended his conduct at Cambridge and Manhattan; he castigated Shippen mercilessly, and insisted that he himself had been unjustly treated. After innumerable delays a Congressional committee investigated his complaints and recommended that Morgan be exonerated. On June 12, 1779, almost two-and-a-half years after his abrupt dismissal, Congress resolved that Morgan had "vindicated his conduct in every respect."[15]

Now that his name was cleared, Morgan could pursue his old rival with a vengeance. Within three days he formally charged Shippen with misconduct and malpractice, and he requested Congress to initiate a trial of the Director General. Complaints about Shippen were so rampant and the charges so serious that Congress ordered a court martial in July. But Washington could not detach scores of medical personnel from the army to testify that summer, so the proceedings were postponed. During the winter of 1779-1780, Morgan and Shippen traveled through Pennsylvania counties gathering deputations and testimonials to support their respective positions. In the process they hurled such a barrage of insults at each other that the venomous dispute demoralized the entire department. Many physicians, surgeons, mates, apothecaries, nurses, stewards, wardmasters, and storekeepers provided information; they corrected, modified, or disavowed previous statements, or, like Potts, some tried to remain neutral in the dispute. Under these circumstances Shippen had little time to supervise the department, his influence with Congress plummeted, budget appropriations were pigeonholed, and Cochran became the de facto head of the department. On January 15, 1780, Washington ordered Shippen to trial and placed under arrest. Shippen was charged on five counts—fraud, speculation in hospital supplies, corrupt financial practices, neglect of duty, and "indecent and infamous conduct as unbecoming an officer and Gentleman . . ." After some legal technicalities were clarified by the Judge Advocate, the case began at Morristown on March 14. For two months a steady stream of witnesses, led by Rush, testified about the horrors of military hospitals in the winter of 1777-1778, stressing Shippen's peculation and his callousness to suffering soldiers.

Although over sixty members of the medical staff testified either for Morgan or for Shippen, Potts did not. The only mention of his name during the trial occurred when Michael Bright, a civilian of Reading, stated that his own home was the temporary storehouse for sugar destined for army hospitals. Bright swore that early in 1778 Shippen had the sugar removed and that he sold it to tavern keepers in Reading, White Horse, and Conestoga Creek. Soon after, stated Bright, Potts called for the sugar to distribute it to the hospitals. As Bright explained the incident:

> On my informing him that it was sold, he was struck with amazement, and exclaimed, God, is it possible! Sold! Yes, said I, it is sold. Sold! said he once again, with an emphasis. Yes, I replied once again, it is sold. Well, he said, shaking his head and hands very significantly, this is more of the same and worse and worse, or words to that effect.[16]

Why Potts did not testify at Morristown or provide Morgan with evidence is unclear. It is even possible that Potts repudiated Bright's statement and that he may have assisted Shippen. On May 12 Shippen forwarded a letter from Potts to Colonel John Laurens, the Judge Advocate, stating: "I enclose a letter I received last night from Dr. Potts, relative to Bright's disposition disclaiming his ejaculations, and I don't know if it will be of any use."[17] Potts had a knack for avoiding controversy. He had managed to remain out of the Stringer-Morgan feud, the Rush-Shippen feud, the Gates-Schuyler feud, and the Morgan-Shippen feud. He was a cautious man, and possibly he was disheartened by the unedifying spectacle of his two former professors, who possessed the best medical minds in America, clawing and flaying each other in the most undignified controversy of the profession in decades.

Although Potts tried to extricate himself from the dispute, he was implicated in a rumored scandal involving the illegal use of government property. On March 15, 1780, Craik wrote him that departmental gossip abounded concerning the purveyor's peculation in hospital stores, and that Potts's conduct would be investigated. According to unnamed accusers, Potts kept wagons and stores at nonexistent hospitals in Chester and Reading, and supposedly he sold himself government provisions at public expense. "My dear Sir," Craik warned, "these things are of a serious nature. How they are found I am entirely ignorant, but I make no doubt that you can make it apparent that you have done nothing but what you have a right to do and can answer for."[18]

Potts quickly refuted the insinuations. In letters to the Medical Committee he insisted that the charges were "entirely groundless," that he hoarded no stores for his own profit, and that he was not even authorized to determine the location of hospitals. Instead of enriching himself by profiteering, Potts asserted that if he had not earned some money by investing in cargo ships (Potts had interests in the brig *Delaware* and the sloop *Queen of France*), he would "have been reduced from a handsome little fortune to misery." Potts was quite ill when he penned these responses; he was distressed at the departmental turmoil and embittered by the false accusations. Stating that he had obligations to his family, and that, because of illness contracted in service, his health was poor, on April 11, 1780, Potts asked to resign from office. "I have a numerous family to maintain," he stated, and "it is my duty to take care of them which I cannot do on my present pay, so that at the present I am incapable of doing it ... For these and other reasons," Potts added, "I must beg you to appoint some other person in my place." After he recuperated at Reading, Potts promised he would be eager for another assignment. "I shall at all times be ready (if I can but crawl) to contribute my [might] toward the full and final winning of our glorious independence."[19] No formal charges of peculation were even filed against Potts, but undoubtedly the unfounded accusations hurt his pride and hastened his decision to retire from the service on October 6, 1780.

At Morristown Morgan paraded his witnesses until May 15, when the court declared a recess, and in June Shippen opened his own defense. The five charges against him were trimmed to two—peculation and neglect of duty. Although speculation in government stores was legal during the war and was a common practice by many public agents, such conduct was indefensible by a Director General, and Shippen undoubtedly enriched himself by selling wine and sugar. The question of whether Shippen was actually indifferent to the plight of his patients was harder to ascertain. Shippen seldom visited the wards, and he rarely indicated the concern for the sick and wounded shown by Morgan, Potts, and Rush. On August 10, 1780, the court acquitted Shippen of all charges, but labeled his conduct with respect to speculation "highly improper and justly reproachable."[20] Washington forwarded the verdict to Congress, and on August 18 Congress voted to acquit Shippen, yet it kept intact the same criticism by the Morristown court of his fraudulent activities. Although Morgan and Rush were outraged at the verdict—especially since Shippen remained as Director General—Morgan had finally won his victory, and Shippen's days as hospital chief were numbered.

Under a cloud of censure, Shippen returned to his post, but his position was untenable, and he had lost the confidence of Congress, Washington, and his own staff. Shippen contributed little to the task of reorganizing the department desired by Congress, and Cochran, not Shippen, had the job of providing personnel and material to Gates's army, and then to Greene's army in the Carolinas. Shippen finally resigned on January 3, 1781, and returned to private practice. Inasmuch as Shippen's resignation seemed to confirm Morgan's charges, Morgan renewed the dispute with another vitriolic pamphlet about his opponent. But the public was weary of this incessant bickering; the controversy exhausted the energies of Morgan and Shippen, and neither recovered the vigor, brilliance, or imagination of his prewar years. Their great days as leaders of the profession were over; their careers were virtually wrecked in this tragic and disgraceful episode that demeaned the medical profession.

Congress tried to reform the dispirited and fragmented department. The Act of September 8, 1780—the third reorganization of hospital administration—designated the Director General as the undisputed authority in military hospitals; it provided him with three deputies, or chief physicians, whom he could assign to any American theater of war, and it abolished the wasteful district department hierarchies. The organization of flying and regimental hospitals remained the same, and no changes occurred with respect to the general hospitals located at New Windsor, Robinson's House (near West Point), West Point, Morristown, Philadelphia, Boston, Fishkill, Trenton, Yellow Springs, and Williamsburg. The staff was slightly reduced, but a major feature of the plan was that the director, as in the British army, could appoint a chief physician to a field army in order to supervise regimental personnel.

On October 6, 1780, Congress selected Cochran as Director General, named Thomas Bond, Jr., as Potts's successor, and reappointed a number of Potts's former staff to new posts—Treat, McKenzie, Craigie, Tilton, Adams, Townshend, and Hagen. Cochran was an able and conscientious administrator, and he was the only successful director of the war.[21] He strove to acquire adequate appropriations from a tight-fisted Congress beset by enormous financial problems; he convinced the delegates to grant his men back pay and suitable pension benefits; he placated disgruntled staff members; and he even managed to persuade some embittered doctors to remain in the service. He was a popular leader, who had Washington's support and the approval of the physicians. Impressed by his talents Congress very slowly granted larger sums of money for the hospitals. But by the spring of 1781, when finances were scrutinized by Robert Morris, the Superintendent of Finances determined to economize, Cochran's department was again nearly destitute of supplies. How the medical department functioned in the south, particularly during Greene's campaign in 1780–1781 against Cornwallis, is outside the limits of this study. Cochran relied heavily on Craik to invigorate his battered department; and for the final major campaign of the war in October 1781 at Yorktown, Cochran tactfully deferred the responsibility of supervising medical arrangements to Craik, one of Washington's favorites and his fellow Virginian.

Potts quickly faded from public life. He attempted a brief return to private practice, but only one patient is cited in his ledger for September 1780; thereafter the pages are bare. On October 11, 1780, he had his last will and testament drawn. Naming Samuel Potts, his brother, and Thomas Mifflin as his executors, Potts gave his wife, Grace, all his household effects, and £3,000 from the sale of his real estate. To his eldest son Benjamin, Potts deeded a gold watch and fifty guineas; to Thomas Dundas his sword, pistols, and one hundred guineas. The proceeds from the sale of his real property were to be assigned to a trust fund for the benefit of his five surviving children, who would receive their shares of the inheritance at the age of twenty-one or on their respective marriages.[22] On October 15, 1781, at the age of thirty-six, Potts died of unknown causes in Reading. He was buried in the family plot at Pottsgrove, without a stone to mark his remains, according to Quaker custom. Decades later, one of his descendents placed a small stone slab over the site, which still remains to mark his grave.

In summary, how does one evaluate Jonathan Potts? The advantages he derived from his superior education and his social standing have been explained. That he was class valedictorian and the first of the medical graduates from the College of Philadelphia to become a member of the American Philosophical Society (1768) suggest a high level of intelligence. Because of his university background and his hospital training, Potts represented a new breed of physicians emerging in the late colonial era who won high positions in the Continental army. Despite the correspondence about Potts that has survived, little of it is personal. One has the impression that Potts was a shy, devout, and reserved man. Little information about his private life is available. Only one portrait of Potts is known, and its authenticity is questionable. The painting, reputedly done by Matthew Pratt, a Philadelphia artist studying in England, was supposedly started in late 1766 when Potts was in London and completed in 1781. The portrait shows a man with a prominent nose, a broad forehead, copious hair, deep-set eyes, and a visage that suggests pride in his achievements. Potts's portrait and private papers became the property of William B. Potts, a nephew. Sometime in the mid-nineteenth century, the descendents donated the Jonathan Potts Papers to the Historical Society of Pennsylvania, apparently after removing personal letters from the correspondence. As a result of Potts's reticence and possibly his inherent Quakerism, one cannot provide an intimate analysis of the man, and it is difficult to speculate about his private life.

With respect to Potts's official career, more information is available. By 1774, after initiating a promising medical practice, Potts became a radical in politics, long before most Pennsylvanians championed the cause of American freedom. His enthusiasm for the Revolution, his involvement with Committees of Safety, his enlistment in a rifle battalion in 1775—all strike notes of patriotic virtue. His first major accomplishment in the army was the supervision of the hospital on Lake George, a task he performed with skill and dedication. Potts's willingness to serve under Washinton during the dark days of 1776 on the Delaware and his participation in the battle of Princeton should endear Potts to his countrymen. The high point of his career came when he directed medical arrangements at Saratoga. In contrast to the usual denunciations of army doctors, Potts was publicly lauded; in the entire war, he was the only member of the medical profession to receive praise from Congress for his performance. He worked in the less responsible post of Purveyor from 1778 until 1780, but this position did not provide him with opportunities for making significant contributions to military medicine. His poor health, the financial difficulties he suffered as a medical officer, and his distaste for the acrimony that wracked the department were factors that let him to resign.

Potts revealed himself as a man of goodwill, one with integrity. He had undeniable charm, and he was quite popular with his medical and military colleagues. Potts shunned bureaucratic bickering, and remarkably enough his name is not linked to the many disputes and scandals that hampered the efficiency of the department. He was a diligent hospital administrator, who was called on in several crises—Lake George, Philadelphia, Ticonderoga, Saratoga, and Valley Forge. Although he was not a Rush, a Morgan, or a Shippen, Potts was a capable medical organizer, who displayed a deep humanitarian concern for sick and wounded troops and who strove to improve the quality of medical care during the Revolution.

Viewed in a broader perspective, it is apparent that Potts's endeavors typified developments in military medicine from 1775 to 1783. The Revolution was a long and bloody struggle. The 1,331 military engagements and 215 naval actions of the war took a heavy toll of human life. About 25,000 servicemen perished in the struggle—6,800 in battle, 8,500 in British prisons, and 10,000 in camps or hospitals. The mortality rate of soldiers was 0.9 percent of the population, second only in the major wars of the United States to the mortality rate of 1.6 percent of the population in the Civil War. Considering that 200,000 men were under arms at various times during the Revolutionary War, the ratio of mortality to the American participants in the Revolution was 12.5 percent, a figure very close to the figure of 13 percent suffered by Union forces during the Civil War. The sickness rate of the Revolutionary War was likewise high. The prevalence of sickness for Washington's army (excluding the southern campaigns and minor engagements) reached 35 percent in December 1776 and 35.5 percent in February 1777. The lowest level of sickness for one month in 1775 was 10.6 percent; for 1777, 9.7 percent; for 1778, 17.7 percent, for 1778, 16 percent; for 1779, 8.7 percent; and for 1780, 8.2 percent. The ratio of troops incapacitated by sickness and wounds for the eight-year war period averaged 18 percent.[23] Clearly the war took a heavy toll of lives, and disease so frequently crippled the American army that it was rendered relatively inactive for many months.

The administration of the hospitals had a direct influence on the efficiency of the Continental army. The medical department was not geared for large-scale warfare in 1776, and because of the pressure exerted by yearly campaigns, it was not until 1779 that some stability appeared in the structure of the department. Suspicious of excessive centralization and inexperienced with hospital arrangements, Congress was unable to decide until late 1780 whether to have a powerful Director General or whether to split his authority among regional directors. Only in the year 1777 were Congressional appropriations generally adequate for the department; except for the aftermath of the 1776 retreat to the Delaware and the 1777 year at Valley Forge, Delegates were usually indifferent to hospital conditions. The composition of the membership of the Medical Committee, one of the least important of thirty-three Congressional committees, frequently changed, and seldom were civilian doctors represented. The effectiveness of the department was plagued not only by politics— Congressmen tried to have their constituents with medical training receive high appointments—but also by the endless disputes between directors and their immediate subordinates, between staff surgeons and regimental surgeons, and between physicians and generals. The chronic shortage of drugs, supplies, and instruments further contributed to the harassed state of the hospital department.

With the exception of the construction of a special building at Yellow Springs and one at Williamsburg, army hospitals were usually converted shelters, inadequately suited for the admittance of patients. But such facilities were typical of those for European armies in the eighteenth century. The evacuation procedures for American casualties from the battlefields seems gruesome and shocking, but one should note that improvements in transporting the wounded humanely and efficiently did not occur until the French Revolution, when in 1792 Dominique Jean Larrey experimented with specially constructed ambulance wagons and with trained medical corpsmen. One can appreciate the limitations of military medicine during the Revolutionary War by realizing that the army did not have an actual medical corps and that the regulations which constituted an embryonic program of preventive medicine emanated not from the doctors but from the orderly books and orders of the day of the military. Although precise comparisons of medical care with other major European armies of the era is very difficult to ascertain, it appears that the level of medicine in the Continental army was roughly equivalent to that in the military forces of advanced European nations.

Did the Revolution have a major impact on the development of preventive medicine in America? One result of the war was to demonstrate the importance of hospitals. Whereas only one private hospital existed in the American colonies in 1775, innumerable shelters were converted into army hospitals during the war. In protecting the health of its soldiers and sailors, the state thus assumed a responsibility in public health that had far-reaching consequences. Owing to the availability of large numbers of patients, about fourteen hundred doctors who enlisted in the services had unusual opportunities for observing diseases on an unprecedented scale. Army doctors discovered that diseases common to armies could be curtailed by controlling certain causative factors related to a soldier's well-being. Although the surgeons were unable to stem communicable diseases, they developed sanitary codes for the generals to enforce, they collected data about pestilence, and they acquired experience in protecting large groups of men from contagious diseases. The war provided medical men with a broad, practical education in treating smallpox, typhus, dysentery, malaria, and numerous respiratory ailments. Yet with the exception of the great victory of mass inoculation over smallpox, little actually changed in preventive-medicine procedures. As the regimental surgeons returned home after demobilization, they used the same treatment—the lancet, the puke, the poly-pharmacy—that characterized their practice for centuries. Physicians still grasped at metaphysical theories; the scientific facts about disease did not emerge until the following century.

Surgery remained at a low ebb during the war, and no novel techniques in operative procedures emerged. Still army doctors witnessed a great variety of operations and had innumerable opportunities for dissections. With ample human material available, surgeons undoubtedly enlarged their skills and anatomical knowledge. John Warren, who performed the first successful operation of the shoulder joint in 1781, remarked that "the military hospitals of the United States furnished a large field for observation and experiment in the various branches of the healing art, and for opportunities in anatomical knowledge."[24] By the war's end fewer amputations probably occurred. "The longer we continued in the war," Tilton remarked, "amputation and cutting became less fashionable. From obstinacy in the patients, we had the opportunity of observing that the limbs might be saved, which the best authorities directed to be cut off. I have seen gunshot wounds through the elbow, knee, or ankle saved without the loss of a limb. It therefore became an axiom with us to take the chance of saving the limb in such cases."[25] Yet no evidence exists to indicate that any significant development in wound surgery occurred in the North Atlantic world until the Napoleonic Wars. Doctor Charles Gilman of New Jersey accidentally discovered the disinfectant properties of alcohol. Wounded at Harlem Heights in the hand, Gilman remarked that his injury was painful and that it continually discharged pus. Soon after, he remembered, "I spilled—quite accidently—for I had had too much rum, some upon the member. I covered it, and in two days, I noticed no odor. I removed the cover and the wound was healing. Thereafter, all wounds were soaked in rum clothes before covering."[26] But information about Gilman's practice is scant, and apparently no other record of this discovery survives from the Revolution.

Potts's Last Years

In pharmacy the Revolution stimulated the domestic production of drugs and the professionalization of the apothecary. Some drugs were manufactured at Carlisle and Yellow Springs in 1778, but the first large-scale production of compounds such as Glauber's Salts and muriate of ammonia was begun in 1786 by Charles and Christopher Marshall—the same firm that had supplied the Pennsylvania line with medical chests in 1776. The emphasis on drug standards and the knowledge required to compound chemicals demonstrated the importance of the twenty-five apothecaries who served in the war. A gradual professional distinction emerged in the postwar era between doctors and pharmacists, as the doctors—usually preoccupied with patients and with mastering the burgeoning materia medica of the day—turned over to the apothecary the task of preparing remedies. The symbol of this occupational specialization was the written prescription for a drug—a device known since the early eighteenth century in colonial America, a practice utilized at the Pennsylvania Hospital, and one continued by apothecaries through the war. Henceforth apothecaries had an expanded role in the dispensing of medicine. After the publication of the "Lititz Pharmacopoeia" in 1778 came the impetus to improve drug standards, demonstrated by the *Massachusetts Medical Society Pharmacopoeia* (1807), the *New York Hospital Pharmacopoeia* (1812), and the first *National Pharmacopoeia* (1817–1819).

In the intellectual realm some changes are apparent. Scientific activity probably declined during the war, the personal and institutional links that American doctors had with Britain and the Continent were temporarily severed, and the normal flow of books and periodicals across the ocean was interrupted by the conflict. Professional clubs and societies on the seaboard were virtually dormant; King's College was closed, and the medical school at the College of Philadelphia had a sharp drop in enrollment. The contact with British, German, and French surgeons may have stimulated the dissemination of advanced professional techniques from Europe, but except for Thacher's commentary in Albany about his European medical colleagues, additional information on this point is lacking. Jean-Francois Coste, the chief physician of the French expeditionary force under Count de Rochambeau, spoke to groups of American doctors, he discussed his experiments in treating venereal disease, and he wrote a pharmacopoeia for military use while in America. In general, however, the influence of foreign doctors from the services is not apparent during the war. More significant in the exchange of ideas among doctors was the gradual erosion of the provincialism in American medicine; surgeons from isolated communities in thirteen states assembled in one great national endeavor to fight epidemic diseases and to learn the rudiments of hygiene. They exchanged ideas, discussed the merits of various therapies, traded medicines and formulas, and presumably commented about unique surgical experiences. The war was a nationalizing factor for the medical profession.

Furthermore six army doctors published accounts of their observations. John Jones wrote the first book on surgery (1775), Rush's essay on hygiene appeared in 1777, and Brown's pharmacopoeia in 1778. Rush commented on smallpox, typhus, and other aspects of preventive medicine in his famous *Medical Inquiries and Observations* (1789), a work republished during the War of 1812 and considered still useful in the Civil War. The most significant work in military preventive medicine of the era was written by Tilton, whose *Economical Observations* was written in 1813. An advocate of high sanitary standards and of a unified medical corps, Tilton became Director General during the War of 1812. Soon after the Revolution, Ebenezer Beardsley wrote about dysentery and Barnabas Binney commented about gunshot wounds. Though these works could not match the contributions in military or naval medicine by Pringle, Monro, Lind, or John Hunter, these books and articles represent an important development in the emergence of an American medical literature.

The war was an impetus to the improvement of the medical profession. In 1775 only a small number of army doctors had university degrees or college training, but it was this select minority that won the high appointments in the medical department. Because of the need to weed out unqualified candidates for surgeoncies, the Director General, Congress, and several northern states established examining boards for applicants. Evidence about the relative success of the college-bred candidates in passing the tests compared to unlettered apprentices is unavailable, but probably the better-educated surpassed their competitors. As a result of the military experience, several states by 1783 enacted licensure legislation to protect the public from quacks. Another effect of the war was to end the traditional dependence upon Edinburgh for advanced medical training and to increase the number of medical graduates from King's, Harvard, and the College of Philadelphia. Medical societies reappeared. In 1781 the Massachusetts Medical Society was organized by fourteen Boston physicians, eight of whom had served in the war, and by 1791 six more medical groups were formed to advance medical knowledge. In 1797 the first American medical journal, the *Medical Respository,* was published in New York, and in 1812 the *New England Journal of Medicine and Surgery* appeared. Clearly the Revolution hastened the professionalization of American medicine.

Within this context, how does one appraise Potts's role? He was a pioneering sanitarian, but he was not an innovator in military medicine. Nor can he be credited with any scientific, medical, or literary achievements. Yet he supervised the largest army hospital of the war, and he directed the first mass inoculation of American troops. If these accomplishments appear relatively modest, so too were those of his wartime colleagues in medicine. Potts represents the dedicated army doctor who toiled under incredible difficulties to ease the misery of sick and wounded soldiers. Placing the work of army surgeons and physicians in perspective, Anthony Wayne, Potts's friend, commented to Congress: "If a long, constant, and faithful attendence to duty—in humanity, in assiduity, and in tender care of the sick have a claim to merit, none are more justly entitled to it than these gentlemen." Citing the many battles in which he participated, Wayne remarked in 1780 that "I do not recall a single instance but what these doctors contended in the field of battle to dress the wounded—frequently in the eye of danger to save the life of a brave officer or wounded soldier."[27] Jonathan Potts truly symbolizes these patriotic doctors of the American Revolution.

Appendix I

A Table of Fees and Rates

For sundry articles and services in medicine and surgery, as agreed on and established by the New Jersey Medical Society, at their general meeting in New Brunswick, July 23d, 1766.

Proclamation Money

	£	s.	d.
Visits in Towns			
Visiting in towns, whereby the physician and surgeon can readily attend the patient without riding, to be charged for according to the duration of the ailment and degree of attendance, viz.: In slight cases whereby a visit or two may be wanted	0	00	0
Per week			
In other cases requiring longer and daily care and attendance: for each week's attendance and in proportion for lesser or more time, exclusive of medicines	0	10	0

Appendix I

	£	s.	d.
Visits in the country			
Visits in the country under half a mile to be charged for as in towns, viz., per week &c	0	10	0
About half a mile & not more than 1½			
Every visit about half a mile and not exceeding a mile and a half	0	1	6
Above 1½ & not more than 15			
Every visit above one and a half miles and not exceeding fifteen miles, for each mile additional	0	1	0
Above fifteen & not more than 25			
Every visit above fifteen miles and not exceeding twenty-five miles, for each mile above fifteen and under twenty-five	0	1	6
Above 25			
Every visit above twenty-five miles, for each mile above twenty-five	0	2	0
Every visit in the night, exclusive of other things	0	5	0
Consultations			
Consultation Fees, viz.: Every first visit and opinion by the consulted physician or surgeon, exclusive of traveling fees	0	15	0
Every succeeding visit and advice by do. (ditto) &c.	0	7	6

A Table of Fees and Rates

Surgical operations and services   £   s.   d.

Fees for surgical operations and services, exclusive of visits and traveling charges, viz.:

	£	s.	d.
Phlebotomy	0	1	6
Extracting a tooth	0	1	6
Cutting an issue	0	2	0
Cupping with scarification	0	2	0

Wounds

	£	s.	d.
As first dressing of all large or deep incised or contused wounds, including ung'ts, &c., except in very extraordinary cases, where the surgeon shall consult the Society, who will adjudge the proper charge in such particular cases	0	7	6
Succeeding dressing of do., each time	0	2	0

Sinuses and Abscesses

	£	s.	d.
Opening large sinuses or abscesses and first dressing	0	7	6
Succeeding dressing of do., each	0	3	0

Inflammations

	£	s.	d.
Advice for large inflammations and abscesses, when attended twice a day, per week, and proportionably for a greater or less time	0	10	0
Do. when attended once a day, per week, &c	0	5	0

Ulcers

	£	s.	d.
Dressing all malignant, putrid or phagadaeme ulcers, each dressing	0	2	0

Appendix I

	£	s.	d.
Dressing small cutaneous or superficial wounds, small and healing ulcers and small abscesses, each dressing	0	1	0
Opening small abscesses and sinuses	0	2	0
Drawing off the urine by the catheter, each time	0	7	6
Administering a clyster	0	3	9

Trepan

Operation of the trepan	3	00	0
Dressing each time	0	3	9

Couching, &c

Couching or extracting the cataract	3	00	0
Cutting the Iris	3	00	0
Fistula Lachrymalis	1	10	0

Couching &c

Each dressing do.	0	1	6
Bronchotomy	1	10	0
Extirpation of the Tonsils	1	00	0
Extraction of the polypus of the nose	1	00	0
Operation for the Hare-lip	1	10	0
Operation for the Wry-neck	1	10	0
Each dressing the five preceding cases	0	1	6

Amputations

Amputations of the breast	3	00	0
Ditto of the fore and back arm	3	00	0
Ditto of the leg or thigh	3	00	0
Each dressing for the first 14 days after the preceding amputations	0	5	0

A Table of Fees and Rates

	£	s.	d.
Each succeeding dressing	0	2	6
Amputation of the fingers or toes, each	0	15	0
Each dressing do.	0	2	0
Suture of the tendons and Gastroraphy, each	1	00	0
Each dressing do.	0	2	6
Bubonocele Epiplocele and Hernia Femoralis, each	3	00	0
Each dressing do.	0	5	0
Exomphalos and Hernia Ventralis	1	10	0
Each dressing	0	2	6
Hydrocle Radical operation	3	00	0
Ditto palliative by puncture	1	10	0
Castration, each Testicle	3	00	0
Each dressing do.	0	5	0
Phymosis and paraphymosis	0	7	6
Each dressing	0	2	0
Paracentisis	1	10	0
Fistula in ano, deep, sinuous and of long standing	3	00	0
Do. small and recent	2	00	0
Each dressing in such Fistulas	0	3	0
Empyema	1	00	0
Each dressing do.	0	2	0
Extirpation of large encysted and large cancerous Tumors	1	10	0
Dressing do., each time	0	3	0
Extirpation of small encysted and small cancerous Tumors	0	15	0
Each dressing do.	0	1	6
Cutting for the stone in the bladder	5	00	0
Each dressing do.	0	5	0

Appendix I

	£	s.	d.
Cutting for the stone in the urethra	1	10	0
Each dressing do.	0	2	0
Assistant Surgeon's fee in all operations			

Midwifery, viz.

	£	s.	d.
Delivering a woman in a natural case	1	10	0
In a preternatural case	3	00	0
In a laborious case, requiring forceps or extrication with the crotchet, &c.	3	00	0

Inoculation

Inoculation of the small pox, including medicine and attendance

Fractures and Dislocations

	£	s.	d.
Reduction of a simple fracture, and depression of the nose, with necessary dressing during the cure	1	7	0
Luxation or fracture of the lower jaw, with do.	1	00	0
Luxation of the neck, with do.	2	00	0
Luxation of the Humerus, and do.	1	10	0
Ditto of the Cubit, and do.	1	10	0
Simple fracture of the Clavicle, and do.	1	10	0
Ditto of the fore and back arm, and do.	1	10	0
Dislocation or fracture of the wrist bones, with do.	1	10	0
Dislocation of the thigh bone, with do.	2	00	0
Ditto of the knee, with do.	1	10	0
Ditto or fracture of the Patella, with do.	0	15	0
Ditto of the ankle, with do.	1	10	0

A Table of Fees and Rates

	£	s.	d.
Simple fracture of the thigh or leg bones, with do.	2	00	0
Simple ditto of the heel, with do.	1	10	0
Dislocation of the fingers or toes, with do.	0	7	6
Compound fractures of all kinds, one-third more than simple, besides the daily dressing, which is to be charged at the rate fixed for large wounds, when the fracture is of the thigh, leg or arm; but at the rate of small wounds when of the fingers or toes, &c.			
Other surgical cases not here mentioned, either to be proposed to the Society for their decision, or to be charged as nearly to the tenor of this table as possible.			
Rates of extemporaneous forms of medicine, exclusive of visiting and traveling fees, viz.:			
Bolus Cathartic or emetic	0	2	0
Ditto with musk	0	3	0
Every other do. alternative for persons above years of age.			
Every do. for persons under years			
Decoction with one ounce Cort. Peruv. and proportionably with greater or less quantity	0	7	6
Other decoctions and wines made with foreign medicaments, per pound	0	7	6
Do. with indigenous or native medicines, per pound	0	3	0
Draughts, each	0	2	2
Electary Cathartic, per ounce	0	7	6
Do. Alternative, per ounce	0	5	0

Appendix I

	£	s.	d.
Elixirs and Essences, per ounce	0	3	9
Emulsions	0	1	0
Epispastic plasters for the neck, side or back	0	3	0
Do. for the arms, wrists or legs, each	0	1	6
Each dressing of the large blisters	0	1	0
Each do. of the lesser	0	0	6
Ingredients for nitrous decoctions, 1 pound	0	7	6
Ingredients foreign for other decoctions, &c., per oz.	0	2	0
Ditto for Glysters	0	3	0
Musk Julap	0	2	6
Julaps, per ounce	0	1	0
Linctus and Lohocs, per ounce	0	2	6
Lozenges, per ounce	0	3	0
Mixtures compounded of aqueous and spirituous and Saline or solid substances, per ounce	0	1	0
Mixtures consisting soley of spirituous substances, such as Tinctures, Elixirs, Essences, &c., per oz.	0	3	9

Ointments, viz.

	£	s.	d.
Mere-fort, per ounce	0	2	6
Do. mit., per ounce	0	2	0

Pills, viz.

	£	s.	d.
Cathart., 1 dose	0	2	0
Mercur., per dose	0	1	6
Anodyn, per dose	0	1	0
Alterative, per dose	0	2	0
Potion cathart., with manna, per ounce	0	4	0

A Table of Fees and Rates

	£	s.	d.
Powders, Cathart, viz.			
Rhubarb, per dose	0	3	0
All others, per dose	0	2	0
Powders Emetic, per dose	0	2	0
Do. Alterative, per dose	0	1	0
Salts Cathartic, per dose	0	1	6
Do. with manna, 1 ounce, per dose	0	3	0
Tartar Cream of, per dose	0	1	6
All medicines charged by the dose to persons under three years of age one-fourth less than to those above that age.			
Tinctures, per ounce	0	3	0
Salivation, including medicines	3	00	0
Simple Gonorrhoea, includ. do.	2	5	0
Gonorrh. attended with Chancres, or particular trouble	3	00	0

All other prescribed forms not here specified, to be submitted to the direction of the Society, and rated as near as possible to the tenor of this Table.

The Society reserves to themselves the right, at all times hereafter, of making all such alterations in and additions to this Table, as shall appear to them just and expedient.

ROBT. McKEAN, President

Appendix II

Illness in the American Ranks during the Revolution

The first table in this appendix shows the percentage of rank and file who were sick from July 1775 through July 1783. The second figure is a graph of this data. This material is reprinted with permission from *The Sinews of Independence: Monthly Strength Reports* of the Continental Army, pp. xxx, xxxi, edited by Charles H. Lesser (Chicago: University of Chicago Press, 1976).

PERCENTAGE OF RANK AND FILE WHO WERE SICK

		Sick Present	Sick Absent	Sick TOTAL	Rank & File TOTAL	Sick %
1775	July	1409	697	2106	19081	11.0
	August	2381	1176	3557	20823	17.1
	September	1908	946	2854	19253	14.8
	October	1476	952	2428	19048	12.8
	November	1490	812	2302	18831	12.2
	December	1216	552	1768	16668	10.6
1776	January	1422	245	1667	13564	12.3
	February	2417	376	2793	18887	14.8
	March	1071	172	1243	7720	16.1
	April	789	698	1487	12205	12.2
	May	588	308	896	9051	9.9
	June	875	217	1092	11227	9.7
	July	2313	259	2572	15529	16.6
	August	1878	998	2876	11389	25.3
	September	8403	4310	12713	39892	31.9
	October	6225	6190	12415	40962	30.3
	November	2825	3306	6131	22735	27.0
	December	600	2580	3180	9125	34.9
1777	January }					
	February }	Missing				
	March }					
	April	199	275	474	2188	21.7
	May	1057	1020	2077	8378	24.8
	June	Missing				
	July	448	481	929	4306	21.6
	August	655	803	1458	6945	21.0
	September	Missing				
	October	1511	4339	5850	33021	17.7
	November	1821	4754	6575	25004	26.3
	December	2087	5008	7095	22047	32.2
1778	January	1455	3598	5053	18033	28.0
	February	3201	3680	6881	19402	35.5
	March	3285	2923	6208	18558	33.5
	April	3798	2311	6109	21848	28.0
	May	3766	1670	5436	20032	27.1
	June	951	5116	6067	22223	27.3
	July	1175	4079	5254	24300	21.6
	August	2270	2927	5197	25422	20.4
	September	2274	4062	6336	30695	20.6
	October	1911	3214	5125	29256	17.5
	November	1749	2979	4728	29483	16.0
	December	1660	3043	4703	28035	16.8
1779	January	1875	2310	4185	27485	15.2
	February	1349	1883	3232	24886	13.0
	March	1265	1283	2548	23288	10.9
	April	1143	993	2136	22279	9.6
	May	975	890	1865	20244	9.2
	June	788	968	1756	18962	9.6

PERCENTAGE OF RANK AND FILE WHO WERE SICK

		Sick Present	Sick Absent	Sick TOTAL	Rank & File TOTAL	Sick %
1779	July	829	1210	2039	21793	9.4
	August	910	754	1664	19052	8.7
	September	1119	844	1963	20077	9.8
	October	1144	1327	2471	24593	10.0
	November	990	932	1922	20394	9.4
	December	931	760	1691	15604	10.8
1780	January	1244	794	2038	18334	11.1
	February	1043	762	1805	16349	11.0
	March	843	598	1441	14843	9.7
	April	660	431	1091	10673	10.2
	May	603	410	1013	10477	9.7
	June	357	572	929	9498	9.8
	July	529	527	1056	12746	8.3
	August	1051	909	1960	20353	9.6
	September	1016	853	1869	21043	8.9
	October	591	581	1172	14317	8.2
	November	465	914	1379	14294	9.7
	December	354	287	641	6723	9.5
1781	January	333	233	566	5468	10.4
	February	248	234	482	4618	10.4
	March	251	293	544	5115	10.6
	April	369	494	863	5804	14.9
	May	406	208	614	7392	8.3
	June	199	271	470	8661	5.4
	July	286	292	578	8737	6.6
	August	Missing				
	September	411	396	807	4995	16.2
	October	1233	805	2038	14240	14.3
	November December	Missing				
1782	January	1676	620	2296	9469	24.3
	February	1752	503	2255	9080	24.8
	March	924	465	1389	8664	16.0
	April	736	320	1056	8853	11.9
	May	677	392	1069	8842	12.1
	June	756	422	1178	9969	11.8
	July	903	340	1243	10414	11.9
	August	792	503	1295	10603	12.2
	September	725	445	1170	9825	11.9
	October	722	411	1133	10165	11.2
	November	656	442	1098	10359	10.6
	December	715	404	1119	10575	10.6
1783	January	726	312	1038	10202	10.2
	February	787	323	1110	10134	11.0
	March	794	285	1079	10115	10.7
	April	813	238	1051	9807	10.7
	May	798	234	1032	9874	10.5
	June	181	131	312	2577	12.1
	July	203	54	257	2328	11.0

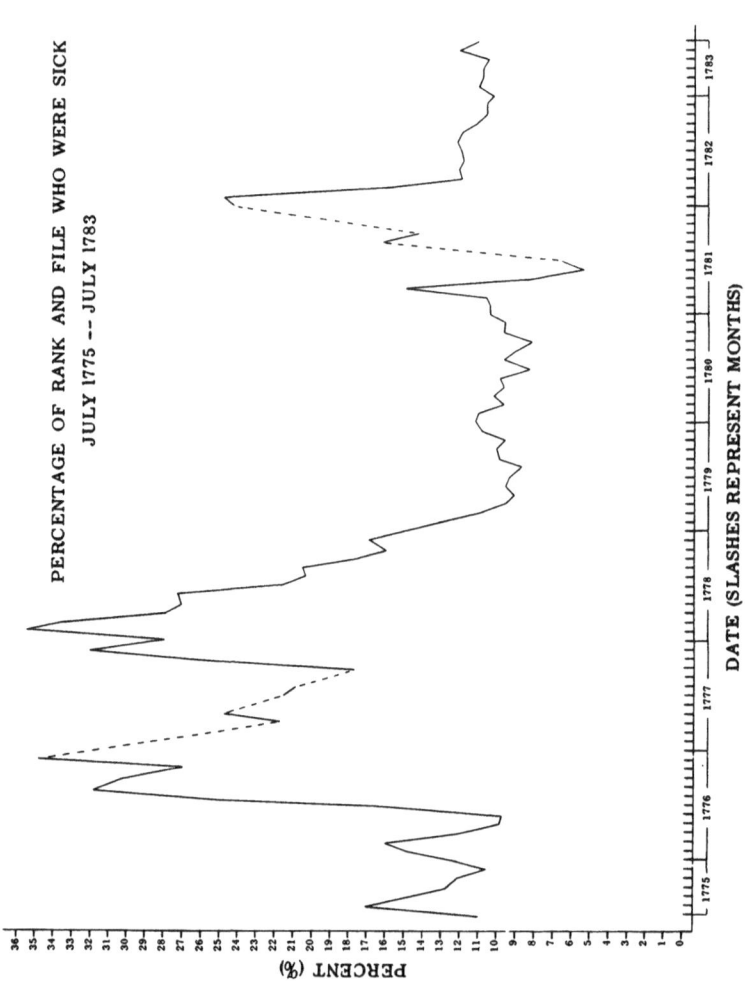

Notes

I. An Apprenticeship in Philadelphia

1. Potts Family Bible, Pottstown Historical Society. For bibliographic information, see Mrs. Thomas James, *Memorial of Thomas Potts, Junior* (Cambridge, Mass., 1874), pp. 170–211; Edward D. Neill, *Biographical Sketch of Dr. Jonathan Potts* (Albany, N.Y., 1863); Howard A. Kelly and Walter L. Burrage, *Dictionary of Medical Biography* (Baltimore: The Norman, Remington Co., 1920), pp. 932–933; Francis R. Packard, *History of Medicine in the United States*, 2 vols. (New York: Paul B. Haeber, Inc., 1931), **1**, pp. 359, 375; Dumas Malone, ed., *Dictionary of American Biography*, 20 Vols., (New York: C. Scribner's Sons, 1928–1936), **7**, p. 137; James Grant Wilson, and John Fiske, *Appleton's Cyclopaedia of American Biography*, 6 vols. (New York: D. Appleton and Co., 1900), **5**, p. 92.
2. Linda McCurdy, *The Potts Family Iron Industry in the Schuylkill Valley* (Pottstown, Pa.: Pottstown Historical Society, 1975), *passim*. See also Paul Chancellor and Marjorie Potts Wendell, *A History of Pottstown* (Pottstown, Pa.: Historical Society of Pottstown, 1953), pp. 1–33.
3. The Pennsylvania Historical and Museum Commission restored Pottsgrove Mansion in 1952. For descriptions of home, see Chancellor and Wendell, pp. 18–23, and McCurdy, pp. 124–125.
4. *Ibid.*, pp. 126–137.
5. Henry Melchior Muhlenberg, *Journals*, translated by Theodore G. Tappert, and John W. Doberstein, 3 vols. (Philadelphia: The Muhlenberg Press, 1945), **2**, p. 107.

Notes

6. McCurdy, pp. 140-142.
7. Eugene E. Doll, *The Ephrata Cloister* (Ephrata, Pa.: Carl Schurz Memorial Foundation, 1948), *passim*.
8. James, p. 183.
9. Five letters of the Bond brothers concerning their examinations of ship passengers are in the Gilbert Collection of Miscellaneous Letters, Library of the College of Physicians of Philadelphia, hereafter cited as Coll. Phys. Phil.
10. Thomas G. Morton, *The History of the Pennsylvania Hospital, 1751-1887*, (Philadelphia, 1897), p. 488; and James Thacher, *American Medical Biography* (Boston, 1828), p. 178.
11. Co-Partnership Ledgers of Thomas and Phineas Bond, 6 vols., 1751-1764, *passim.*, Coll. Phys. Phil.
12. Caspar Wistar, "State of Medicine from the first Settlement of Pennsylvania to the year, 1762," *The Eclectic Repertory and Analytical Review*, 7 (1818), 273-277.
13. Although I have been unable to find a medical apprentice's contract for Pennsylvania in this era, I have tried to reconstruct what may have been a typical one from Wyndham B. Blanton, *Medicine in Virginia in the Eighteenth Century* (Richmond, Va.: Garrett and Masie, 1931), pp. 77-78; Morton, p. 481 (an apothecary's indenture); J. William Frost, *The Quaker Family in Colonial America* (New York: St. Martins Press, 1973), p. 138; and a cordwainer's indenture (which is almost identical to the apothecary apprentice's contract) in Indentures of Apprentices, Society Miscellaneous Collections, Historical Society of Pennsylvania, hereafter Soc. Misc. Coll., and HSP. For a summary, see Genevieve Miller, "Medical Apprenticeships in the American Colonies," *Ciba Symposium*, 8 (1947), 502-510, hereafter *Ciba*. A New Jersey contract for a period of four years and eight months is described by Fred R. Rogers and A. Reasoner Sayre, *The Healing Art. A History of the Medical Society of New Jersey* (Trenton, N.J.: The Medical Society of New Jersey, 1966), p. 15.
14. *Pennsylvania Gazette,* July 3, 1740.
15. The Casebooks of Jonathan Elmer and Benjamin Duffield, Potts's fellow students, are in the Manuscript Collection, Coll. Phys. Phil.
16. George W. Corner, ed., *The Autobiography of Benjamin Rush* (Princeton, N.J.: Princeton University Press, 1948), p. 38.
17. Carl Bridenbaugh and Jessica Bridenbaugh, *Rebels and Gentlemen. Philadelphia in the Age of Franklin* (New York: Reynal

I. An Apprenticeship in Philadelphia

and Hitchock, 1942), pp. 263-303, *passim.*, and Carl Bridenbaugh, *Cities in Revolt. Urban Life in America, 1743-1776* (New York: Alfred A. Knopf, 1955), pp. 199-201, 409-410.
18. For Shippen's early life, see Betsy C. Corner, *William Shippen, Jr., Pioneer in American Medical Education* (Philadelphia: American Philosophical Society, 1951), and Herbert Thomas, "William Shippen, Jr., The Great Pioneer in American Obstetrics," *American Journal of Obstetrics and Gynecology,* **37** (1939), 512-517.
19. Jonathan Elmer, Lecture Notes (1766) with William Shippen, Manuscript Collection, National Library of Medicine.
20. L. H. Butterfield, ed., *The Diary and Autobiography of John Adams,* 4 vols. (Cambridge, Mass.: Harvard University Press, 1962-1968), **2**, p. 116.
21. For Morgan's career, see Whitfield Bell, Jr., *John Morgan. Continental Doctor* (Philadelphia: University of Pennsylvania Press, 1965).
22. Anon., "A Biographical Sketch of John Archer, M.B.," *Bulletin of the Johns Hopkins Hospital,* **10** (1899), 141-147, p. 145. See also Bell, "An Eighteenth Century American Manuscript. The Clinical Notebook of John Archer, M.B., 1768," *The Library Chronicle,* **22** (1956), 222-226.
23. Notebook of John Archer, ff. 5-6, 12; the Charles Patterson Van Pelt Library, the University of Pennsylvania.
24. James E. Gibson, *Dr. Bodo Otto and the Medical Background of the American Revolution* (Springfield, Ill.: Charles C. Thomas, 1937), p. 191. See also Toby Gelfand, "The Origins of a Modern Concept of Medical Specialization: John Morgan's *Discourse* of 1766," *Bulletin of the History of Medicine,* **50** (1976), 511-535, hereafter *Bull. Hist. Med.*
25. For a brief summary of Bond's career, see Elizabeth H. Thomson, "Thomas Bond, 1713-84, First Professor of Clinical Medicine in the American Colonies," *Journal of Medical Education,* **33** (1958), 614-624.
26. Bond's speech is cited in Morton, pp. 462-476.
27. For information about the Pennsylvania Hospital, see William H. Williams, *America's First Hospital, the Pennsylvania Hospital, 1751-1841* (Wayne, Pa.: Haverford House, Publishers, 1975), and Williams, "Independence and Early American Hospitals, 1751-1812," *Journal of the American Medical Association,* **236** (1976), 35-38, hereafter *J.A.M.A.*
28. Williams, *First Hospital. . . .,* p. 66.

29. Cited by Philip Padelford, ed., *Colonial Panorama. 1775: Dr. Robert Honyman's Journal for March and April* (San Marino, Ca.: The Huntington Library, 1939).
30. Butterfield, **2**, p. 116.
31. Williams, *First Hospital.* . . ., p. 67.
32. Minutes of the Board of Managers, 10 vols. 1751–1860, **3**, f. 159, Pennsylvania Hospital Historical Library, hereafter, Minutes.
33. Archer Notebook, f. 145.
34. Minutes, **4**, f. 72.
35. *Ibid.*, **3**, ff. 205–209.

II. A Term in Edinburgh

1. J. F. Watson, *Annals of Philadelphia*, 3 vols. (Philadelphia, 1899), **2**, p. 378.
2. I have extracted much information about the state of medicine in Philadelphia and in Edinburgh from George Corner, *Two Centuries of Medicine. A History of the School of Medicine* (Philadelphia: J. B. Lippincott Co., 1965), pp. 1–31; Betsy C. Corner, *Shippen, passim.;* Bell, *Morgan*, pp. 18–69; Bell, *The Colonial Physician and Other Essays* (New York: Science History Publications, 1975); and Francis R. Packard, "How London and Edinburgh Influenced Medicine in Philadelphia in the Eighteenth Century," *Annals of Medical History*, 4 (1932), 229–244, hereafter *Ann. Med. Hist.*
3. Thomas Ruston Journal, 1762–65, Thomas Ruston Papers, Manuscript Room, Library of Congress, hereafter, Lib. Cong.
4. For the Richardson family, see Martha Gandy Fales, *Joseph Richardson and Family, Philadelphia Silversmiths* (Middletown, Conn.: Wesleyan University Press, 1974).
5. L. H. Butterfield, ed., *The Letters of Benjamin Rush*, 2 vols. (Princeton, N.J.: Princeton University Press, 1951), **1**, p. 26.
6. Diary of Jonathan Potts, Private Source, Pottstown, hereafter Diary. For a summary of this diary, see Richard L. Blanco, "The Diary of Jonathan Potts: A Quaker Medical Student in Edinburgh (1766–67)," *Transactions and Studies of the College of Physicians of Philadelphia*, 44 (1977), 119–130.
7. Benjamin Rush. Journal Commencing August 31, 1766, Manuscript Room, Lilly Library, Indiana University, hereafter, Rush Journal.

II. A Term in Edinburgh

8. Diary.
9. Rush Journal, f. 13.
10. Diary.
11. James, p. 176.
12. Rush Journal, f. 13.
13. Cited by Bell, *Colonial Physician* . . ., p. 46.
14. See Betsy C. Corner, "Dr. Fothergill's Friendship with Benjamin Franklin," *American Philosophical Society Proceedings,* **102** (1958), 413-419; and Richard Hingston Fox, *Doctor John Fothergill and Friends* (London: Macmillan and Co., Ltd., 1919).
15. Diary.
16. Rush Journal, ff. 21-22.
17. Diary.
18. Manuscript Collection, American Philosophical Society, hereafter Mss. Coll., and APS.
19. Leonard W. Labaree, ed., *The Papers of Benjamin Franklin,* 18 vols. (New Haven, Conn.: Yale University Press, 1960), **13**, pp. 387, 404.
20. James, p. 172; Labaree **13**, p. 517.
21. I. Minis Hays, ed., *Calendar of the Papers of Benjamin Franklin,* 5 vols., (Philadelphia: American Philosophical Society, 1908) **3**, p. 463; and Labaree, **13**, p. 532.
22. Labaree, **13**, pp. 531-532.
23. I am indebted to Charles Finalyson, Keeper of Manuscripts, Edinburgh University Library, for providing me with data from the Matriculation Album about Potts's professors.
24. Walter Jones Letters, Roger Jones Family Papers, Lib. Cong.
25. Cited by Bell, "Medical Students and Their Examiners in Eighteenth Century America," *Transactions and Studies of the College of Physicians of Philadelphia,* **21** (1953), 13-25, p. 15, hereafter *Trans. Stud.*
26. Walter Jones Letters.
27. Butterfield, *Rush,* 1, p. 41.
28. James, p. 176.
29. Butterfield, *Rush,* 1, pp. 31-32
30. Diary.
31. James, p. 178.
32. *Ibid.*
33. Rush Journal, f. 35.
34. Diary.
35. Soc. Coll., HSP.
36. Autograph Collection, HSP, hereafter Auto. Coll.

Notes

37. Mss. Coll., APS.
38. Diary. The major work of Alexander Monro, *primus* (1697–1767), was *The Anatomy of the Humane Bones* (1726); Robert Whytt (1714–1766), President of the Royal College of Physicians of Edinburgh, published works on hysteria disorders and tuberculous meningitis that became medical classics. Thomas Sydenham (1624–1689), "the English Hippocrates," was a venerated clinician and an authority on internal medicine; his major works were translated from Latin by 1699. Potts may have purchased John Swain's edition of *The Whole Works of Thomas Sydenham*, printed in 1749 and in 1753. Pringle's pioneering study on military medicine, *Observations on Diseases of the Army in Camp and Garrison*, was published in 1752, and was available in many editions. Carl von Linné (Linnaeus), (1707–1778), the writer of innumerable scientific works, was the founder of the modern system of botanical nomenclature.
39. Frost, pp. 150–168, 172–174, 180.
40. Soc. Coll., HSP.
41. I am grateful to J. William Frost, Director of the Friends Historical Library, Swarthmore College, for providing me with a photostat copy of a page from the Minutes of the Philadelphia Monthly Meeting (October 30, 1767), and for additional information about the ramifications of the Potts marriage ceremony.
42. Potts is listed only once (May 5, 1767) in a manuscript by John E. Eshelman, Records of Quakers in Berks County Historical Society. For information about the Quakers in Berks, see Eshelman, "The Society of Friends and Their Meeting House in Berks County," *Berks County Historical Review*, **29** (1954), 104–109, 117–123, hereafter *Berks Cty. Hist. Rev.*
43. Butterfield, *Rush*, 1, p. 64.

III. The Medical World of Jonathan Potts

1. For discussions of contemporary medical concepts, see Blanton, pp. 1–7; Richard H. Shryock, "Eighteenth Century Medicine in America," *American Antiquarian Society*, **59** (1949), 275–292; and especially, Lester S. King, *The Medical World of the Eighteenth Century* (Chicago: University of Chicago Press, 1963).

III. The Medical World of Jonathan Potts

2. James Tilton, *Economical Observations on Military Hospitals* (Wilmington, Del., 1813), pp. 52-53.
3. Rush is cited by Cecil K. Drinker, *Not So Long Ago. A Chronicle of Medicine and Doctors in Colonial Philadelphia* (New York: Oxford University Press, 1937), pp. 145-147.
4. William Buchan, *Domestic Medicine, or the Family Physician* (Boston, 1778), pp. 411-412.
5. I have extracted information about disease from Blanton, pp. 60-68; John Duffy, *Epidemics in Colonial America* (Baton Rouge, La.: Louisiana State University Press, 1953); Gordon W. Jones, "Medicine in Virginia in Revolutionary Times," *Journal of the History of Medicine and Allied Sciences,* 31 (1976), 250-270, hereafter *J. Hist. Med.;* John B. Blake, "Disease and Medical Practice in Colonial America," in Felix Marti-Ibañez, ed., *History of American Medicine* (New York: M.D. Publications, Inc., 1958), pp. 34-37; E. B. Krumbhaar, "The State of Pathology in the British Colonies of North America," *Yale Journal of Biology and Medicine,* 19 (1946-1947), 801-815, hereafter *Yale J. Bio. Med.;* J. Worth Estes, "As Healthy a Place as Any in America: Revolutionary Portsmouth, N. H." *Bull. Hist. Med.,* 50 (1976), 636-652; David L. Cowen, *Medicine and Health in New Jersey* (Princeton, N.J.: D. Van Nostrand, Inc., 1964); Cowen, *Medicine in Revolutionary America* (Trenton, N.J.: New Jersey Historical Commission, 1976); and Ernest Caulfield, "Some Common Diseases of Colonial Children," *Publications of the Colonial Society of Massachusetts,* 35 (1942-1946), 4-65.
6. The background of smallpox is covered by John B. Blake, *Public Health in the Town of Boston, 1630-1822* (Cambridge, Mass.: Harvard University Press, 1959).
7. For information on surgery, see Blanton, pp. 11-18, and John Duffy, *The Healers: The Rise of the Medical Establishment* (New York: McGraw-Hill Book Co., 1976), pp. 13-18.
8. Potts Day Book, 1767-1772, *passim,* HSP.
9. *Ibid.*
10. Marion E. Brown, "Adam Kuhn: Eighteenth Century Physician and Teacher," *J. Hist. Med.,* 5 (1950), 163-177.
11. Cited in Frederick P. Henry, *Standard History of the Medical Profession of Philadelphia* (Chicago, 1897), p. 65. For the B.M. degree, see Frederick C. Waites, "The Degree of Bachelor of Medicine in the American Colonies and the United States," *Yale J. Bio. Med.,* 10 (1937-1938), 309-333.

12. James, pp. 106–115.
13. Potts Day Book.
14. Potts Journal, 1767–1775, *passim,* HSP; Cowen, *Medicine and Health,* pp. 10–14. The Bonds' fees are in Drinker, p. 145, and in Bell, *Morgan,* p. 153. Archer's are in Bell, "Archer ... ," and Mercer's are in Henry Woodhouse, "Colonial Medical Practice," *Ciba,* **1** (1940), 379–389.
15. Stephen Wickes, *History of Medicine and Medical Men in New Jersey* (Newark, 1879), pp. 9–13; and Medical Society of New Jersey, *Transactions of the Medical Society of New Jersey* (Newark, 1858), pp. 8–9.
16. Jonathan Potts, *Intermittent Fever Especially Those of the Tertian Type* (Philadelphia: 1776). The dissertation was translated from Latin into English by Maria Wilkins Smith in 1964, Coll. Phys. Phil.
17. Bell, "Medical Students ... ," pp. 14–24.
18. Labaree, **19**, p. 64.
19. Johann David Schoepf, "Travels Through Berks County in 1783," *Pennsylvania Magazine of History and Biography,* **5** (1881), 74–81, p. 76, hereafter *PMHB*.
20. *Ibid.*
21. Potts Day Book.
22. For income levels, see Jackson Turner Main, *The Social Structure of Revolutionary America* (Princeton, N.J.: Princeton University Press, 1965), pp. 99–100, 113, 144–46.
23. *Pennsylvania Gazette,* September 28, 1772.
24. See Harold B. Gill, Jr., *The Apothecary in Colonial Virginia,* (Charlottesville, Va.: University Press of Virginia, 1972); Cowen, *America's Pre-Pharmaceutical Literature* (Madison, Wisc.: American Institute of the History of Pharmacy, 1961); and Glenn Sonnedecker, *Kremers and Urgang's History of Pharmacy* (New York: J. P. Lippincott, 1976), pp. 145–171.
25. Cited in Bridenbaugh, *Rebels,* p. 296.
26. James, pp. 183–184.
27. David C. Humphreys, "The King's College Medical School and the Professionalization of Medicine in Pre-Revolutionary New York," *Bull. Hist. Med.,* **49** (1975), 206–234.
28. Henry K. Beecher, and Mark D. Altschule, *Medicine at Harvard. The First Hundred Years* (Hanover, N.H.: University Press of New England, 1977), pp. 3–19.
29. Richard H. Shryock, *Medical Licensing in America, 1650–1965* (Baltimore: Johns Hopkins University Press, 1967), pp. 3–19.

IV. The Doctor as a Patriot

1. Cited in Raymond Albright, *Two Centuries of Reading, Pennsylvania, 1748-1948* (Reading: Historical Society of Berks County, 1948), p. 64; and in Morton L. Montgomery, *History of Berks County* (Reading, 1894), pp. 23-24.
2. *Pennsylvania Archives*, 2nd Ser., 3, pp. 470-478, hereafter *Pa. Arch.*
3. Cited in Merrill Jensen, *The Founding of a Nation* (New York: Oxford University Press, 1969), p. 495.
4. For Miller's role, see Arthur D. Graeff, "The Relations Between the Pennsylvania Germans and the British Authorities," *Pennsylvania-German Society Proceedings*, 47 (1939), 20-31; Daniel Miller, "Early German American Newspapers," *Ibid.*, 18-19, (1907-1908), 5-33.
5. Potts Papers, ff. 1-4, HSP, hereafter P.P.
6. Soc. Misc. Coll., HSP.
7. Montgomery, pp. 30-31.
8. P.P., f. 56.
9. Albright, pp. 65-69; Montgomery, pp. 32-38; *Pa. Arch.* 2nd, Ser., 10, pp. 35-36; John Linn and William H. Egle, *Pennsylvania in the War of the American Revolution.* 2 vols. (Harrisburg, 1880), 1, pp. 321-323.
10. Cited by William G. Clemens, "Nagle's Company. First to Cambridge," *Berks Cty. Hist. Rev.*, 7 (1942), 107-110, p. 108.
11. *Ibid.*, p. 110. The actual date of the arrival of the first rifle company and that of subsequent rifle companies remain a puzzle. The Orderly Book of Edward Burd of Nagle's Company (Lib. Cong.) begins on July 3, 1775, and ends on September 24, 1775.
12. Cited by Kenneth Roberts, ed., *March to Quebec* (New York: Doubleday, Doran and Co., 1938), p. 509.
13. Soc. Misc. Coll., HSP.
14. Mss. Coll., APS.
15. The Edward Hand Papers, Manuscript Room, New York Public Library, hereafter, N. Y. Pub. Lib.
16. Mss. Coll., Berks County Historical Society; and Jonathan Potts Account Book, HSP.
17. For information about Boston, I have relied heavily on Philip Cash, *Medical Men at the Siege of Boston, April, 1775-April, 1776* (Philadelphia: American Philosophical Society, 1973). A useful article is J. Worth Estes, "Medical Letters from the Siege of Boston," *J. Hist. Med.*, 31 (1976), 271-291.

18. John Hennen, *Military Surgery* (London: 1820), p. 30. For the background of the British army medical department in the eighteenth century, see Richard L. Blanco, *Wellington's Surgeon-General: Sir James McGrigor* (Durham, N.C.: Duke University Press, 1974), pp. 8-24. Some information about the French army medical department is in Lee Kennett, *The French Armies in the Seven Year's War* (Durham, N.C.: Duke University Press, 1967), pp. 13-17.
19. Benjamin Rush, *Medical Inquiries and Observations,* 2 vols. (Philadelphia, 1794), 1, p. 260.
20. John Ranby, *Method of Treating Gunshot Wounds* (London, 1781, 3rd ed.), pp. 21, 30, 121.
21. John Jones, *Plain Concise Practical Remarks On the Treatment of Wounds and Fractures.* (Boston, 1776).
22. Richard Brocklesby, *Oeconomical and Medical Observations in Two Parts, From the Year 1758 to the Year 1764, Inclusive. Tending to the Improvement of Military Hospitals and to the Cure of Camp Diseases Incident to Soldiers* (London, 1764).
23. Donald Monro, *An Account of the Diseases which were most frequent in the British Military Hospitals in Germany* (London, 1764). An expanded edition is Monro, *Observations on the Means of Preserving the Health of Soldiers and of Constituting Military Hospitals and On the Diseases Incident to Soldiers,* 2 vols. (London, 1780).
24. John Pringle, *Observations on Diseases of the Army in Camp and Garrison* (London, 1752). The casualty figure is cited by Henry Steele Commager and Richard B. Morris, eds., *The Spirit of Seventy-Six,* 2 vols. (Indianapolis, Ind.: Bobbs-Merrill, 1958), **2**, p. 815.
25. Tilton, p. 9.
26. James Thacher, *A Military Journal During the American Revolutionary War from 1775-1783* (Boston, 1827), pp. 35-36.
27. Papers of the Continental Congress, National Archives. Item 152, Roll 166, vol. 1, f. 39. Hereafter P.C.C., and N.A.
28. Cited by Louis C. Duncan, *Medical Men in the American Revolution, 1775-1783* (Carlisle Barracks, Pa.: Medical Field Service School, 1931), p. 16.
29. Cash, p. 105.
30. Pa. Arch., 1st Ser., 4, pp. 679, 696; 5, pp. 77, 112; and *Journals of the Continental Congress,* 34 vols. (Washington, 1904-37), 4, pp. 229, 271, hereafter *J.C.C.*
31. P.C.C., Item 78, Roll 100, vol. 18, ff. 56-57.

V. The Canadian Campaign and Fort Ticonderoga

32. Peter Force, *American Archives,* 4th Ser., **6**, pp. 1699, 1067, hereafter Force.
33. James, p. 186.
34. Potts Papers, Fort Ticonderoga Museum, hereafter, P.P. at FTM.

V. The Canadian Campaign and Fort Ticonderoga

1. P.P., ff. 68–69.
2. Roberts, p. 205. For a summary of the early phase of the Canadian campaign, see Philip Cash, "The Canadian Military Campaign of 1775–1776: Medical Problems and Effects of Disease," *JAMA,* **236** (1976), 52–56.
3. Schuyler Letterbooks, July 31, 1775, Reel 29, Philip Schuyler Papers, N. Y. Pub. Lib., Hereafter S.P.
4. Cited by Morris H. Saffron, *Surgeon to Washington. Dr. John Cochran (1730–1807)* (New York: Columbia University Press, 1977), p. 272.
5. Stringer to Schuyler, July 2, Albany; October 6, 8, 10, Fort George, Letters to Schuyler, 1772–75, Box 24, Reel 12, S.P.
6. Benjamin Trumbull, "A Concise Journal or Minutes of the Principal Movements Toward St. John in 1775," *Connecticut Historical Society Collections,* **7** (1899), 139–173, p. 146.
7. Montgomery to Schuyler, October 9, Camp near St. Jean's Letters to Schuyler, 1772–75, Box 24, Reel 12, S.P.
8. Trumbull, p. 160.
9. Roberts, p. 484.
10. *Ibid.,* p. 230.
11. *Ibid.,* p. 574.
12. *Ibid., p. 443.*
13. *Ibid.,* p. 238.
14. P.C.C., Item 161, Roll 197, ff. 309–311.
15. Thomas to Congress, May 5, 1775, copy, Letters, Box 40, Reel 20, S.P.
16. Butterfield, *Adams,* **2**, pp. 65–66.
17. Frederick R. Kirkland, ed., "Journal of a Physician on the Expedition Against Canada, 1776," *PMHB,* **59** (1935), 321–361, p. 327.
18. Force, 5th. Ser., **1**, 129.

Notes

19. *Ibid.,* 4th Ser., **6**, 589–593.
20. P.C.C., Item 153, Roll 172, Vol. 2, f. 215.
21. Kirkland, p. 333.
22. Arnold to Schuyler, June 10, 1776, Letters, Box 39, Reel 19, S.P.
23. Stringer to Schuyler, June 7, 12, and 22, Letters to Schuyler, Box 27, Reel 13, *ibid..*
24. For an imaginative account of this episode, see Kenneth Roberts, *Rabble in Arms* (New York: Doubleday and Co., Inc., 1950), pp. 162–164, 199–200.
25. Kirkland, p. 336.
26. Force, 4th ser., **6**, p. 1220.
27. Cited by Theodore Sizer, *The Autobiography of Colonel John Trumbull, Patriot-Artist, 1756–1843* (New Haven, Conn.: Yale University Press, 1953), p. 27.
28. L. H. Butterfield, Wendell D. Garrett, and Margaret Sprague, eds., *Adams Family Correspondence,* 2 vols. (Cambridge, Mass.: Belknap Press of Harvard, 1963), **2**, pp. 37–38; and Force, 4th Ser., **6**, p. 1083.
29. P.C.C. Item 152, Roll 166, vol. 2, f. 237.
30. Charles Henry Jones, *The Campaign for the Conquest of Canada* (Philadelphia, 1882), p. 97.
31. Arnold to Schuyler, Albany, June 25, Reel 36, S.P.
32. Butterfield, *Adams,* **2**, p. 65.
33. Force, 5th Ser., **1**, p. 607.
34. P.P., f. 70.
35. Force, 5th Ser., **1**, p. 607.
36. Harold E. Brown, *The Medical Department of the Army from 1775 to 1873* (Washington, 1873), p. 21; and Revolutionary War Papers, Item 135, Roll 137, f. 170, N.A. hereafter Rev. War P.
37. Force, 5th Ser., **1**, pp. 651–652, 857.
38. Potts to Gates, August 8, Fort George, Box 4, Reel 2, Gates Papers, New-York Historical Society, hereafter, G.P., and N.Y.H.S.
39. P.P., f. 86.
40. Morgan to Potts, P.P. at FTM. See also Mss. 1962, Fort Ticonderoga Museum, hereafter, FTM. See also Morgan to Stringer, June 24, 1776, Mss. 1093, New York Academy of Medicine.
41. Morgan to Potts, July 12, P.P. at FTM.
42. P.P., f. 77.
43. Force, 5th Ser., **1**, pp. 919–922.

V. The Canadian Campaign and Fort Ticonderoga

44. Gibson, p. 108.
45. Force, 5th Ser., 1, 651-652.
46. *Ibid.*, 5th Ser., 1, 1146.
47. Mss. 1967, FTM.
48. Force, 5th Ser., 2, 277.
49. James Sullivan, ed., *Minutes of the Albany Committee of Correspondence* 2 vols., (Albany, N.Y.: University of the State of New York, 1923), 1, pp. 531-55. The Albany Committee also dispatched two medical chests from civilian sources.
50. Gibson, pp. 108-109.
51. *Ibid.*, p. 110.
52. Cited by Silas R. Coburn, *History of Dracut, Massachusetts* (Lowell: Press of the Courier-Citizen, 1922), p. 22.
53. Force, 5th Ser., 2, 574.
54. *Ibid.*, 5th Ser., 1, 653-655, 800, 1128, 1270-1271.
55. Force, 5th Ser., 1, 1114.
56. Soc. Mis. Coll., H.S.P.
57. P.C.C., Item 171, Roll 190, ff. 13-14.
58. Duncan, p. 110.
59. "Letters from Dr. Samuel Kennedy to His Wife in 1776," *PMHB*, 8 (1884), 111-116, p. 115.
60. Kirkland, p. 346.
61. Thomas William Baldwin, ed., *The Revolutionary Journal of Colonel Jeduthan Baldwin, 1775-1778* (Bangor, Maine: DeBurians, 1906), p. 63.
62. Sizer, p. 28.
63. James Wilkinson, *Memoirs of My Own Times,* 3 vols. (Philadelphia, 1816), 1, p. 86.
64. P.P., f. 94.
65. P.P., ff. 102-106, 108-111, 114, 119, and Force, 5th Ser., 1, p. 1266. For details on the drug inventory, see George A. Griffenhagen, "Drug Supplies in the American Revolution," *National Museum Bulletin,* No. 225, (1961), 110-133.
66. Ammi Robbins, *Journal of Ammi R. Robbins, Chaplain in the American Army in the Northern Campaign of 1776* (New Haven, Conn., 1850), p. 33.
67. Orderly Book of Horatio Gates Commanding the Northern Army of the United States From 10 June, 1776 to 3 June, 1777, f. 24, N.-Y. Hist. Soc.
68. P.C.C., Item 152, Roll 166, vol. 2, ff. 205-207.
69. Butterfield, 2, pp. 61-62.

70. Force, 5th Ser., 1, p. 28. See also *Ibid.*, 5th Ser., 1, pp. 145, 399–400.
71. Thacher, p. 51.
72. Force, 4th Ser., 6, p. 820.
73. P.C.C., Item 191, Roll 190, ff. 13–14.
74. Box 4, Reel 2, G.P.
75. Force, 5th Ser., 1, p. 1203, and S.P., August 17, Reel 29.
76. Gibson, p. 102.
77. P.C.C., Item 154, Roll 174, f. 59.
78. Force, 5th Ser., 1, 1146.
79. *Ibid.*, 1197.
80. Gibson, p. 101.
81. October 25, 1775, Box 4, Reel 2, G.P.
82. Force, 5th Ser., 2, 67–68, and 5th Ser., 1, 1079–1080. See also Charles H. Lesser, *The Sinews of Independence* (Chicago: University of Chicago Press, 1976), p. 30.
83. September 1, 1776, Box 4, Reel 2, G.P.
84. "Letters from Ticonderoga, 1776," *Bulletin of the Fort Ticonderoga Museum* 10 (1961), 386–398; 11 (1962), 450–459, p. 452.
85. Adams to Sally Adams, November 9, 1776, Dr. Samual Adams Letters, Sol Feinstone Collection, Boston Public Library.
86. Thacher, p. 66.
87. Cited by Charles J. Stillé, *Major-General Anthony Wayne and the Pennsylvania Line in the Continental Army* (Port Washington, New York: Kennikat Press, 1968), p. 41.
88. Mss. 1974, FTM, and Gates Orderly Book, f. 73.
89. Mss. 1952, FTM.
90. Force, 5th Ser., 1, 1129.
91. Mss. 1961, FTM.
92. Mss. 130, FTM, and McNeill, p. 11.
93. Thacher, p. 64.
94. John Trumbull, *Autobiography, Reminiscences, and Letters of John Trumbull from 1756 to 1811* (New York, 1811), p. 36.
95. Brown, p. 28.
96. Force, 5th Ser., 3, 1592–93.
97. P.P., f. 136. See also *Ibid.*, f. 138, and Stringer to Schuyler, November 7, 1776, Mss. 1976, FTM.
98. Miscellaneous Bound Manuscripts, Massachusetts Historical Society. The unsigned return indicates that before the fleet action in October, 324 died in the hospitals, 1,127 were returned to duty, and 1,892 were discharged.
99. Mss. 195, FTM.

VI. With Washington on the Delaware

1. For an account of the hygienic problems encountered by the army in New York City, see Morris H. Saffron, "Rebels and Disease: The New York Campaign of 1776," *Academy of Medicine of New Jersey Bulletin,* **13** (1967), 107–118. Some information about the 1776 campaign in lower New York and in New Jersey is in Duncan, pp. 111–188, and in Bell, *Morgan,* pp. 187–205.
2. Cited by Saffron, p. 111.
3. John Morgan, *Vindication of His Public Character in the Station of Director-General of the Military Hospital* (Boston, 1777), p. 103.
4. John C. Fitzpatrick, ed., *The Writings of George Washington from the Original Manuscript Sources, 1745–1799,* 39 vols. (Washington, D.C.: U.S. Government Printing Office, 1931–1944), **6**, p. 113.
5. Thomas J. Fleming, *1776. The Year of Illusion* (New York: W. W. Norton and Co., Inc., 1975), p. 292.
6. Cited by Duncan, p. 135.
7. Cited by Saffron, p. 107
8. Robert G. Albion, and Leonidas Dodson, eds., *Philip Vickers Fithian, Journal, 1775–1776* (Princeton, N.J.: Princeton University Press, 1934), p. 193.
9. Rufus Rockwell Wilson, *Heath's Memoirs of the American War* (New York, 1904), p. 61.
10. Fitzpatrick, **4**, p. 477.
11. Richard K. Showman, ed., *The Papers of Nathanael Greene,* 1 vol. (Chapel Hill, N.C.: University of North Carolina Press, 1976), **1**, pp. 234, 238.
12. Francisco Guerra, *American Medical Biography* (New York: Lathrop C. Harper, Inc., 1962), p. 588.
13. Ebenezer Beardsley, "History of a dysentery in the 22nd regiment of the late continental army," *The American Museum,* **5** (1789), 249–250.
14. Fitzpatrick, **5**, p. 285; **6**, pp. 53–54.
15. Estimates are in Saffron, p. 112; Duncan, pp. 130–136, 143, 148; Fleming, p. 291; and Lesser, p. xxxi. For a summary of sickness rates, see Appendix 2.
16. Duncan, pp. 150–151.
17. Morgan, pp. 20–21.
18. Fitzpatrick, **13**, p. 480–482.
19. Showman, **1**, pp. 312–313.

Notes

20. Alfred L. Elwyn, ed., *Letters by Josiah Bartlett, William Whipple and Others* (Philadelphia, 1889), p. 58.
21. Force, 5th Ser., **2**, pp. 1099-1100.
22. Pa. Arch., 1st Ser., **5**, p. 630.
23. Henry Phelps Johnson, *Memoir of Colonel Benjamin Tallmadge* (New York, 1904), p. 20.
24. Wilkinson, **1**, p. 117.
25. Tilton, p. 29.
26. Fitzpatrick, **13**, p. 482.
27. *Ibid.*, **6**, pp. 327-328.
28. Pa. Arch., 1st Ser., **5**, pp. 78-79.
29. *Ibid.*, 1st Ser., **5**, pp. 89-90. See also Joseph M. Toner, *The Medical Men of the Revolution* (Philadelphia, 1876), pp. 52-53.
30. Thomas Wharton to Potts, December 5, Potts Papers, Lib. Cong., and Wharton to Potts, Dec. 10, P.P., f. 139, HSP.
31. Morgan, p. 19, and P.P., f. 14.
32. William Duane, ed., *Extracts from the Diary of Christopher Marshall Kept in Philadelphia and Lancaster During the American Revolution, 1774-1781* (Albany, N.Y., 1877), p. 295; and Duncan, pp. 170-171.
33. Howard Kendell Sanderson, *Lynn in the Revolution* (Boston: W. B. Clark Co., 1909), pp. 156-157.
34. Tilton, p. 63.
35. Butterfield, Adams, **2**, p. 209.
36. Ethel Ames, *Nancy Shippen, Her Journal Book* (Boston: Lippincott, 1909), pp. 156-157.
37. Duncan, pp. 172-174. John W. Jordon, "Bethlehem During the Revolution. Extracts from the Moravian Archives at Bethlehem," *PMHB*, **12** (1888), 385-406.
38. Force, 5th Ser., **3**, p. 1119.
39. *Ibid.*, 5th Ser., **3**, pp. 1258-59.
40. Cited by Saffron, p. 27.
41. Cited by Duncan, p. 176.
42. William S. Stryker, *The Battles of Trenton and Princeton* (Boston and New York, 1898), p. 431.
43. Corner, *Rush*, pp. 128-129.
44. Catherine Williams, *Biographies of Revolutionary War Heroes* (Providence, R.I., 1839), pp. 196-197.
45. Benjamin Cowell, *Spirit of '76 in Rhode Island* (Boston, 1850), p. 305.
46. Sergeant R., "The Battle of Princeton," *PMHB*, **20** (1896), 515-519, p. 515.

VII. With Gates at Saratoga

47. Corner, *Rush,* pp. 128-129.
48. Wilkinson, 1, p. 141.
49. Sergeant R., p. 517.
50. Stryker, p. 445. The original document is in P.C.C., Item 78, Roll 100, vol. 18, ff. 121-122.
51. Stryker, pp. 449-452.
52. *Ibid.,* p. 445. See also Edward D. Neill, "Death of Anthony Morris," *PMHB,* 1 (1877), 175-180, p. 177. For a vivid, contemporary description of the fighting and of the treatment of the wounded on the Clark homestead, see Varnum Lansing Collins, *A Brief Narrative of the Ravages of the British and Hessians at Princeton in 1775-1776* (Princeton, N.J.: The University Library, 1906).
53. P.P., f. 209. Robert Townshend, another surgeon, submitted an expense account to Potts for services rendered at the Head of the Elk and at Bristol from December 17, 1776, to January 12, 1777. P.P., Lib. Cong.
54. Brown to Rush, December 27, 1776, Rush Papers, HSP.
55. Isaac Foster Papers, Lib. Cong.
56. Richard Henry Lee, *Memoir of the Life of Richard Henry Lee,* 2 vols. (Philadelphia, 1825), 2, p. 169.
57. James Curtis Ballagh, ed., *The Letters of Richard Henry Lee,* 2 vols. (New York: The Macmillan Co., 1912-14), 1, pp. 166-167.
58. Edmund C. Burnett, ed., *Letters of the Members of the Continental Congress,* 8 vols. (Washington, D.C.: The Carnegie Institute of Washington, 1921-1936), 2, pp. 211-212.
59. Cited in Gibson, pp. 135-136.
60. The George Washington Papers, Shippen to Washington, January, 25, 1777, Reel 39, Lib. Cong., hereafter G.W.P.
61. Butterfield, *Adams,* 2, p. 209.
62. *Pennsylvania Evening Post,* June 5, 1777.
63. *Pennsylvania Packet,* April 22, 1777.
64. Duncan, p. 153; Gibson, p. 131; Howard H. Peckham, *The Toll of Independence* (Chicago: University of Chicago Press, 1974), p. 28.

VII. With Gates at Saratoga

1. Fitzpatrick, **6**, p. 473.
2. Trumbull to Washington, February 24, 1777, Reel 40, G.W.P.

3. Joseph H. Jones, *The Life of Ashbel Green* (New York, 1849), p. 90.
4. Hugh Thursfield, "Smallpox in the American War of Independence," *Ann. Med. Hist.*, 3rd Ser., 4 (1942), 312–318, p. 316; and Gibson, p. 84.
5. Cited by Saffron, p. 35.
6. Butterfield, *Adams*, 2, p. 219.
7. P.C.C., Item 170, Roll 189, f. 123.
8. Wayne to Schuyler, February 2, 1777, transcript in FTM.
9. P.C.C., Item 170, Roll 189, ff. 141–142.
10. Letterbook IV, 1775–78, Reel 29, S.P.
11. P.P., f. 152; and James, pp. 191–192.
12. Mss. 2134, FTM.
13. Jordan, p. 398.
14. P.P., f. 154.
15. *Ibid.*, f. 16.
16. *Ibid.*, f. 199.
17. Thacher, p. 79.
18. Mss. 2132, FTM.
19. James, pp. 194–196.
20. *Ibid.*, pp. 193–194.
21. *Ibid.*, pp. 195–196.
22. Potts to Wayne, April 21, Albany, Wayne Papers, HSP.
23. James, pp. 196–197.
24. P.P., f. 182.
25. *Ibid.*, f. 144.
26. Mss. 2109, FTM.
27. Baldwin, p. 100.
28. "Diary of Enos Hitchcock, D.D. A Chaplain in the Revolutionary Army," *Publications of the Rhode Island Historical Society*, 7 (1889), 105–225, p. 113.
29. Schuyler Letters, Reel 28, S.P.
30. "Trial of Major General St. Clair," *Revolutionary and Miscellaneous Papers, 3, Collections of the New York Historical Society for the Year 1880* (New York, 1881), p. 29.
31. James, pp. 198–199.
32. *Ibid.*, p. 195.
33. Pa. Arch., 1st Ser., 5, p. 350.
34. Varick to Schuyler, April 7 and 12, Letters to Schuyler, Box 32, Reel 15, S.P.
35. Mss. 2122, FTM.
36. Schuyler to Congress, June 21, 1777, Letterbook, Reel 29, S.P.

VII. With Gates at Saratoga

37. Schuyler to Potts, June 21, Schuyler Letters, Reel 28, *ibid.*
38. Thacher, p. 85.
39. James, pp. 200–201.
40. *Trumbull Letters, Massachusetts Historical Collections,* 5th Ser., **10** (1898), p. 141.
41. Schuyler to Washington, July 24, Provision Returns, Box 49, Reel 24, S.P.
42. P.P., ff. 263, 266.
43. *Ibid.,* f. 249.
44. *Ibid.,* f. 284.
45. *Ibid.,* f. 269.
46. *Ibid.,* f. 247.
47. Jonathan Potts to Samuel Potts, July 28, 1777, Soc. Coll., HSP.
48. P.P., f. 281.
49. *Ibid.,* f. 287.
50. Mss. 1957 FTM, and the Papers of Benjamin Lincoln, vol. 2, Reel 2, f. 194, Mass. Hist. Soc.
51. P.P., ff. 295, 298, 307.
52. *Ibid.,* f. 279.
53. *Ibid.,* f. 300.
54. Lloyd A. Brown and Howard W. Peckham, ed., *Journal of Henry Dearborn, 1776–1783* (Chicago: Caxton Club, 1939), p. 111.
55. Mss. 20897, Roll 67, M859, RG 93, National Archives.
56. Varick to Schuyler, September 19, Stillwater, Reel 19, S.P.
57. See Allen C. Wooden, "The Wounds and Weapons of the Revolutionary War from 1775 to 1783," *Delaware Medical Journal,* **33** (1972), 59–65. The best summary of battlefield surgery in the eighteenth century is by Donald M. Vess, *Medical Revolution in France 1789–1796* (Gainesville, Fl., 1975), pp. 117–136.
58. Cited by Duncan, pp. 120–121.
59. Ranby, p. 19
60. John Jones, p. 93.
61. Cited in Robert Graves, *Sergeant Lamb's America* (New York: Alfred A. Knopf, 1962), p. 315.
62. Box 7, Reel 3, G.P.
63. Wilkinson, **1**, p. 282.
64. *Ibid.*
65. Box 8, Reel 4, G.P.
66. James, p. 203.
67. P.P., f. 339.
68. Sullivan, **1**, pp. 186, 823.
69. P.P., ff. 372, 384.

Notes

70. Thacher, pp. 113–115.
71. Marvin L. Brown, Jr., *Baroness Von Riedesel and the American Revolution. Journal and Correspondence for a Tour of Duty, 1776–1783* (Chapel Hill, N.C.: University of North Carolina Press, 1965), p. 58.
72. Graves, p. 322.
73. Wilkinson, **1**, p. 282.
74. James, p. 203.
75. Mss. 2123 FTM; and P.P., ff. 315, 331, 346.
76. Cited by Hiram Bingham, Jr., *Five Straws Gathered from Revolutionary Fields* (Cambridge, Mass., 1901), p. 11.
77. Wilkinson, **1**, p. 267.
78. Duncan, p. 259; P.P., f. 273.
79. Wilkinson, **1**, p. 243.
80. P.P., f. 388.
81. *Ibid.*, f. 293.
82. Rush to Washington, February 28, Princeton, Reel 47, G.W.P.
83. Mss. 2103 FTM; October 20, Reel 44, G.W.P.
84. J.C.C., **9**, pp. 870–871.

VIII. The Valley Forge Hospitals

1. Cited by John Smith Hanna, *A History of the Life and Services of Captain Samuel Dewees* (Baltimore, 1885), p. 94.
2. Journal of Major Joseph Bloomfield, Library, New Jersey Historical Society.
3. Muhlenberg, **2**, pp. 82–84.
4. Tilton, p. 29.
5. Cited by Commager, **2**, pp. 832–833.
6. Cited by Worthington Chauncey Ford, *Defense of Philadelphia in 1777* (New York: DeCapo, 1971), pp. 167–168.
7. Fitzpatrick, **10**, p. 150.
8. Jordan, p. 405.
9. Cited by James M. Beck, *Bethlehem and Its Military Hospitals* (Bethlehem, Pa., 1897), p. 13.
10. Francis Alison, Jr. A List of Soldiers and Attending Nurses in the Court House Hospital and the Brick House Hospital at Reading, Pa., Nov. 17, 1777, M-29-25, Coll. Phys. Phil.
11. P.P., f. 383.
12. Cited by John B. B. Trussell Jr., *Birthplace of an Army. A Study*

VIII. The Valley Forge Hospitals

of the Valley Forge Encampment (Harrisburg, Pa.: Pennsylvania Historical and Museum Commission, 1976), p. 41.
13. Cited by George L. Heiges, "Letters Relating to the Continental Military Hospitals in Lancaster County," *Lancaster County Historical Papers,* **52** (1948), 73–96, p. 94.
14. *Ibid.,* p. 94.
15. *Ibid.*
16. Lesser, p. xxxi. See Appendix II.
17. Gibson, p. 153.
18. Tilton, pp. 14–15.
19. Rush, *Medical Inquiries,* **1**, p. 258.
20. Tilton, pp. 59–60.
21. Fitzpatrick, **10**, p. 233.
22. Cited by John F. Reed, *Valley Forge, Crucible of Victory* (Monmouth Beach, N.J.: Philip Freneau Press, 1969), p. 5.
23. Butterfield, *Rush,* pp. 195–196.
24. Cited by Heiges, p. 95
25. P.C.C., Item 78, Roll 100, vol. 18, f. 367.
26. Butterfield, *Rush,* pp. 154–176, *passim.*
27. *Ibid.,* **1**, pp. 182–183.
28. *Ibid.,* **1**, p. 185.
29. Butterfield, *Adams,* **2**, pp. 377–378.
30. P.C.C., Item 78, Roll 102, f. 171.
31. Butterfield, *Adams,* **1**, p. 205.
32. P.C.C., Item 78, Roll 102, vol. 21, f. 212.
33. Tilton, p. 12.
34. I have extracted much information about Valley Forge from Trussell; Reed; John Joseph Stoudt, *Ordeal at Valley Forge* (Philadelphia: University of Pennsylvania Press, 1963); George Weedon, *Valley Forge Orderly Book* (Philadelphia: Dodd, Mead and Co., 1902); and Harry Block, "Medical Conditions at Valley Forge," *New York State Medical Journal,* **70** (1970), 3010–3012.
35. Cited by Reed, p. 5.
36. Jeanette D. Black and William Greene Roelker, *A Rhode Island Chaplain in the Revolution* (Providence: Rhode Island Society of the Cincinnati, 1949), p. 73.
37. Albigence Waldo, "Diary of Surgeon Albigence Waldo, of the Connecticut Line," *PMHB,* **21** (1897), 299–323.
38. Friedrich Kapp, *The Life of John Kalb* (New York, 1870), p. 137.
39. Waldo, pp. 306–309.
40. George E. Scheer, ed., *Private Yankee Doodle. Being a Narrative*

of Some of the Adventures, Dangers, and Sufferings of a Revolutionary Soldier (Boston: Little, Brown, 1962), pp. 100–101.
41. Cited by Trussell, p. 36.
42. *Ibid.*, p. 7.
43. *Ibid.*, pp. 37–38.
44. Weedon, pp. 185, 242–243, 251, 254–255, 285, 288–289, 305–306.
45. P.P., f. 447.
46. Kapp, pp. 139–140.
47. Weedon, pp. 181, 186, 190.
48. Scheer, p. 110.
49. P.P., f. 452.
50. Bingham, p. 12.
51. Cited by Trussell, p. 7.
52. Waldo, p. 312.
53. Cited by William S. Middleton, "Medicine at Valley Forge," *Ann. Med. Hist.*, Ser. 3, 3 (1941), 481–486, p. 483.
54. Cited in Wickes, p. 65.
55. Weedon, p. 204.
56. Trussell, p. 41; Lesser, p. xxxi.
57. Ricardo Torres-Reyes, *1779–80 Encampment, A Study of Medical Services* (Washington, D.C.: National Park Service, 1971), p. 30.
58. Cited by Bell, *Morgan,* p. 283, n. 20.
59. Monro, pp. 120, 135–136.
60. Cited by Stoudt, p. 108.
61. Rev. War P., Item 135, f. 10.
62. For a good summary of Yellow Springs, see Carol Shiels Roark. "Historic Yellow Springs: The Restoration of an American Spa," *Pennsylvania Folklife,* Autumn 1974, 28–38.
63. P.P., f. 440.
64. Journal of James Sproat, 1753–1786, April, 1777, HSP.
65. P.P., f. 467.
66. Rev. War P., Item 135, no. 28.
67. P.P. ff. 24, 400, 424, 427, 436, 446, 476.
68. Letterbook of Captain Samuel Morris, Jr., Eleutherian Mills Library.
69. Greene to Potts, April 16, 1776, Mss. Coll., Valley Forge Historical Society. See also Greene to ——, March 16, 1778, Mss. Coll., New York State Library.
70. P.P., ff. 46, 460.
71. *Ibid.*, f. 444.

IX. Potts's Last Years

72. *Ibid.*, f. 462.
73. *Ibid.*, f. 454.
74. *Ibid.*, f. 29.
75. P.C.C., Item 142, Roll 155, f. 63.
76. P.P., ff. 419-420, 430.
77. *Ibid.*, ff. 431, 441, 467, 481.
78. See Edward Kremers, "The Lititz Pharmacopoeia," *The Badger Pharmacist*, **22-24** (1938), 1-70; Griffenhagen, pp. 123-130; and Cowen, *The Colonial and Revolutionary Heritage of Pharmacy in America* (Trenton, N.J.: New Jersey Pharmaceutical Association, and Institute of the History of Pharmacy, Trenton, New Jersey, and Madison, Wisconsin, 1976), pp. 16-21.
79. Cited by Toner, p. 51.
80. Tilton, p. 38.
81. Charles J. Bushnell, *Memoirs of Samuel Smith, A Soldier of the Revolution* (New York, 1860), p. 14.
82. Scheer, p. 131.
83. Dr. Samuel Adams Diary, July 29, 1778, N.Y. Pub. Lib.
84. "Reminiscences of William Read," in R. W. Gibbes, *A Documentary History of the American Revolution*, 3 vols. (New York, 1857), **2**, 256-260, p. 257.
85. P.P., f. 485.
86. Lesser, p. xxxi. See Appendix II.
87. Tilton, p. 114.

IX. Potts's Last Years

1. Fitzpatrick, **13**, p. 344.
2. Thacher, p. 158.
3. For the 1778-1779 encampment, see Peter Angelakos, "The Army at Middlebrook, 1778-1779," *New Jersey Historical Society Proceedings*, **70** (1952), 97-120.
4. Fitzpatrick, **14**, p. 221.
5. Torres-Reyes, p. 30; Lesser, p. xxxi. See Appendix II.
6. Thacher, p. 191.
7. Kapp, p. 183.
8. Scheer, p. 124. A good summary of the 1779-1780 encampment is by George J. Svejda, *Quartering, Disciplining, and Supplying the Army at Morristown, 1779-1780* (Washington, D.C.: National Park Service, 1970).

Notes

9. P.P., f. 509.
10. Cited by Saffron, pp. 227–228.
11. Torres-Reyes, p. 30; Lesser, p. xxxi. See Appendix 2.
12. Tilton, pp. 49, 55.
13. James, pp. 206–207.
14. Cited by Gibson, p. 260.
15. Cited by Bell, p. 219.
16. *Ibid.*, p. 229.
17. *Pennsylvania Packet,* September 9, 1780.
18. Shippen to Laurens, May 12, 1780, John Laurens Papers, N.-Y. Hist. Soc.
19. P.P., Lib. Cong.
20. Bell, *Morgan,* pp. 235–246.
21. Saffron, pp. 6–79, *passim.*
22. James, p. 211.
23. Lesser, p. xxxi; Peckham, 131–133. See Appendix II. See also James E. Gibson, "The Role of Disease in the 70,000 Casualties in the American Revolutionary Army," *Trans. Stud.,* 4th Ser., **17** (1941), 121–130, who estimates a 25 percent annual loss from sickness and wounds. Duncan, p. 371, estimates a 20 percent annual loss.
24. Cited by Edward Warren, *The Life of John Warren, M.D.* (Boston, 1874), p. 227.
25. Tilton, p. 62.
26. C. Malcolm Gilman, "Military Surgery in the American Revolution," *Journal of the Medical Society of New York,* **57** (1960), 492–496.
27. Wayne to Samuel Huntington, September 13, 1780, P.C.C., Item 161, Roll 179, ff. 226–227.

Bibliography

MANUSCRIPTS

American Antiquarian Society
 1. General Hospital Return, by Samuel Stringer
 2. Henry B. Livingston Orderly Book (microfilm)
American Philosophical Society
 1. Miscellaneous Manuscripts
Berks County Historical Society
 1. John E. Eshelman, Records of Quakers in Berks County, manuscript
 2 Revolutionary War Collection (microfilm)
Boston Public Library
 1. Sol Feinstone Collection (microfilm)
College of Physicians of Philadelphia Library
 1. Casebooks of Benjamin Duffield and Jonathan Elmer
 2. Francis Alison, Jr., A List of Soldiers
 3. Gilbert Collection of Letters
 4. Ledger Books of Thomas and Phineas Bond
Delaware Hall of Records
 1. Francis Theodore Tilton, Dr. James Tilton of Delaware (1747–1822), 7 vols., typescript
Eleutherian Mills Library
 1. Letterbook of Captain Samuel Morris, Jr.
Fort Ticonderoga Museum
 1. Jonathan Potts Papers
 2. Miscellaneous Manuscripts and Transcripts

Bibliography

Henry Huntington Library
    1. Philip Schuyler Letterbook (microfilm)
Historical Society of Pennsylvania
    1. American Physicians Collection
    2. Anthony Wayne Papers
    3. Autograph Collection
    4. Benjamin Rush Papers
    5. Dreer Collection
    6. Gratz Collection
    7. James Sproat Journal
    8. Jonathan Potts, Day Book, Ledger Books, and Journal Books
    9. Jonathan Potts Papers
    10. Phineas Bond Daybook
    11. Society Miscellaneous Collections
Indiana University, Lilly Library
    1. Benjamin Rush Journal (microfilm)
John F. Reed Collection (King of Prussia)
    1. Nathanael Greene Letter, April 16, 1776
Library of Congress
    1. Edward Hand Papers
    2. George Washington Papers (microfilm)
    3. Isaac Foster Papers
    4. James McHenry Papers
    5. Jonathan Potts Papers
    6. Joseph Toner Collection
    7. Peter Force Collection
    8. Richard Montgomery Orderly Book
    9. Roger Jones Family Papers
    10. Thomas Ruston Papers
Massachusetts Historical Society
    1. Benjamin Lincoln Papers (microfilm)
    2. John Warren Papers
    3. Miscellaneous Bound Manuscripts
    4. William Eustis Papers
    5. William Heath Papers (microfilm)
    6. William Livingston Papers
Morristown National Park
    1. John Cochran Letterbook (microfilm)
    2. Lloyd W. Smith Collection (microfilm)
National Archives
    1. Miscellaneous Manuscripts (microfilm)

2. Papers of the Continental Congress (microfilm)
   3. Revolutionary War Records (microfilm)
National Library of Medicine
   1. Jonathan Elmer, Lecture Notes (1766) with William Shippen (microfilm)
New Jersey Historical Society
   1. Journal of Major Joseph Bloomfield
New York Academy of Medicine
   1. John Morgan Letter, June 24, 1776
New-York Historical Society
   1. James Duane Papers
   2. John Laurens Papers (microfilm)
   3. Horatio Gates Orderly Book (microfilm)
   4. Horatio Gates Papers (microfilm)
New York Public Library
   1. Dr. Samuel Adams Diary (microfilm)
   2. Edward Hand Papers (microfilm)
   3. Emmett Collection
   4. Philip Schuyler Papers (microfilm)
New York State Library
   1. Letter of Nathanael Greene, March 16, 1778
Pennsylvania Hospital Historic Library
   1. Minutes of the Board of Managers, 1751–1860
Pottstown, Private Source
   1. Diary of Jonathan Potts
Princeton University Library
   1. Atkinson Autograph Collection
University of Pennsylvania, Charles Peterson Van Pelt Library
   1. Clinical Notebook of John Archer (microfilm)
Valley Forge Historical Society
   1. Nathanael Greene Letter, April 16, 1778

PERIODICALS

Pennsylvania Evening Post
Pennsylvania Gazette
Pennsylvania Journal and Weekly Advertiser
Pennsylvania Packet

Bibliography

PRIMARY PRINTED SOURCES

Albion, Robert G., and Leonidas, Dodson, eds., *Philip Vickers Fithian: Journal, 1775-1776*. Princeton, N.J.: Princeton University Press, 1934.

Ames, Ethel, *Nancy Shippen. Her Journal Book*. Philadelphia: Lippincott, 1934.

Baldwin, Thomas William, ed., *The Revolutionary Journal of Colonel Jeduthan Baldwin*. Bangor, Maine: DeBurians, 1906.

Ballagh, James Curtis, ed., *The Letters of Richard Henry Lee*, 2 vols. New York: The Macmillan Co., 1912-1914.

Beardsley, Ebenezer, "History of a Dysentery in the 22nd regiment of the late continental army," *The American Museum*, 5 (1789), 245-250.

Bingham, Hiram, *Five Straws Gathered From Revolutionary Fields*. Cambridge, Mass.: 1901.

Black, Jeanette D., and William Greene Roelker, *A Rhode Island Chaplain in the Revolution*. Providence: Rhode Island Society of the Cincinnati, 1949.

Brocklesby, Richard. *Oeconomical and Medical Observations in Two Parts, From the year 1758 to the year 1764 Inclusive. Tending to the Improvement of Military Hospitals and to the Cure of Camp Disease Incident to Soldiers*. London: 1764.

Brown, Lloyd A., and Howard W. Peckham, eds., *The Journal of Henry Dearborn, 1776-1783*. Chicago: Caxton Club, 1939.

Brown, Marvin L., ed., *Baroness von Riedesel and the American Revolution. Journal of Tour of Duty, 1776-1783*. Chapel Hill, N.C.: University of North Carolina Press, 1965.

Buchan, William, *Domestic Medicine, or the Family Physician*. Boston: 1778.

Burnett, Edward C., *Letters of the Members of the Continental Congress*. 8 vols. Washington, D.C.: The Carnegie Institute of Washington, 1921-1930.

Bushnell, Charles J., *Memoirs of Samuel Smith, A Soldier of the Revolution*. New York: 1860.

Butterfield, Lyman H., ed., *The Letters of Benjamin Rush*, 2 vols. Princeton, N.J.: Princeton University Press, 1951.

———, ed., *The Diary and Autobiography of John Adams*, 5 vols. Cambridge, Mass.: Harvard University Press, 1961-1966.

———, Wendell D. Garrett, and Margaret Sprague, eds., *Adams*

Primary Printed Sources

Family Correspondence, 4 vols. Cambridge, Mass.: Belknap Press of Harvard, 1963-1973.
Collins, Varnum Lansing, *A Brief Narrative of the Ravages of the British and Hessians at Princeton in 1775-1776.* Princeton, N.J.: The University Library, 1906.
Commager, Henry Steele, and Richard Brandon Morris, eds., *The Spirit of Seventy-Six.* 2 vols. Indianapolis, Ind.: Bobbs-Merrill, 1958.
Corner, George W., *The Autobiography of Benjamin Rush.* Princeton, N.J.: Princeton University Press, 1948.
Duane, William, ed., *Extracts from the Diary of Christopher Marshal Kept in Philadelphia and Lancaster During the American Revolution, 1774-1781.* Albany, N.Y.: 1877.
Elwyn, Alfred L., ed., *Letters by Josiah Bartlett, William Whipple, and Others.* Philadelphia: 1889.
Fitzpatrick, John C., ed., *The Writings of George Washington from the Original Manuscript Sources, 1745-1799.* 39 vols. Washington, D.C.: U.S. Government Printing Office, 1931-1944.
Force, Peter, ed., *American Archives,* 9 vols. Washington, D.C.: 1837-1853.
Ford, Worthington Chauncey, ed., *Journals of the Continental Congress, 1774-1789.* 34 vols. Washington, D.C.: U.S. Government Printing Office, 1904-1937.
Fraser, Persifor, "Letters from Ticonderoga, 1776," *Bulletin of the Fort Ticonderoga Museum.* **10** (1961), 386-398; **11** (1962) 450-459.
Gibbes, R. W., ed., *A Documentary History of the American Revolution.* 3 vols. New York: 1867.
Graves, Robert, *Sergeant Lamb's America.* New York: Alfred A. Knopf, 1962.
Guerra, Francisco, *American Medical Bibliography,* New York: Lathrop C. Harper, Inc., 1962.
Hanna, John Smith, *A History of the Life and Services of Captain Samuel Dewees.* Baltimore: 1885.
Hays, I. Minis, ed., *Calendar of the Papers of Benjamin Franklin in the Library of the American Philosophical Society,* 5 vols. Philadelphia: American Philosophical Society, 1908.
Heiges, George L. "Letters Relating to the Continental Military Hospitals in Lancaster County." *Lancaster County Historical Society Papers,* **52** (1948), 73-96.

Bibliography

Hennen, John, *Military Surgery.* London: 1820.
Hitchcock, Enos, "Diary of Enos Hitchcock, D.D., A Chaplain in the Revolutionary War," *Publications of the Rhode Island Historical Society.* **7** (1889), 105–225.
James, Mrs. Thomas Potts, *Memorial of Thomas Potts, Junior.* Cambridge, Mass.: 1894.
Johnson, Henry Phelps, *Memoir of Colonel Benjamin Tallmadge.* New York: 1904.
Jones, John, *Plain Concise Practical Remarks On the Treatment of Wounds and Fractures.* Philadelphia: 1775.
Jordan, John W., "Bethlehem During the Revolution. Extracts from the Moravian Archives at Bethlehem," *Pennsylvania Magazine of History and Biography,* **21** (1896), 515–519.
Kennedy, Samuel, "Letters of Dr. Samuel Kennedy to His Wife in 1776," *Pennsylvania Magazine of History and Biography,* **8** (1885), 111–116.
Kirkland, Frederick F., ed., "Journal of a Physician on the Expedition Against Canada, 1776," *Pennsylvania Magazine of History and Biography,* **59** (1935), 321–361.
Labaree, Leonard W., ed., *The Papers of Benjamin Franklin,* 20 vols. New Haven, Conn.: Yale University Press, 1957–
Lee, Richard Henry, *Memoirs of the Life of Richard Henry Lee,* 2 vols. Philadelphia: 1825.
Medical Society of New Jersey. *Transactions of the Medical Society of New Jersey.* Newark: 1858.
Monro, Donald, *An Account of the Diseases which were most frequent in the British Military Hospitals in Germany.* London: 1764.
———, *Observations on the Means of Preserving the Health of Soldiers and of Constituting Military Hospitals and on the Diseases Incident to Soldiers,* 2 vols. London: 1780.
Morgan, John, *Vindication of his Public Character in the Station of Director-General of the Military Hospital.* Boston: 1777.
Muhlenberg, Henry Melchior, *Journals.* Trans. by Theodore G. Tappert and John W. Doberstein, 3 vols. Philadelphia: The Muhlenberg Press, 1945.
Neill, Edward D., "Death of Anthony Morris," *Pennsylvania Magazine of History and Biography,* **1** (1877), 175–180.
New-York Historical Society, "Trial of Major-General St. Clair," *Collections of the New-York Historical Society for the year 1880.* New York: 1881.
Padelford, Philip, ed., *Colonial Panorama. 1775: Dr. Robert Hon-*

Primary Printed Sources

yman's Journal for March and April. San Marino, Cal.: The Huntington Library, 1939.

Pennsylvania Archives. 1st Ser., 11 vols.; 2nd Ser., 19 vols.; 4th Ser., 21 vols.; 5th Ser., 8 vols. Philadelphia and Harrisburg: 1852-1906.

Potts, Jonathan, *On Intermittent Fever.* Philadelphia: 1776.

Pringle, John, *Observations on Diseases of the Army in Camp and Garrison.* London: 1752.

Ranby, John, *Method of Treating Gun-shot Wounds.* London: 1781.

Robbins, Ammi, *Journal of Ammi R. Robbins, Chaplain in the American Army in the Northern Campaign of 1777.* New Haven, Conn.: 1850.

Roberts, Kenneth, ed., *March to Quebec.* New York: Doubleday, Doran and Co., 1938.

Rush, Benjamin, *Medical Inquiries and Observations,* 2 vols. Philadelphia: 1794.

Scheer, George, ed., *Private Yankee Doodle, Being a Narrative of Some of the Adventures, Dangers, and Sufferings of a Revolutionary Soldier.* Boston: Little Brown, 1962.

Schoepf, Johann David, "Travels Through Berks County in 1783," *Pennsylvania Magazine of History and Biography,* 5 (1881), 74-81.

Sergeant, R., "The Battle of Princeton," *Pennsylvania Magazine of History and Biography,* 21 (1896), 175-180.

Showman, Richard K., ed., *The Papers of Nathanael Greene,* 1 vol. Chapel Hill, N.C.: University of North Carolina Press, 1976-

Sizer, Theodore, *The Autobiography of Colonel John Trumbull. Patriot-Artist, 1765-1813.* New Haven: Yale University Press, 1953.

Sullivan, James, ed., *Minutes of the Albany Committee of Correspondence,* 2 vols. Albany, N.Y.: University of the State of New York, 1923.

Thacher, James, *A Military Journal During the American Revolutionary War, from 1775 to 1783.* Boston: 1827.

———, *American Medical Biography.* Boston: 1828.

Tilton, James, *Economical Observations on Military Hospitals.* Wilmington, Del.: 1813.

Trumbull, Benjamin, "A Concise Journal or Minutes of the Principal Movements Toward St. John in 1777," *Connecticut Historical Society Collections,* 7 (1899), 139-173.

Bibliograpohy

Trumbull, John, *Autobiography, Reminiscences, and Letters of John Trumbull, 1756-1811.* New York: 1811.
Trumbull, Jonathan, *Letters. Massachusetts Historical Society Collections,* 5th Ser., **10** (1898).
Van Sweiten, Baron Gerhard, *The Diseases Incident to Armies, With the Method of Cure.* Boston: 1777.
Waldo, Albigence, "Valley Forge, 1777-78. Diary of Surgeon Albigence Waldo, of the Connecticut Line," *Pennsylvania Magazine of History and Biography,* **21** (1897) 199-323.
White, Joseph, *Narrative of Events.* Boston: 1833.
Wilkinson, James, *Memoirs of My Own Times,* 3 vols. Philadelphia: 1818.
Wilson, Rufus Rockwell, *Heath's Memoirs of the American War.* New York: 1904.
Wistar, Caspar, "State of Medicine from the first Settlement of Pennsylvania, to the year 1762," *The Eclectic Repertory and Analytical Review,* **7** (1818), 273-277.

SECONDARY SOURCES

Albright, Raymond, A., *Two Centuries of Reading, Pennsylvania, 1748-1948.* Reading: Historical Society of Berks County, 1948.
Angelakos, Peter, "The Army at Middlebrook, 1778-79," *New Jersey Historical Society Proceedings,* **70** (1952), 97-120.
Anon, "A Biographical Sketch of John Archer, M.B.," *Bulletin of the Johns Hopkins Hospital* **10** (1899), 141-147.
Bell, Whitfield, Jr., "Medical Students and Their Examiners in Eighteenth Century America," *Transactions and Studies of the College of Physicians of Philadelphia,* **21** (1953), 13-25.
———, "An Eighteenth Century American Medical Manuscript. The Clinical Notebook of John Archer, M.B. 1767," *The Library Chronicle,* **22** (1956), 222-226.
———, *John Morgan. Continental Doctor.* Philadelphia: University of Pennsylvania Press, 1965.
———, *The Colonial Physician and Other Essays.* New York: Science History Publications, 1975.
Beck, Herbert M., "The Military Hospitals at Lititz, 1777-78," *Historical Papers and Address of the Lancaster County Historical Society,* **23** (1919), 5-14.

Secondary Sources

Beck, James M., *Bethlehem and Its Military Hospitals*. Bethlehem, Pa.: 1897.
Blake, John B., *Public Health in the Town of Boston, 1630-1822*. Cambridge, Mass: Harvard University Press, 1951.
Blanco, Richard L., "The Diary of Jonathan Potts: A Quaker Medical Student in Edinburgh (1766-67)," *Transactions and Studies of the College of Physicians of Philadelphia* 44 (1977), 119-130.
――, *Wellington's Surgeon-General: Sir James McGrigor*. Durham, N.C.: Duke University Press, 1974.
Blanton, Wyndham B., *Medicine in Virginia in the Eighteenth Century*. Richmond, Va.: Garrett and Masie, 1931.
Block, Harry, "Medical Conditions at Valley Forge," *New York State Medical Journal*, 70 (1970), 3010-3012.
Bridenbaugh, Carl. *Cities in Revolt. Urban Life in America, 1743-1776*. New York: Alfred A. Knopf, 1955.
――, and Jessica Bridenbaugh, *Rebels and Gentlemen. Philadelphia in the Age of Franklin*. New York: Reynal and Hitchcock, 1942.
Brown, Harold, E. *The Medical Department of the United States Army from 1775 to 1873*. Washington, D.C.: 1873.
Brown, Marion E., "Adam Kuhn: Eighteenth Century Physician and Teacher," *Journal of the History of Medicine*, 5 (1950), 163-177.
Cash, Philip, *Medical Men at the Siege of Boston, April, 1775-April, 1776*. Philadelphia: American Philosophical Society, 1973.
――, "The Canadian Military Campaign of 1775-1776: Medical Problems and Effects of Disease," *Journal of the American Medical Association*, 236 (1976), 52-56.
Caulfield, Ernest, "Some Common Diseases of Colonial Children," *Publications of the Colonial Society of Massachusetts*, 35 (1942-1946), 4-65.
Chancellor, Paul, and Marjorie Potts Wendell, *A History of Pottstown, Pennsylvania*, Pottstown: Historical Society of Pottstown, 1953.
Clemens, William G., "Nagel's Company. First at Cambridge," *Berks County Historical Review*, 7 (1949), 107-110.
Coburn, Silas R., *A History of Dracut, Massachusetts*. Lowell, Mass.: Press of the *Courier-Citizen*, 1922.
Codman, John R., *Arnold's Expedition to Quebec*. New York: 1903.
Corner, Betsy C., "Dr. Fothergill's Friendship with Benjamin Franklin," *American Philosophical Society Proceedings*, American Philosophical Society, 102 (1958), 413-419.

Bibliography

———, *William Shippen: Pioneer in American Medical Education*, Philadelphia: 1951.

Corner, George W., *Two Centuries of Medicine. A History of the School of Medicine.* Philadelphia: J. B. Lippincott Co., 1965.

Cowell, Benjamin, *The Spirit of '76 in Rhode Island.* Boston: 1850.

Cowen, David L., *America's Pre-Pharmaceutical Literature.* Madison, Wis.: American Institute of the History of Pharmacy, 1961.

———, *Medicine and Health in New Jersey.* Princeton, N.J.: D. Van Nostrand, Inc., 1964.

———, *Medicine in Revolutionary New Jersey.* Trenton, N.J.: New Jersey Historical Commission, 1976.

———, *The Colonial and Revolutionary Heritage of Pharmacy in America*, Trenton, N.J., and Madison Wis.: New Jersey Pharmaceutical Association, and Institute of the History of Pharmacy, Trenton, New Jersey, and Madison, Wisconsin, 1976.

Doll, Eugene E., *The Ephrata Cloister.* Ephrata, Pa.: Carl Schurz Memorial Foundation, 1958.

Drinker, Cecil K., *Not So Long Ago. A Chronicle of Medicine and Doctors in Colonial Philadelphia.* New York: Oxford University Press, 1937.

Duffy, John, *Epidemics in Colonial America.* Baton Rouge, La.: Louisiana State University Press, 1953.

———, *The Healers: The Rise of the Medical Establishment.* New York: McGraw-Hill Book Co., 1976.

Duncan, Louis C., *Medical Men in the American Revolution, 1775–1783.* Carlisle, Pa.: Medical Field Service School, 1931.

Eshelman, John, "The Society of Friends and Their Meeting House in Berks County," *Berks County Historical Review*, 29 (1954), 117–123.

Estes, J. Worth, "As Healthy a Place as Any in America: Revolutionary Portsmouth, N. H." *Bulletin of the History of Medicine*, 50 (1976), 636–652.

———, "Medical Letters from the Siege of Boston," *Journal of the History of Medicine and Allied Sciences*, 31 (1961), 271–291.

Fales, Martha Gandy, *Joseph Richardson and Family. Philadelphia Silversmiths.* Middletown, Conn.: Wesleyan University Press, 1974.

Fleming, Thomas J., *1776. The Year of Illusion.* New York: W. W. Norton and Co., Inc., 1975.

Ford, Worthington Chauncey, *Defense of Philadelphia in 1777.* New York: DeCapo, 1971.

Secondary Sources

Fox, Richard Hingston, *Dr. John Fothergill and Friends*. London: Macmillan and Co., Ltd., 1919.

Frost, J. William, *The Quaker Family in Colonial America*. New York: St. Martin's Press, 1973.

Gelfand, Toby, "The Origins of a Modern Concept of Medical Specialization. John Morgan's Discourse of 1765" *Bulletin of the History of Medicine*, **50** (1976), 511–535.

Gibson, James E., *Bodo Otto and the Medical Background of the American Revolution*. Springfield, Ohio: Charles C. Thomas, 1937.

———, "The Role of Disease in the 70,000 Casualties in the American Revolutionary Army" *Transactions and Studies of the College of Physicians of Philadelphia*, **17** (1941), 121–127.

Gill, Harold, Jr., *The Apothecary in Colonial Virginia*. Williamsburg: University Press of Virginia, 1972.

Gilman, Malcolm C., "Military Surgery in the American Revolution," *Journal of the Medical Society of New Jersey*, **57** (1960), 492–496.

Graef, Arthur D., "The Relations Between the Pennsylvania Germans and the British Authorities," *Pennsylvania German Society Proceedings*, **47** (1939), 222–248.

Griffenhagen, George D., "Drug Supplies in the American Revolution," *National Museum Bulletin*, **225** (1961), 110–133.

Henry, Frederick P., *Standard History of the Medical Profession of Philadelphia*. Chicago: 1897.

Humphreys, David C., "The King's College Medical School and the Professionalization of Medicine in Pre-Revolutionary New York," *Bulletin of the History of Medicine*, **49** (1975), 206–234.

Jensen, Merrill, *The Founding of a Nation*. New York: Oxford University Press, 1969.

Jones, Charles Henry, *The Campaign for the Conquest of Canada*. Philadelphia: 1882.

Jones, Gordon W., "Medicine in Virginia in Revolutionary Times," *Journal of the History of Medicine and Allied Sciences*, **31** (1976) 250–270.

Jones, John H., *The Life of Ashbel Green*. New York: 1849.

Jordon, John W., "The Military Hospitals at Bethlehem and Lititz During the Revolution," *Pennsylvania Magazine of History and Biography*, **12** (1888), 385–406.

Kapp, Frederick, *The Life of John Kalb*. New York: 1870.

Bibliography

Kelley, Howard A., and Walter L. Burrage, *Dictionary of Medical Biography*. Baltimore: The Norman, Remington Co., 1920.
Kennett, Lee, *The French Armies in the Seven Years War*. Durham, N.C.: Duke University Press, 1967.
King, Lester S., *The Medical World of the Eighteenth Century*. Chicago: University of Chicago Press, 1958.
Lesser, Charles, ed., *The Sinews of Independence*. Chicago: University of Chicago Press, 1976.
Linn, John, and William H. Egle, *Pennsylvania in the War of the Revolution*, 2 vols. Harrisburg: 1880.
Main, Jackson Turner, *The Social Structure of Revolutionary America*. Princeton, N.J.: Princeton University Press, 1965.
Malone, Dumas, ed., *Dictionary of American Biography*, 20 vols. New York: C. Scribner's Sons, 1928–1936.
Martí-Ibañez, Felix, ed., *History of American Medicine. A Symposium*. New York: M.D. Publications, Inc., 1958.
McCurdy, Linda, *The Potts Family Iron Industry in the Schuylkill Valley*. Pottstown, Pa.: Pottstown Historical Society, 1975.
Middleton, William S., "Medicine at Valley Forge," *Annals of Medical History*, 3rd Ser., **3** (1941), 48–486.
Miller, Daniel, "Early German American Newspapers," *Pennsylvania German Society Proceedings,* **18-19** (1947), 502–510.
Miller, Genevieve, "Medical Apprenticeships in the American Colonies," *Ciba Symposium,* **8** (1947), 502–510.
Montgomery, Morton L., *History of Berks County*. Reading, Pa.: 1894.
Morton, Thomas G., *The History of the Pennsylvania Hospital, 1751-1895*. Philadelphia: 1897.
Neill, Edward D., *Biographical Sketch of Doctor Jonathan Potts*. Albany, N.Y.: 1863.
———, "Death of Anthony Morris," *Pennsylvania Magazine of History and Biography,* **1** (1877), 175–180.
Packhard, Francis R., "How London and Edinburgh Influenced Medicine in Philadelphia in the Eighteenth Century," *Annals of Medical History*, 3rd Ser., **4** (1932), 229–244.
Peckham, Howard H., *The Toll of Independence*. Chicago: University of Chicago Press, 1974.
Reed, John F., *Valley Forge. Crucible of Victory*. Monmouth Beach, N.J.: Philip Freneau Press, 1969.
Richards, Henry Melchior Muhlenberg, "The Pennsylvania Germans in the Revolutionary War, 1775-1783," *Pennsylvania German Society Proceedings,* **17** (1906), 21–31.

Secondary Sources

Roark, Carol Shiels, "Historic Yellow Springs: The Restoration of an American Spa," *Pennsylvania Folklife,* Autumn (1974), 28–38.
Roberts, Kenneth, *Rabble in Arms.* New York: Doubleday and Co., Inc., 1950.
Rogers, Fred R., and Sayre A. Reasoner, *The Healing Art. A History of the Medical Society of New Jersey.* Trenton, N.J.: Medical Society of New Jersey, 1966.
Saffron, Morris H., "Rebels and Disease. The New York Campaign of 1776," *Academy of Medicine of New Jersey Bulletin,* **13** (1967), 107–118.
———, *Surgeon to Washington. Dr. John Cochran (1730–1807).* New York: Columbia University Press, 1977.
Sanderson, Howard Kendell, *Lynn in the Revolution.* Boston: W. B. Clark Co., 1909.
Shryock, Richard H., "Eighteenth Century Medicine in America," *American Antiquarian Society Proceedings,* **59** (1949), 275–292.
———, *Medical Licensing in America, 1650–1965.* Baltimore: Johns Hopkins University Press, 1967.
Sonnedecker, Glenn, *Kremers and Urgang's History of Pharmacy.* New York: J. P. Lippincott, 1976.
Stillé, Charles J., *Major-General Anthony Wayne and the Pennsylvania Line in the Continental Army.* Port Washington, N.Y.: Kennikat Press, 1968.
Stoudt, John Joseph, *Ordeal at Valley Forge.* Philadelphia: University of Pennsylvania Press, 1963.
Stryker, William S., *The Battles of Trenton and Princeton.* New York: 1898.
Svejda, George J., *Quartering, Disciplining, and Supplying the Army at Morristown, 1779–1780.* Washington, D.C.: National Park Service, 1970.
Thomas, Herbert, "William Shippen, Jr., The Great Pioneer in American Obstetrics," *American Journal of Obstetrics and Gynecology,* **37** (1939), 512–517.
Thomson, Elizabeth H., "Thomas Bond, 1713–84. First Professor of Clinical Medicine in the American Colonies," *Journal of Medical Education,* **33** (1958), 614–624.
Thursfield, Hugh, "Smallpox in the American War of Independence," *Annals of Medical History,* 3rd. Ser., **4** (1942), 312–318.
Toner, Joseph M., *The Medical Men of the Revolution.* Philadelphia: 1876.
Torres-Reyes, Ricardo, *1779–80 Encampment. A Study of Medical Services.* Washington, D.C.: National Park Service, 1971.

Bibliography

Trussell, John B. B., Jr., *Birthplace of an Army. A Study of the Valley Forge Encampment.* Harrisburg, Pa.: Pennsylvania Historical and Museum Commission, 1976.
Vess, David M., *Medical Revolution in France, 1789-1796.* Gainesville, Fla.: University of Florida Press, 1975.
Waite, Frederick C., "The Degree of Bachelor of Medicine in the American Colonies and the United States," *Yale Journal of Biology and Medicine,* **10** (1937), 309-333.
Warren, Edward, *The Life of John Warren, M.D.* Boston: 1874.
Watson, J. F., *Annals of Philadelphia.* 3 vols. Philadelphia: 1898.
Weedon, George, *Valley Forge Orderly Book.* Philadelphia: 1902.
Wickes, Stephen, *History of Medicine and Medical Men in New Jersey.* Newark, N.J.: 1879.
Williams, Catherine, *Biographies of Revolutionary Heroes.* Providence, R.I.: 1875.
Williams, William H., *America's First Hospital. The Pennsylvania Hospital, 1745-1841.* Wayne, Pa.: Haverford House, Publishers, 1975.
———, Independence and Early American Hospitals, 1751-1812," *Journal of the American Medical Association,* **236** (1976), 35-38.
Wilson, James Grant, and John Fiske, *Appleton's Cyclopaedia of American Biography,* 6 vols. New York: D. Appleton and Co., 1920.
Wooden, Allen C., "The Wounds and Weapons of the Revolutionary War from 1775 to 1783," *Delaware Medical Journal,* **33** (1972), 59-65.
Woodhouse, Henry. "Colonial Medical Practice," *Ciba Symposium,* **1** (1940), 379-89.

Index

Abercromby, General James, 86
Acland, Lady Christian Henrietta, 155–156
Acland, Major John, 154, 156
Adams, Dr. Samuel, 106–107, 190–191
Adams, John, 12, 17, 64, 94, 103, 123, 129, 130, 134
Adams, Samuel, 129
Albany, 85, 133, 140, 154, 185
Alexandria, 133
Alison, Benjamin, 102
Allentown, 123, 166, 183
American Philosophical Society, 6, 203
Apprenticeships, medical, 6–9
Archer, John, 13, 18, 49
Arnold, Colonel Benedict, 84, 88, 89–90, 92, 94, 108–109, 147, 152, 155
Associators, 63
Assumpsink Creek, 125

Baer, Hans, 167
Baldwin, Colonel Jeduthan, 101, 138
Baltimore, 5, 133, 185
Bangs, Lieutenant Isaac, 115–116
Bard, Dr. John, 58
Bard, Dr. Samuel, 58, 59
Bartlett, Dr. Josiah, 119
Bartlett, Jonathan, 144-145
Basking Ridge, 195
Battery, The (N.Y.), 115
"Battle of the Clouds," 184
Baum, Colonel Fredrich, 145
Beardsley, Ebenezer, 117, 120
Beebe, Lewis, 90, 92, 93, 101, 102
Bemis Heights, 147, 148
Bennington, 145
Berks County, 2, 23, 61, 64, 80
Bethlehem, 123, 125, 163, 166
Bettering House (Phila.), 122, 164
Biddle, Clement, 46, 48, 66, 139
Biddle, Edward, 48, 69
Biddle, John, 68, 122
Biddle, Owen, 128
Binney, Dr. Barnabas, 197, 210
Binney, Dr. Thomas, 138
Bird, Mark, 52

Index

Black, Joseph, 27, 46
Blaine, Ephraim, 186
Bloomfield, Major Moses, 163, 171
Board of War, 140, 143
Boerhaave, Herman, 21, 36–37, 49
Bond, Colonel William, 101
Bond, Dr. Phineas, 6–7, 18
Bond, Dr. Thomas, Jr., 121, 202
Bond, Dr. Thomas, Sr., 6–8, 15–16, 18, 46, 49, 51, 121
Boone, Jedah, 48, 88
Boston, 131, 202
Boston Medical Society, 58
Boston Port Acts, 61
Bowery, 113
Braddock, General Edward, 48
Brandywine, battle of, 161–162, 163
Brewer, Colonel Samuel, 138
Bright, Michael, 199
British army,
  medical department, 70–71
  surgery in, 72–73
  preventive medicine in, 73–75
Brocklesby, Richard, 73–74
Brodhead, Daniel, 52
Brooklyn Heights, 115, 118
Bronholt, Susanah, 15
Brown, Dr. William, 129, 130, 170, 171, 187, 194, 210
Browne, Surgeon John, 144, 157–158
Brunswick, 119, 121, 127, 194
Bryant, William, 128
Buchan, Dr. William, 38, 56, 115
Buckingham, 166
Bunker Hill, 68, 69, 77
Burd, Edward, 52, 64, 67, 68–69

Burgoyne, General John, 90, 92, 140, 143, 147–148, 153, 156
Burlington, 125, 163
Buttonmould Bay, 108

Cadwalader, General John, 124, 125
Cambridge, 67, 68
Cape Henlopen, 23
Carleton, Sir Guy, 88, 90–91, 101, 109, 110, 156
Carlisle, 3, 51, 68, 187, 209
Carroll, John, 91
Castleton, 142
Chambly, 87, 92, 107
Charlestown (Hampshire Grants), 104
Chase, Samuel, 91
Chaudiere River, 84, 85
Chesapeake Bay, 161
Chesnut, Nathaniel, 45
Chester, 163
Chew, Benjamin, 7
Christian ABC Book, 5
Church, Dr. Benjamin, 78
City Hospital (N.Y.), 113
City Tavern (Phila.), 63
Claremont, N.H., 104
Clark, David, 26
Clark, William, 126
Clarke, Sir Francis, 154
Clecknor, Adam, 45
Clinton, General Henry, 144, 156, 189
Clymer, Richard, 110
Cochran, Dr. John, 124–125, 126, 130, 134, 180, 182, 190, 195, 198, 202–203
Colchester, Va., 133

Index

College of New Jersey, 8
College of Philadelphia, 13, 46–48, 50–51, 58, 203, 209
Committee of Correspondence, 63
Committee of Safety, 61, 80, 121, 122
Committee of Safety (Albany), 98, 144
Committee of Safety (New Hampshire), 99
Committee of Safety (Reading), 166
Conestoga, 199
Conner, Morgan, 48, 52, 67, 68
Continental Association, 64
Continental Congress, 77, 81, 110
Cornwallis, Earl, Charles, 122, 124, 125
Coste, Jean François, 210
Craigie, Andrew, 76, 97, 99, 156, 183, 186, 187
Craik, Dr. James, 70, 130, 183, 185, 186, 200, 203
Crown Point, 85, 93, 94, 108–109
Crummer, Jane, 155–156
Cullen, William, 26–28, 37
Cummins, James, 24
Cushing, Lieutenant Charles, 91
Cutting, John B., 186

Danbury, 193
Darby, Pa., 122
Davis, Ebenezer, 175
Dead River, 84
Dearborn, Captain Henry, 148

Declaration of Rights and Grievances, 64
Delaware, 200
Delaware River, 120, 161
Dewees, Captain Samuel, 163
Dewees, Thomas, 45
Dewees, William, 174
Deschambault, 91
Dettingen, battle of, 73
Dick, Sir Alexander, 26
Dimsdale, Thomas, 79–80
Diseases
 diarrhea, 40
 dysentery, 40, 117
 typhoid, 40
 typhus, 40–41, 74–75, 115, 158, 168
 smallpox, 40–43
 yellow fever, 41
 respiratory, 41
 dietary, 41
 childhood, 42
 scurvy, 42, 179
 at Boston, 77–80
 in Canadian campaign, 89–106, *passim*
 at Manhattan, 114–117
 venereal, 115, 180
 at military hospitals in N.J. and Pa., 118–123, *passim*
 at Valley Forge, 178–185
 scabies, 179–180
 at Middlebrook, 194
 at Morristown, 195–196
 impact on campaigns, 205–206
Dorchester Heights, 73
Dover, 185
Drowne, Dr. Solomon, 113, 116
Drugs, 53–54, 166–167

Index

Drummond, Colin, 26
Dumfries, 133
Dundas, Thomas, 42, 45, 53, 203

East River, 115
Easton, 3, 123
Edinburgh Meeting of Friends, 30, 31–32
Edinburgh University, 19, 21–29
Elizabeth, N.J., 119, 121, 122, 128
Elmer, Jonathan, 11
Ephrata, 5, 167, 183
Erwing, General James, 124
Ettwein, Reverend John, 165
Evansburg, 163
Exeter Monthly Meeting, 33

Faulkner's Swamp, 163
Fermoy, General Matthias Roche de, 158
First Continental Congress, 63, 64
Fisher, Private Elijah, 177, 178, 181
Fisher's Island, 6
Fishkill, 119, 133, 202
Fitzpatrick, George, 23
Flatbush, 118
Fothergill, Dr. John, 13
Fothergill, Samuel, 25
Fort Anne, 138, 142, 143
Fort Dayton, 146
Fort Edward, 138, 142, 143, 144
Fort George, 83, 85, 86, 94, 110
Fort Island, 131
Fort Lee, 115, 119, 121

Fort Mercer, 164
Fort Mifflin, 164
Fort Miller, 138
Fort Stanwix, 138, 140, 146
Fort Ticonderoga, 67, 78, 82, 85, 86, 94–95, 107, 109, 110, 111, 117, 135, 140–141, 142
Fort Washington, 84, 115, 119
Foster, Isaac, 70, 129, 197
Franklin, Benjamin, 3, 7, 10, 26–27, 37, 51, 91, 107
Frazer, Colonel Persifor, 106
Freeman's Farm, battle of, 148, 153
French Creek, 168
Friendship, 23–24

Gage, General Thomas, 47
Galen, 47
Galloway, Joseph, 26
Gates, General Horatio, 83, 94, 95, 98, 100, 101, 103, 104, 105–106, 111, 124, 133, 140, 147, 153, 156, 158, 200
German Flats, 138
Germantown, 5, 162
Gilman, Dr. Charles, 208
Glover, Colonel John, 138
Governor's Island, 115
Gowanus Marsh, 115
Great German Bible, 5
Green, Colonel Ashbel, 134
Greene General Nathanael, 116, 117, 119, 164, 170, 177, 186, 189, 201
Gregory, James, 28
Grub, Jacob, 48
Gulph Mills, 167

268

Index

Hackensack, 119, 120, 124
Hagen, Surgeon Francis, 145–146
Haller, Henry, 52
Hallowell, Henry, 122
Hampshire Grants, 103
Hancock, John, 82, 119, 130, 135
Hand, Colonel Edward, 70, 89
Hand-in-Hand Fire Insurance Company, 6
Hanover, 133, 163
Harlem Heights, 117, 119
Harvard Corporation, 58
Haskell, Caleb, 88
Hayes, Dr. John McNamara, 153–154
Head of Elk, 161, 163
Heath, General William, 116, 118
Height of the Land, 84
Henry, Governor Patrick, 171
Henry, John, 88
Herkimer, Colonel Nicholas, 146–147
Hessians, 124–125, 128
Highlands, 191
Hildreth, Micah, 99
Hitchcock, Chaplain Enos, 139
Hocker, Ludwig, 5
Hockley, James, 45
Honyman, Dr. Robert, 17
Hoover, Jacob, 48
Hope, John, 27
Hospital Bill of 1776, 77
Hospital Bill of 1777, 130
Howe, General Sir William, 79, 118, 124, 141, 147, 161–162, 174, 189
Howland, Private John, 126
Hubbardton, 142

Hudson, River, 115
Huff, Jacob, 53
Hunter, John, 210
Hunter, William, 22

Inflexible, 108
Inoculation, 43, 56–57, 89, 91, 102–106, 133–135, 180–181
Intolerable Acts, 61, 63, 64
Isle aux Noix, 87, 92

Jenner, Dr. Edward, 43
Jesuit's bark, 42
Jockey Hollow, 195
Johnston, Robert, 102, 144, 146–147
Jones, John, 70, 73, 158, 210
Jones, Walter, 28

Kalb, Baron Johann de, 176, 179, 194, 195
Kearsley, John, 10
Keene, 104
Kennebec River, 84
Kennedy, Samuel, 100–101, 199
Kimmel, Joseph, 167
King's College (N.Y.), 58, 113
Knox, General Henry, 127–128
Kuhn, Adams, 46

Lafayette, Marie Joseph, Marquis de, 177, 193
Lake Champlain, 82, 84, 92
Lake George, 82, 84
Lake Megantic, 85

269

Index

Lamb, Sergeant Roger, 156
Lancaster, 80, 163, 167, 177
Lancaster County, 170
Larry, Dominique-Jean, 207
Laurens, Henry, 172
Laurens, Colonel John, 199
Lechmere Point, 79
Lee, Alice, 11
Lee, Arthur, 28
Lee, General Charles, 69, 118, 189
Lee, Richard Henry, 124, 129
Lexington and Concord, 61
Leyden, 21
Library Company, 3
Licensure laws, 58–59
Lincoln, General Benjamin, 146
Lincoln, Mordecai, 52
Lind, James, 41
Linneus, 32, 46
Lititz, 166, 167, 185, 187
"Lititz Pharmacopoeia," 187–188, 209
Liverpool, 24
Livingston, Governor William, 169
Lloyd, Captain Charles, 167
Long Island, 118

Manatawny, 3
Manchester, Vt., 145
Manhattan, battle of, 113–118
Mannheim, 187
Marshall, Christopher, 53, 122, 209
Martin, Private Joseph Plum, 177, 179–180, 195
Massachusetts Charter, 64
Massachusetts Medical Society, 211

Massachusetts Medical Society Pharmacopoeia, 209
Massachusetts Provincial Congress, 75
Mawhood, Colonel Charles, 126–127
McCall, Arch, 45
McCrae, Jane, 144–145
McCrae, Dr. Stephen, 108, 109, 111
McHenry, Dr. James, 97, 99, 114, 182
McKenzie, Dr. Colin, 22
McKenzie, Surgeon Samuel, 146
McKonkey's Ferry, 124
Mease, James, 185
Medical Committee of the Continental Congress, 121, 186, 195, 197, 200
Medical department, Continental army, 77–78
Medical Repository, 211
Medical Society of Edinburgh, 29
Medicine
 practice of, 35, 37–40
 theory of, 36–37
Mendham, 166, 195
Mercer, General Hugh, 48, 70, 117, 120, 126–127, 128
Middlebrook, 191, 193–194
Middleton, Dr. Peter, 58
Mifflin, General Thomas, 67, 122, 124, 125
Miller, John Heinrich, 65
Miller, William, 25, 30
Mohawk River, 138, 140
Mohawk Valley, 85
Monmouth, battle of, 189, 190
Monro, Donald, 74, 183
Monro, Alexander II, 32

Index

Montgomery County, 4
Montgomery, General Richard, 87–88, 89
Montreal, 91
Moore, Charles, 25
Moravians, 123
Morgagni, 23, 29
Morgan, Dr. John, 6, 10, 12, 14–15, 26, 46, 50, 70, 78, 80, 87, 88, 89, 96, 97, 98, 99, 100, 106, 113–114, 118, 119–120, 121, 122, 125, 129, 150, 172, 184, 198–200, 201
Morris, Captain Anthony, 185
Morris, Arthur, 128
Morris, George, 68
Morris, Gouverneur, 86
Morris, Susannah, 46
Morristown, 119, 124, 128, 131, 193, 194–195, 202
Moses Creek, 142
Moultrie, Dr. John, 22
Mt. Independence, 100, 107
Muhlenberg, Reverend Henry Melchior, 4, 163, 168

Nagle, George, 52, 67–68
National Pharmacopoeia, 209
New Castle, 122
New England Journal of Medicine and Surgery, 211
New Jersey Medical Society, 49, 59
Newark, 119
New Windsor, 202
New York Hospital Pharmacopoeia, 209
New York Packet, 116
Norridgenock Falls, 84

Nixon, Colonel John, 138
Northampton, 163
Northern department of Continental army, 81
Northumberland, 51
Norwich, 119
Nova Scotia, 79

Obstetrics, 12
O'Hara, Captain Henry, 135
Olney, Captain Stephen, 126
Oriskany, 146
Oswego, 140

"Palatine Fever," 6
Paoli, 162
Paramus, 121, 193
Parsons, General Samuel Holden, 133
Paton, Colonel John, 52
Patton and Williams, 53
Paulus Hook, 115
Peekskill, 119, 131, 133
Pemberton, James, 13
Pemberton, John, 25
Penn, Governor John, 63
Penn, Thomas, 13
Penn, William, 5
Pennsylvania Chronicle, 56
Pennsylvania Coffee House (London), 31
Pennsylvania Gazette, 53
Pennsylvania Hospital, 3, 6, 12, 16–17, 18, 122, 164
Pennsylvania Staatbote, 65
Pennypacker, Derek, 48
Pennypacker's Mill, 163
Perth Amboy, 119, 121, 128

Index

Philadelphia, 9–11, 161, 162, 163, 165, 202
Philadelphia Academy, 5, 26
Philadelphia Monthly Meeting, 33, 34
Philadelphia Yearly Meeting, 25
Pine Street (Phila.), 122
Ploughed Hill, 69
Pluckemin, 128, 195
Polly, 83
Poor, Colonel Enoch, 102
Porter, Colonel Elisha, 102
Potter, Colonel James, 120
Potter's Field, 123
Potts, Benjamin, 203
Potts, David, 5
Potts, Grace Richardson, 23, 31, 32–33, 203
Potts, Isaac, 174
Potts, Israel, 45
Potts, John, Jr., 47
Potts, John, Sr., 2–4, 45, 47
Potts, Dr. Jonathan
  birth, 2
  early education, 4–5
  apprenticeship, 7–8
  attends Shippen's lectures, 11
  attends Pennsylvania Hospital, 16–18
  at Edinburgh University, 26–34
  departs for England, 23
  engaged to Grace Richardson, 23
  storm at sea, 24
  arrival at Liverpool, 24
  visits Samuel Fothergill, 25
  travels to Scotland, 25–26
  correspondence with Benjamin Franklin, 26–27

Potts, Jonathan *(cont'd)*
  experiences in Edinburgh, 29–30
  attending Edinburgh Meeting of Friends, 30–31
  leaves England, 31
  purchases books in London, 31
  marriage, 32–33
  practices in Pottsgrove, 45–48, 51
  returns to Philadelphia, 46–47
  receives Bachelor of Medicine degree, 47
  bequest from father, 47–48
  returns to Pottsgrove, 48
  fees, 48
  dissertation on malaria, 49–50
  receives M.D. degree, 50–51
  practices in Reading, 51–52
  income from practice, 48, 52–53
  sells drugs, 53–55
  advises on smallpox, 56–57
  serves on Berks County Committee of Correspondence, 64–67
  urges support to Continental Congress, 64–66
  on Committee of Observation, 66
  enlists in rifle battalion, 67–68
  activities in late 1775, 80–81
  petitions Congress, 81
  arrives at Fort George, 94
  difficulties at Fort George Hospital, 95–97
  visits Fort Ticonderoga, 102–103

Index

Potts, Jonathan *(cont'd)*
  involved in Morgan-Stringer feud, 96-98
  link in smallpox precautions, 105
  ordered to Mt. Independence, 107
  assists Benedict Arnold, 108
  furlough home, 111
  cooperates with Pennsylvania Council of Safety, 122
  joins Washington at Trenton, 125
  at battle of Princeton, 126-128
  appointed Deputy Director General for Northern Department, 130
  prepares for new assignment, 135-136
  arrives in Albany, 136
  hospital preparation in upper N.Y., 137-139
  conversations with Richard Varick, 140
  ordered to remove hospital from Ticonderoga, 141
  at Moses Creek, 143
  preparations before Saratoga, 144-146
  at battle of Saratoga, 148-154
  evacuates wounded, 154-155
  receives praise for accomplishments at Saratoga, 157-159
  receives Shippen's plea, 166-167
  praised by Benjamin Rush, 171
  appointed Purveyor General, 173-174
  supplies Yellow Springs, 184

Potts, Jonathan *(cont'd)*
  supplies Valley Forge Hospitals, 185-186
  receives praise of colleagues, 186
  acquires drugs, 185-186
  reports to Board of War, 191
  Cochran requests supplies from, 195
  Potts's requests to Medical Committee, 196-197
  mentioned in Shippen trial, 199
  implicated in a scandal, 200
  resignation from army, 200-201
  death and bequests, 203
  evaluation of Potts's career, 204-205, 211-212.
Potts, Joseph, 5
Potts, Mary Francis, 32
Potts, Ruth Savage, 2
Potts, Samuel, 68, 139, 145, 203
Potts, William B., 204
Pottsgrove, 45, 46, 203
Pottsgrove Manor, 2-4
Poultner, Thomas, 4
Pratt, Matthew, 204
Princeton, 125, 168
Pringle, Sir John, 22, 32, 74-75
Proclamation of 1763, 62
Prospect Hill, 68
Province Island, 131
Provincial convention of 1775 (Phila.), 64
Proze, J., 102

Quebec, 83, 85, 88, 89
Queen of France, 200

Index

Ranby, John, 72–73, 151
Raritan River, 120
Read, Dr. William, 191
Reading, 3–4, 51–54, 56–57, 63, 80, 162, 163, 164, 166, 183, 184, 187, 199, 203
Red Bank, 164
Red Hook, 115
Red Lion (Lionville), 168
Redman, Dr. John, 8, 21, 46
Reed, Joseph, 82
Reedy Island, 23
Revere, Paul, 62, 63, 64, 68
Rheimstown, 166
Rhenish Palatinate, 5
Rhoads, Samuel, 7
Rice, Nathan, 90, 94
Richardson, Francis, 7, 46
Richardson, Joseph, 23
Richelieu River, 87
Riedesel, Baroness Frederick von, 155
Rittenhouse, David, 10
Robbins, Reverend Ammi, 102
Robertson, William, 27
Robinson's House, 202
Rosebloom, Dr. Jacob, 98
Ross, Dr. John, 102
Royal Savage, 108, 109
Rush, Dr. Benjamin, 8, 17–18, 22–24, 25, 29, 34, 38, 46, 72, 125, 126, 128, 130, 131, 158, 164, 169, 170, 171, 172, 210
Ruston, Thomas, 22
Rutland, 142
Rutter, Martha, 32
Rutter, Thomas, 32, 45

St. Charles River, 88
St. Clair, Colonel Arthur, 80, 138–139, 141, 142

St. Jean's, 87, 92, 107, 141, 142
St. Lawrence River, 82
St. Leger, Colonel Barry, 147
St. Paul's Church (N.Y.), 115
St. Rogue's Gate, 88
St. Thomas's Hospital, 22
Salisbury, 98
Sandy Hook, 190
Saratoga, battle of, 147–157
Savannah, 194
Schenectady, 138
Schenectady Council of Safety, 138
Schoepf, Dr. Johann David, 51
Schuyler, General Philip, 81, 85–87, 91, 92, 94, 104, 110, 133, 134, 135, 136, 139–140, 141, 144, 147
Schuylkill, 189
Scott, Dr. Moses, 166
Scott, Thomas, 25
Scull, Edward, 52
Scull, Nicholas, 147
Scull, Peter, 52
Second Continental Congress, 65, 67
Second Provincial Congress (Pa.), 66
Senter, Isaac, 84, 88–89
Sergeant R., 126–127
Seventh Day Baptists, 5
Shaeferstown, 166
Shippen, Dr. William, Jr., 11–15, 21, 23, 38, 47, 120–121, 123–124, 130–131, 139, 157, 163, 164–165, 166–167, 170, 171, 172, 173, 181, 198, 199, 200, 201
Shippen, Dr. William, Sr., 21
Shippen, Edward, 51
Shippen, Joseph, 173

Index

Shippen, Nancy, 123
Sickness and mortality rates
  at Boston, 80
  in Canadian campaign, 94
  Manhattan, 117
  for 1776, 132
  at Saratoga, 157
  at Valley Forge, 168, 182, 183
  after Monmouth, 191-192
  at Middlebrook, 194
  at Morristown, 195-196
  summary for the war,
    205-206.
Single Brethrens' House, 123, 166
Sisters' House, 166
Skenesboro, 85, 94, 103, 104, 135, 142, 143
Skippack, 163
Smallpox, 76
  at Boston, 79-80
  in Candian campaign, 89-106
  Washington's concern about, 133
  on Lake Champlain, 135
  Ashbel Greene's description of treatment, 137
Smallpox Hospital (Phila.), 164
Smallwood, General William, 120, 177
Smith, Lieutenant Samuel, 190
Smith, Provost William, 6, 50, 53
Smyth, George, 131
Society of Friends, 4, 25
Somerset Court House, 128
Sorel, 88, 91
Springfield, 104
Sproat, Reverend James, 184
Stamford, 119
Stamp Act, 62, 65
Stark, General John, 102, 145

Steuben, Baron Frederick Wilhelm von, 188
Stockton, Richard, 110
Stoney Brook, 126
Stony Point, 194
Strettle, Mollison, 30
Stringer, Dr. Samuel, 70, 81, 86-87, 92, 95, 96-98, 100, 106, 110, 129
Suffolk County Resolves, 64
Sullivan, General John, 82, 91-92, 93, 94, 126-127, 189, 194
Sunbury, 51
Surgery, 37, 43-45, 71-72, 107, 128
  at Oriskany, 146-147
  at Saratoga, 148-153, 208
Sutton, Benjamin, 80
Syndenham, Thomas, 32, 49

Tallmadge, Colonel Benjamin, 120
Tea Act, 63
Tea Party, 63
Tennant, John, 56
Test Act, 22
Thacher, James, 76-77, 102, 104, 107, 137, 142, 154-155, 209
Thomas, General John, 90, 91
Thompson, General William, 68, 91
Thomson, Charles, 26
Three Rivers, 88, 91
"Tilton Hut," 176
Tilton, James, 37, 75, 120, 123, 166, 167, 168, 171, 173, 196, 208, 210
Townshend Acts, 62, 65
Trappe, 163

Index

Treat, Dr. Malachi, 171
Trenton, 121, 124, 125, 131, 133, 163, 202
Trumbull, Benjamin, 87–88
Trumbull, Colonel John, 93, 109
Trumbull, Governor Jonathan, 86, 94, 103, 134
Trumbull, Jonathan, Jr., 101, 144
Tufts, Dr. Cotton, 93
Turner, Philip, 197

Uwchlan, 168

Valcour Island, 108
Valley Forge, 162, 168, 174–189
Van Ingen, Dirk, 138
Varick, Richard, 140, 149
Virginia Club (Edinburgh), 29
Voltaire, 23

Wadsworth, Jeremiah, 185
Waldo, Surgeon Albigence, 175, 176–177
Wallabout Bay, 115
Warren, Dr. John, 114, 124, 125, 126, 186, 197, 208
Warwick, 162, 166
Washington, General George, 67–69, 77, 82, 94, 100, 104, 105, 111, 113–114, 116–117, 119, 121, 124, 125, 127, 133, 144, 164, 169, 174, 175, 178, 181, 184, 187
Watchung Mts., 128
Waterbury, General David, 105–106, 108

Wayne, Colonel Anthony, 80, 107, 111, 135, 136, 137, 177, 211–212
Weehawken, 117
Weeks, Paymaster William, 157, 180
Wesley, John, 56
West Point, 202
Wharton, Samuel, 7, 27
White Horse, 199
White Plains, 117, 190
Whyatt, Robert, 32
Wigglesworth, Colonel Samuel, 99
Wilkinson, Major James, 101, 120, 154, 157
Williamsburg, 202, 206
Williamstown, 104, 126
Wilmington, 122, 123, 163, 177
Wilson, James, 52
Wind Mill Point, 108
Wingate, Colonel Elisha, 102
Wistar, Dr. Casper, 7
Workhouse (N.Y.), 113
Wood Creek, 142, 143
Wood, Thomas, 58
Wood, Surgeon Vincent, 153
Wooster, General David, 88–90
Worcester, 104

Yale, 51
Yellow Springs, 48, 180, 184, 188, 191, 206, 209
York, Pa., 80, 170
Young, Surgeon Joseph, 136
Younglove, Surgeon Moses, 146

For Product Safety Concerns and Information please contact our EU
representative GPSR@taylorandfrancis.com
Taylor & Francis Verlag GmbH, Kaufingerstraße 24, 80331 München, Germany